Intelligence in an Insecure World

Peter Gill: for Jake, Rosa, Shai, Tomas and Ty
Mark Phythian: to my parents Vic and Mary Phythian

Intelligence in an Insecure World

Peter Gill and Mark Phythian

polity

First published in 2006 by Polity Press

Polity Press
65 Bridge Street
Cambridge CB2 1UR, UK

Polity Press
350 Main Street
Malden, MA 02148, USA

ISBN-10: 0-7456-3244-0
ISBN-13: 978-07456-3244-5
ISBN-10: 0-7456-3245-9
ISBN-13: 978-07456-3245-2

A catalogue record for this book is available from the British Library.

Typeset in 10.5 on 13pt Swift
by Servis Filmsetting Ltd, Manchester
Printed and bound in Great Britain
by MPG Books Ltd, Bodmin, Cornwall

The publisher has used its best endeavours to ensure that the URLs for external websites referred to in this book are correct and active at the time of going to press. However, the publisher has no responsibility for the websites and can make no guarantee that a site will remain live or that the content is or will remain appropriate.

For further information on Polity, visit our website: www.polity.co.uk

Contents

Detailed Contents

List of Figures, Tables and Boxes

Figures

Tables

Boxes

Preface

Today, intelligence is never far from the news headlines. A subject traditionally seen as ethereal and elusive in view of the secrecy surrounding it is now more obviously central to our lives than at any time previously. The stories in which it features demonstrate the importance, vulnerabilities and risks associated with intelligence. In this book we aim to provide an informative and relevant introduction to the whole subject of security intelligence for readers who want to place recent events and controversies, such as the 2003 invasion of Iraq and the 7 July 2005 London bombings (7/7), into some broader context. Since we first conceived this book three years ago, its shape has changed somewhat. Initially, we intended to range more widely in terms of countries, in order to illuminate what was similar and what was different about intelligence under various regimes. At the same time we intended to discuss just how much has changed in the world of intelligence because of the 11 September 2001 attacks on New York and Washington, DC. But, as we worked on the book, controversy over intelligence on Iraq's supposed Weapons of Mass Destruction (WMD) and subsequent inquiries demanded greater attention. In order to do justice to the issues involved, and to the voluminous material that has been published in their wake, the scope of the book has narrowed to essentially the UK and the USA.

In chapter 1 we briefly survey the historical evolution of intelligence and discuss the key components of the intelligence cycle, in order to develop a definition of intelligence on which to base the discussion that follows. Chapter 2 proceeds from the premiss that the literature on intelligence may well be full of fascinating stories, some true, many untrue, but that if we are to move the study of intelligence beyond 'story-telling', then it needs to be placed within the broader context of the study of government and society. In North America there has been much discussion of how governments organize intelligence; by contrast, most of the UK literature is historical. Here, we look to place intelligence on a more secure conceptual grounding. We suggest how research, whether comparative or single country, might best proceed, based on the concept of surveillance.

Chapter 3 discusses the organizations involved in producing intelligence. State agencies are commonly distinguished by the area of their activity – foreign or domestic – or the form of information they gather – for example, signals,

imagery or human intelligence. Since states are not the only 'players' in the intelligence 'game', we also discuss the growing involvement of corporate security
providers and other non-governmental and community organizations. We
discuss the interaction of these different sectors in the context of developing
security intelligence networks. Chapters 4 and 5 discuss what intelligence agencies actually do – what is often described as the intelligence 'process'. We examine the various ways in which they gather information, how they decide what it
actually 'means', how and to whom the intelligence is sent, and, finally, what is
done with it: how intelligence informs policy (or not) or provides the basis for
military or police action.

The success of the 'surprise' attacks on the Twin Towers and Pentagon on 9/11,
the 7/7 suicide bombings in London, and the failure to find WMD in Iraq since
the war of 2003, have all given the impression that intelligence is bound to fail.
If failures of such magnitude occur, then why should we continue to maintain
intelligence agencies? In chapter 6 we consider earlier intelligence failures, as
well as those of 9/11 and 7/7. Chapter 7 is devoted to a detailed discussion of Iraq
and the US, UK and Australian inquiries into erroneous pre-war intelligence
estimates, and analyses what these contribute to our understanding of the
nature of intelligence failure.

The issues of politicization and intelligence failure discussed here raise
crucial questions for all states as they seek to make sense of increasingly asym-
metric security threats. But they also remind us that security panics can be
corrosive of the very democratic values that governments claim to be protecting. The last twenty years or so have witnessed an unprecedented democratization of intelligence, as former authoritarian states in Eastern Europe, Latin
America and South Africa have been replaced by regimes attempting (some
more energetically than others) to subject intelligence agencies to greater
democratic control. In the older democracies, too, there has been a move to
greater parliamentary oversight of intelligence. In chapter 8 we review these
progressive developments and consider the threat of the so-called global war on
terror to their continuation.

We have both accumulated many intellectual debts in the lead-up to and
process of writing this book. We would like to express our gratitude to the
following (in alphabetical order): Hans Born, Charlotte Bretherton, Tom
Bruneau, Marina Caparini, Marco Cepik, Alan Doig, Ken Dombrowski, Stephen
Dorril, Martin Durham, Stuart Farson, Michael Herman, Loch Johnson, Ian
Leigh, Stephen Marrin, John Morrison, Martyn Nightingale, Paul Rogers,
Shlomo Shpiro, Joe Sim, Mick Smith, Andy Tattersall, Dennis Töllborg, Steve
Tombs, Reg Whitaker, and several others who would prefer to remain anonymous. A number of the ideas herein have been aired at various conferences and
workshops over the last couple of years, and we are grateful to all those participants whose contributions helped shape our thinking – they know who they
are! Many thanks to Pen Gill and Diane Evans who have provided unstinting
support throughout the whole enterprise. We would also like to thank the two

anonymous referees who commented on the draft manuscript and, last but not least, Louise Knight, Ellen McKinlay and Jean van Altena at Polity Press for their help. Portions of the material in chapter 3 were previously published in an article 'Not just joining the dots . . .' in *Policing & Society*, 16, 1 (2006), pp. 26–48, and are reproduced here by permission of Routledge.

Needless to say, any errors are a consequence of our own methods of collection and analysis.

Peter Gill
Mark Phythian
December 2005

Abbreviations

7/7	7 July 2005 London suicide bombings
9/11	11 September 2001 suicide attacks on New York and Washington
ARVN	Army of the Republic of Vietnam
ASIO	Australian Security Intelligence Organisation
ASIS	Australian Secret Intelligence Service
ATCSA	Anti-terrorism, Crime and Security Act, 2001 (UK)
AWACS	Airborne Warning and Control System
BND	Bundesnachrichtendienst (Germany)
BW	biological warfare
CBRN	chemical, biological, radiological and nuclear
CBW	chemical and biological weapons
CIA	Central Intelligence Agency (USA)
CIG	Current Intelligence Group (UK)
COINTELPRO	Counter-Intelligence Programs (FBI, 1950–60s)
COS	Chief of Station (CIA, USA)
CSE	Communications Security Establishment (Canada)
CSIS	Canadian Security Intelligence Service
CTAC	Counter-Terrorist Analysis Centre (UK, 2001–3)
CTC	Counterterrorist Center (USA)
CTG	Counterterrorist Group (EU plus others)
CW	chemical warfare
DCI	Director of Central Intelligence (USA, 1947–2004)
DEA	Drug Enforcement Administration (US Department of Justice)
DIA	Defense Intelligence Agency (USA)
DIO	Defence Intelligence Organisation (Australia)
DIS	Defence Intelligence Staff (UK)
DNI	Director of National Intelligence (USA since 2005)
DSD	Defence Signals Directorate (Australia)
ECHR	European Convention on Human Rights
ECtHR	European Court of Human Rights
EPIC	Electronic Privacy Information Center (USA)
FBI	Federal Bureau of Investigation (USA)
FEMA	Federal Emergency Management Agency (USA)
FOIA	Freedom of Information Act (USA)
FRU	Force Research Unit (UK)

FSB	Federal Security Service (Russia)
GCHQ	Government Communications Headquarters (UK)
GRU	military intelligence agency (USSR)
HMIC	Her Majesty's Inspectorate of Constabulary (UK)
HUMINT	human intelligence
IAIP	Information Analysis and Infrastructure Protection (US Department of Homeland Security)
ICT	Information and Communication Technology
IMINT	imagery intelligence
INR	Bureau of Intelligence and Research (US State Department)
ISA	Intelligence Services Act 1994 (UK)
ISC	Intelligence and Security Committee (UK)
ISI	Inter-Services Intelligence (Pakistan)
ISP	internet service provider
JIC	Joint Intelligence Committee (UK)
JTAC	Joint Terrorism Analysis Centre (UK, since 2003)
KGB	Committee of State Security (Soviet Union)
MI5	Security Service (UK)
MI6	Secret Intelligence Service (UK)
MoD	Ministry of Defence (UK)
NCCL	National Council for Civil Liberties (now, Liberty, UK)
NCIS	National Criminal Intelligence Service (UK)
NCTC	National Counter Terrorism Center (USA)
NGA	National Geospatial Agency (US Defense Department)
NGO	non-governmental organization
NIC	National Intelligence Council (USA)
NIE	National Intelligence Estimate (USA)
NOC	non-official cover (USA)
NRO	National Reconnaissance Office (US Defense Department)
NSA	National Security Agency/ National Security Adviser (USA)
NSC	National Security Council (USA)
ONA	Office of National Assessments (Australia)
ONE	Office of National Estimates (USA)
OSP	Office of Special Plans (USA)
OSS	Office of Strategic Services (USA)
PDB	Presidential Daily Brief (USA)
PFLP	Popular Front for the Liberation of Palestine
PIRA	Provisional Irish Republican Army
PMC	private military companies
PSC	private security companies
RCMP	Royal Canadian Mounted Police
RIPA	Regulation of Investigatory Powers Act 2000 (UK)
SAS	Special Air Service (UK)
SBS	Special Boat Service (UK)
SEIB	Senior Executive Intelligence Brief (USA)
SIA	Single Intelligence Account (UK)
SIGINT	signals intelligence

SIRC	Security Intelligence Review Committee (Canada)
SIS	Secret Intelligence Service (also known as MI6, UK)
SNA	social network analysis
SNIE	Special National Intelligence Estimate (USA)
SOCA	Serious Organised Crime Agency (UK)
SOCOM	Special Operations Command (USA)
SSCI	Senate Select Committee on Intelligence (USA)
TCG	Tasking and Co-ordinating Group (UK)
TRANSEC	Department of Transport Security Division (UK)
UDA	Ulster Defence Association (UK)
UNSCOM	United Nations Special Commission (on Iraqi WMD)
WMD	Weapons of Mass Destruction

chapter 1

What is Intelligence?

All the business of war, and indeed all the business of life, is to endeavour to find out what you don't know by what you do.

Duke of Wellington, 1828, in Lathrop, *The Literary Spy*

Defining Intelligence

ONCE we attempt to define intelligence, it soon becomes apparent that, as a concept, intelligence is as elusive as the daring fictional agents who have cemented it in the popular imagination – partly because any worthwhile definition needs to embrace the full range of activities in which intelligence agencies engage and the purposes underpinning these.

Our starting point should be to recognize that intelligence is a means to an end. This end is the security, and even prosperity, of the entity that provides for the collection and subsequent analysis of intelligence. In the contemporary international system, states are the principal customers of intelligence and the key organizers of collection and analysis agencies. However, a range of sub-state actors, commercial, non-commercial and criminal, also perceive a need to collect and analyse intelligence and guard against the theft of their own secrets. In the contemporary world, this need even extends to sports teams. For example, ahead of the November 2003 Rugby Union World Cup final against hosts Australia, the England team swept their changing room and training base for electronic surveillance equipment, concerned that in 2001 espionage had allowed an Australian team to crack the codes employed by the British Lions, helping secure their dominance in line-outs and go on to win the series.[1]

Once we define intelligence in terms of security, it becomes clear that intelligence is an inherently competitive pursuit. Security is relative, and therefore the purpose of intelligence is to bestow a relative security advantage. Moreover, security is a broad concept which goes beyond preventing military surprise or terrorist attack. In Britain, MI5's[2] own *Statement of Purpose and Values* talks of protecting 'national security and economic well-being'.[3] In other words, a key dimension of security is preserving relative economic advantage and, from there, assisting in advancing it through the collection of financial and commercial intelligence on competitors – whether foreign states or competitor companies.

Ideally, intelligence will enhance security by bestowing on the wise collector, perceptive analyst and skilled customer a predictive power on which basis policy can be formulated. However, customers need to be aware of the limits of intelligence if it is to be most effective as a basis of policy. This was the clear message contained in gently admonitory passages in the UK Butler Report which arose out of the apparent intelligence failure over the question of Iraq's WMD, discussed more fully in later chapters. The Butler Report warned that

> These limitations are best offset by ensuring that the ultimate users of intelligence, the decision-makers at all levels, properly understand its strengths and limitations and have the opportunity to acquire experience in handling it. It is not easy to do this while preserving the security of sensitive sources and methods. But unless intelligence is properly handled at this final stage, all preceding effort and expenditure is wasted.[4]

Similarly, the 2004 Flood Report into Australia's intelligence agencies warned that while its customers would like intelligence to possess the characteristics of a science, and despite the benefit of decades of technological innovation, it stubbornly remains more of an art:

> In so far as it seeks to forecast the future, assessment based on intelligence will seldom be precise or definitive. This is particularly so when it seeks to understand complex developments and trends in future years. Greater precision is sometimes possible in relation to intelligence's warning function – highlighting the possibility of a specific event in the near term future. . . . But even in this field, precision will be hard to achieve. Intelligence will rarely provide comprehensive coverage of a topic. More often it is fragmentary and incomplete.[5]

In defining 'intelligence', we need to recognize that it is an umbrella term – a fact that renders precise definition problematic – covering a chain or cycle of linked activities from the targeting and collection of data (only half-jokingly defined by former US senator Daniel Patrick Moynihan as 'the plural of anecdote'[6]), through analysis to dissemination and the actions, including covert ones, which can result.[7] The intelligence process is usually explained by reference to the concept of the intelligence cycle, typically held to comprise five stages:

- Planning and direction
- Collection
- Processing
- All-source analysis and production
- Dissemination

Figure 1.1 shows how the CIA describes the intelligence process.

While useful as a means of introducing the different stages of the intelligence process, the notion of a *cycle* fails to capture fully the fact that the end product of intelligence is an assessment designed for the customer that the customer

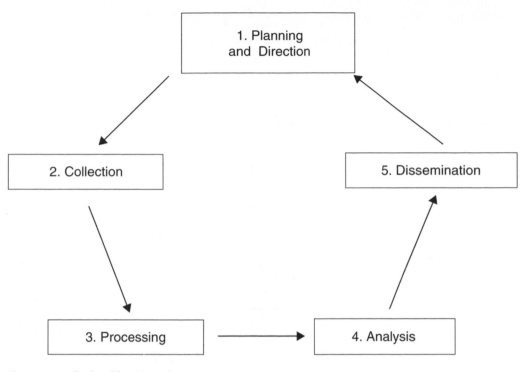

Figure 1.1 The intelligence cycle

then uses in formulating policy or operations. It feeds into, and has the capacity to alter, the very environment in which information was collected and analysis undertaken. The concept of a cycle cannot, in other words, capture the dynamic nature of intelligence's impact on the external environment. A better way of viewing the intelligence process in order to capture this dynamic fully is to adopt the concept of a system that includes feedback, as in the 'funnel of causality'[8] (see figure 1.2). Moreover, the funnel shape illustrates the point that not all information is necessarily translated via analysis into policy, and that much is filtered out.

Intelligence is more than the organized collection of targeted information. Processing can include technical issues such as transcribing and translating intercepted telephone conversations and verifying the reliability of information. Analysis is the process of determining what the information 'means'. It is the analytical process (examined in more detail in chapter 5) that transforms the information, however acquired, into usable intelligence.

The CIA defines this stage of the intelligence process as involving:

> the conversion of basic information into finished intelligence. It includes integrating, evaluating, and analyzing all available data – which is often fragmented and even contradictory – and preparing intelligence products. Analysts, who are subject-matter specialists, consider the information's

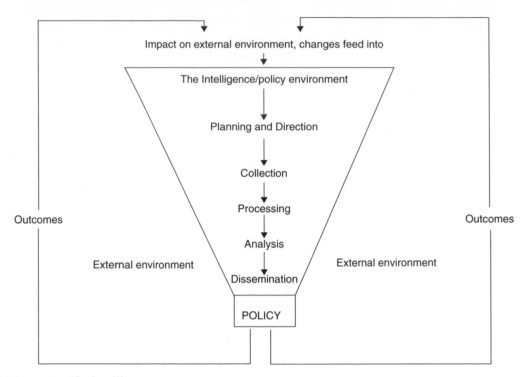

Figure 1.2   The intelligence process

reliability, validity, and relevance. They integrate data into a coherent whole, put the evaluated information in context, and produce finished intelligence that includes assessments of events and judgments about the implications of the information.[9]

For the CIA, at least, those carrying out these analytic functions are assisted by computer software that searches through the databases held across the US intelligence community to produce a daily electronic read file tailored to each analyst's specific area of responsibility.[10] Nevertheless, it is important for both observers and users to recognize that, despite such impressive resources, 'Intelligence analysis is not a perfect science and we should not expect perfection. . . . It is entirely possible for an analyst to perform meticulous and skilful analysis and be completely wrong. Likewise, it is also possible to perform careless and unskilled analysis and be completely right.'[11]

The language employed in the finished product is crucial. In a field which deals with estimates and probabilities, it is essential to convey accurately to the policymaker the degree of certainty underpinning judgements. It needs to be calibrated according to a commonly understood scale. But, unfortunately, no such scale exists, a fact exposed by inquiries into intelligence on Iraq's WMD. As Sherman Kent wrote, the language used should 'set forth the community's findings in such a way as to make clear to the reader what is certain knowledge and what is reasoned judgment, and within this large realm of judgment what varying degrees of certitude lie behind each key statement'.[12]

Intelligence is not just passive. Some intelligence agencies – for example, the Canadian Security Intelligence Service (CSIS) – are charged just with advising government, but many are called upon to implement the policy response arising from their own collection and analysis. Are the necessarily secret activities of intelligence agencies in implementing policy – that is, covert actions – also a part of the intelligence process, or does covert action represent a separate body of activity?

While some authors see covert action as intrinsic to intelligence,[13] it has also been characterized as an 'allied activity', somewhat separate from the core business of intelligence.[14] Hence, for Michael Herman, 'Intelligence is information and information gathering, not *doing* things to people; no-one gets hurt by it, at least not directly. Some agencies do indeed carry out covert action, which confuses the ethical issues, but this is a separable and subsidiary function.'[15] However, the extent and regularity of recourse to covert actions, and the nature of these, help to define the wider security and intelligence culture and, to an extent, reflect the form of government that intelligence agencies serve.[16] In this respect, separation of covert action from intelligence is artificial. More broadly, if police or security agencies do not act in some way on the basis of intelligence, or at least consider its implications for their policies and practices, then one might ask, what is the point of intelligence?

Covert action also raises the question of the relationship between ethics and intelligence. The question of ethics relates not solely to covert responses based on intelligence, but also to covert methods of collection where these involve, for example, communications interception, deception, blackmail, the use of 'honey-traps' and threats or torture. The question of 'spying on friends' raises particular ethical issues. Nevertheless, it is with regard to covert operations that ethical issues are most acute, and the higher up the ladder of escalation covert responses ascend, the more acute they become.[17]

While, in contrast to the CIA, MI5's mission is centred around domestic security, its role, as presented on its website, clearly does embrace covert actions to frustrate entities considered hostile and/or threatening. The role of MI5, it tells us, is to:

- **investigate** – to obtain and then to collate, analyse and assess secret intelligence about threats;
- **counter** – to act, and enable others to act, to counter specific threats;
- **advise** – to keep government, and others as appropriate, informed of the threats, and to advise on the response to those threats, including protective security measures;
- **assist** – to provide assistance to other agencies, organizations and departments in combating threats to national security.

Our aim is to gain the advantage over the targets of our investigations by covertly obtaining information about them, which we can use to counter their activities.

> Over time, we try to obtain detailed knowledge about target organizations, their key personalities, infrastructure, plans and capabilities.[18]

Similarly, the FBI identifies in its Intelligence Program both developing intelligence and action to counter threats:

> The mission of the Intelligence Program is to optimally position the FBI to meet current and emerging national security and criminal threats by:
> – Aiming core investigative work pro-actively against threats to U.S. interests,
> – Building and sustaining enterprise-wide intelligence policies and capabilities, and
> – Providing useful, appropriate, and timely information and analysis to the national security, homeland security and law enforcement communities.[19]

As an area of academic inquiry, intelligence is still in its infancy. Existing definitions of intelligence can generate as many questions as answers. In the CIA's in-house intelligence journal, *Studies in Intelligence*, Michael Warner has pointed out that despite a long history, even in the early years of the twenty-first century, 'we have no accepted definition of intelligence'. This has led to problems, because 'intelligence' 'is defined anew by each author who addresses it, and these definitions rarely refer to one another or build off what has been written before. Without a clear idea of what intelligence is, how can we develop a theory to explain how it works?'[20]

As Warner points out, there are many competing definitions of intelligence. In the 1947 US National Security Act, 'foreign intelligence' 'means information relating to the capabilities, intentions, or activities of foreign governments or elements thereof, foreign organizations, or foreign persons'.[21] The definition arrived at by the Brown–Aspin Commission in 1996 showed that governmental thinking about how intelligence can best be defined had not evolved much despite the passage of fifty years and vast increases in budgets: 'The Commission believes it preferable to define "intelligence" simply and broadly as information about "things foreign" – people, places, things, and events – needed by the Government for the conduct of its functions.'[22]

The definition offered by Loch Johnson, that intelligence is 'the knowledge – and, ideally, foreknowledge – sought by nations in response to external threats and to protect their vital interests, especially the well-being of their own people',[23] represents an advance. This definition brings the security purpose centre-stage, and also introduces the vital ingredient of *prior knowledge*. If intelligence is worth having, it is because analysis will provide customers with prior warnings of potential developments (that is, potential surprises) affecting their security/relative advantage. However, this definition does not distinguish between the collection of targeted information and the subsequent analysis that frames it, thereby providing decision-makers with policy options.

At the end of his discussion of the definitional poverty surrounding intelligence, Warner offers his own definition: 'Intelligence is secret, state activity to understand or influence foreign entities.'[24] But this itself is frustratingly incomplete. It risks elevating a feature of it – secrecy – above its purpose. There is no explicit reference to the purpose of intelligence as lying in security; nor is there any reference to the essential element of providing foreknowledge. Moreover, it is a very *American* definition, in that its focus is *foreign entities*, reflecting political debates at the time of the creation of the CIA and the basic American suspicion of secret police activity at home, but ignoring a significant sphere of potential intelligence activity.

Is secrecy essential to a definition of intelligence? Warner goes so far as to suggest that 'Without secrets it is not intelligence.' We also think that secrecy is important to intelligence. A lack of secrecy endangers the comparative advantage sought from the intelligence. If a target is aware that information is being collected on it, that knowledge could impact on the process by allowing the target to feed (dis)information into it, or adopt other counter-measures. Even knowledge of the range or balance of sources that inform assessments could allow a target to attempt an assessment of the state of this intelligence, and engage in counter-intelligence activities aimed at affecting the conclusions drawn. Clearly, analysis must also be secret, however much the information that feeds into it is open source.[25]

However, secrecy also raises key issues of legality, morality and accountability. It creates an unchallengeable political space for its customers, because they base their actions on supposedly superior analysis. Because this is secret, it is denied to others and so cannot easily be challenged.[26]

To summarize the discussion thus far, any definition of intelligence needs to make reference to the following factors:

- It is more than merely information collection.
- It covers a range of linked activities.
- Intelligence is security-based.
- It aims to provide advance warning.
- It encompasses the potential for intelligence agencies or other entities to engage in covert actions as a possible response.
- Secrecy is essential to the comparative advantage being aimed for.

We can bring these factors together to form our own definition of intelligence:

> *Intelligence is the umbrella term referring to the range of activities – from planning and information collection to analysis and dissemination – conducted in secret, and aimed at maintaining or enhancing relative security by providing forewarning of threats or potential threats in a manner that allows for the timely implementation of a preventive policy or strategy, including, where deemed desirable, covert activities.*

There is a sense in which an emphasis on the intelligence function of states and the consequent intelligence competition between them can lead us to view international affairs through the state-centric and security-driven emphases of neo-realist analyses of international relations. From this perspective, there is no real need for a separate body of definitional and particularly theoretical work on intelligence, because the operation of state intelligence agencies is no more than a logical expression of the broader neo-realist reality that states are the core actors in international politics, searching for security in an anarchical and inherently competitive environment. Perhaps this is just as well because, as historian of intelligence David Kahn has observed, 'Intelligence has been an academic discipline for half a century now. Almost from the start, scholars have called for a theory of intelligence. None has been advanced. Although some authors entitle sections of their work "theory of intelligence", to my knowledge no one has proposed concepts that can be tested.'[27] Suitably warned, we shall turn our attention to the theoretical landscape in chapter 2 and consider the intelligence process more conceptually within the broader context of social science. First, however, we sketch out the manner in which intelligence as we know it today has evolved.

Evolution

Today's global intelligence networks (as discussed in chapter 3) are a product of the Cold War era. However, just as students of terrorism can trace the antecedents of terrorism back to the activities of the Sicarii of Palestine (AD 66–73) and then the Assassins,[28] and students of warfare the early use of chemical weapons to the use of pitch and sulphur to create toxic fumes during the Peloponnesian War,[29] so too the rise of intelligence as a means of providing security can be traced back to antiquity and before.

Indeed, enterprising scholars have gone so far as to trace the practice of intelligence collection back to the Bible, beginning in the Old Testament when 'the Lord spake unto Moses' telling him to send spies into Canaan, raising the awkward theological question of why those blessed with omniscience require the espionage assistance of mere mortals. Spies and agents appear elsewhere, from Delilah to Judas. In the early fourth century BC, the Chinese general Sun-Tzu recognized that 'A hundred ounces of silver spent for information may save ten thousand spent on war,' and wrote in *The Art of War* of the importance of advance intelligence. Intelligence also plays a role in Thucydides' account of the Peloponnesian War.[30]

Just as in Aristotle's model of political development constitutional change followed military innovation, so we would argue that developments in intelligence follow from the emergence of threat situations, either real or perceived. Historically, awareness of, or a perception of, vulnerability[31] – what might be termed the 'security deficit' – can be linked to developments in intelligence designed to improve preparedness to meet that threat. Because the bigger an actor is, the more it stands to lose, and the more it can invest in preventive intelligence to safeguard its relative advantage, the most advanced intelligence networks are found among the wealthiest players in any given state or corporate segment of concurrent global intelligence contests.[32] These are conducted on various levels – politico-military, criminal and commercial.

With the rise of the modern state system, intelligence requirements became more permanent, collection and analysis began to assume a more professional character, and the stakes became larger, focused on the protection of the state and the monarch at its head. In Britain, the development of systems of intelligence was rooted in the protection of the Crown and the uncovering of plots against it. Following the excommunication of Queen Elizabeth I by Pope Pius V in 1570, the threat increased, and so an intelligence effort that up to that point had been configured to uncover domestic treason suddenly required a continental dimension. This was provided by Sir Francis Walsingham, the Queen's Secretary of State from 1573. Walsingham's spies targeted Catholics to uncover potential threats to the Queen, and amongst his successes may be counted advance knowledge of Spanish plans to send an Armada against England. With Walsingham's death and the passing of this threat, intelligence atrophied, but none the less later revived to deal with crises relating, for example, to Jacobite plots and instability in the American colonies.

Throughout the sixteenth century, French intelligence was developing in parallel – for example, with the establishment in 1590 of the *Poste aux Lettres*, employing resealing experts alongside early analysts to open, read, and then reseal private letters. Similarly, as soon as postal services started in the UK, governments started to intercept mail, relying on the traditional royal prerogative power.[33] Given the threatening environment in which it emerged, it should come as little surprise that the newly independent United States soon saw the benefit of intelligence. In 1790 George Washington established a Contingency Fund over which Congress had only limited oversight.[34]

In the nineteenth century, industrialization, the creation of a large urban working class, large-scale immigration, and the dissemination of doctrines and ideas challenging the existing order, increased the significance of intelligence on internal threats to order. In Britain, threats ranged from those posed by Fenians, leading to the creation of the Metropolitan Police Special Branch,[35] to anarchists. In the USA, an anarchist, Leon Czolgosz, shot dead President McKinley. In Russia, revolutionary activity would culminate in the overthrow of the state.[36]

However, it was the spectre of war in Europe at the beginning of the twentieth century that led to the creation of further modern state intelligence agencies. In Britain, this was a need highlighted by the Boer War, and finally given form by the establishment of a Secret Service Bureau in 1909, in the midst of German spy fever. No sooner was World War I over than a new threat – Bolshevism – was identified to justify the continuation of institutionalized intelligence, to be formally divided into MI5 and MI6, whose most famous agent of the period, Sidney Reilly, cemented his reputation for derring-do against the Soviet Union. There certainly was a concerted Soviet effort to gain intelligence on the intentions of those powers such as Britain that had displayed such hostility to the newly formed Soviet state.[37] Counter-intelligence aimed at this effort, subsequently joined by the lesser imperative of needing to keep the indigenous fascist right under surveillance, constituted MI5's main workload during the twenty years' crisis of the inter-war period. The exposure of the Arcos affair in 1927, and the defection and debriefing of Soviet intelligence officer Walter Krivitsky gave MI5 a good idea of the scale of the Soviet operation.[38]

In Russia, foreign intelligence collection under the Czars had been rudimentary, and may be said to have contributed to the débâcle of the Russo–Japanese War. Lenin's creation of the Cheka was meant to go some way towards rectifying this, and to securing the Soviet state and its leaders by gaining intelligence on internal and external threats to the state. Doing so involved the Cheka in eliminating many (one estimate puts the figure killed as a result of Cheka counter-intelligence at 250,000 by 1925) and imprisoning many more in camps in Siberia and similarly remote outposts of the Soviet land mass.

Since the 1920s intelligence agencies had been intercepting the communications and breaking the codes even of allies.[39] Yet liberal sensitivities were still in evidence: the US Secretary of State Henry Stimson tried to halt US interceptions by closing its Black Chamber with the immortal words, 'Gentlemen do not read each other's mail.'[40] In similar vein, consider former director general of MI5 Sir Percy Sillitoe's account of the Klaus Fuchs case:

> I would like to point out that MI5 is not a supernatural organization. I have sometimes felt that many people, not knowing accurately what its methods are, have come to expect that its representatives must all be endowed with a sixth sense. The fact is that there was absolutely no valid reason why anyone's suspicions should reasonably have been aroused about Fuchs. . . .
>
> Given then, that we had never had any grounds for suspecting Fuchs, what should we have done? Should we have, all the same, arranged for him to be shadowed night and day? In that case we should have had logically to follow the same procedure in the case of all the other apparently quite innocent men who were engaged on secret work – and their number was fairly large. . . .
>
> Apart from the obvious practical impossibility of employing such tactics, inevitably some of the scientists would come to sense or somehow suspect that they were being watched. And then you would have a violent outcry, for these men, ninety-nine percent of whom would be entirely blameless, would, very reasonably, protest most strongly. Their lives would have become a nightmare once they realized that their every action was being spied upon.[41]

However, the Fuchs case, the whole question of atomic espionage, and the successful Soviet testing of an atomic bomb well in advance of the US's most pessimistic estimates, all served to make the sense of threat both greater and more immediate than ever before. Sillitoe's strictly constitutionalist approach would soon be unrecognizable as the intelligence world became the arena where the Cold War was at its most intense, and in which the sense of threat was held to justify stretching the bounds of the ethically acceptable.

It was against this background that, in the UK, cinema appeared to bring the world of intelligence into the open. In the wake of Fuchs, the Burgess and Maclean scandals, the construction of the Berlin Wall and the Cuban missile crisis, the emergence of James Bond – armed and gadget-laden successor to

Sherlock Holmes, Richard Hannay and Bulldog Drummond – came to represent all that the British public wanted to know, and because of the operation
of the D-Notice system, all they were likely to discover, about intelligence.[42] The
filmic version of James Bond gave the impression of being rooted in reality by
virtue of loosely mirroring Cold War antagonisms. It also left audiences pre-
disposed to believe in individual villains with a global reach. In this respect,
Osama bin Laden was preceded by a cast that included Dr No, Blofeld, Zorin,
Stromberg, Drax et al., and which may have contributed to Western public's
receptivity to official representations of bin Laden and a highly organized
entity called al-Qaeda.

The Bond films eschewed a focus on the mundane world of signals intelligence
and analysis for the high-octane world of covert operations. In the Cold War-era
films in the series there is no sense of ambivalence or doubt – Bond would not
have made sense or worked at the box office in the desired way if he had been
anything less than an inveterate cold warrior, confirming for the watching
public the necessity of the Cold War struggle, the evil ingenuity of the enemy,
and the global role that Britain's intelligence services afforded it.[43] In short,
through Bond, intelligence was feel-good, reassuring and, of course, invariably
successful. To demonstrate that this fiction could be mistaken for reality,
we need look no further than KGB defector Oleg Gordievsky, who has claimed
that the Central Committee of the Soviet Communist Party watched Bond films,
that the KGB requested that he try to obtain the devices used by Bond in the
films, and that Bond helped shape the Soviet leadership's perception of British
intelligence.[44]

While the British public has remained intrigued by the secret world of intelligence ever since, this fascination has been qualified and shaped by a continual stream of allegations concerning the behaviour and penetration of the
intelligence services. The Burgess and Maclean defections, the Profumo affair
and the defection of Kim Philby (which occurred concurrently) all produced
bestsellers, testimony to the British public's appetite for spy stories. But they
were just the beginning. Writers like Chapman Pincher, described by historian
E. P. Thompson as 'a kind of official urinal in which, side by side, high officials
of MI5 and MI6, Sea Lords, Permanent Under-Secretaries . . . and others, stand
patiently leaking in the public interest',[45] popularized the intelligence exposé,
the best known being his Peter Wright-informed account of the case against
former MI5 director general Sir Roger Hollis, *Their Trade is Treachery*.[46] This was
followed up with further bestsellers offering slight variations on the theme.[47]
More significantly, by the 1970s, MI5's focus on the 'enemy within' led to allegations concerning a wide range of dubious domestic activities, ranging from
the targeting of the leadership of the Campaign for Nuclear Disarmament and
National Council for Civil Liberties (NCCL),[48] to a range of questionable activities in Northern Ireland,[49] its alleged role in the 1984–5 miners' strike,[50] and
the involvement of MI5 officers in a plot to undermine Labour prime minister
Harold Wilson, as recounted by Peter Wright in *Spycatcher*.[51]

By the time British politics textbooks came to cover intelligence matters, it was in the context of such concerns. To give a flavour from the time, one of the first to do so provided the following end-of-chapter summary on the security services:

> The security services are the most secret part of the secret state and their activities are generally hidden from view by the need to preserve 'national security'. This level of secrecy precludes the possibility of effective accountability to Parliament or anyone else. Virtually a law unto themselves, the security services mount surveillance on both real and imagined enemies of the state, and this has even extended to operations mounted against an elected Labour Prime Minister. The security services represent a major worry for those concerned about erosion of civil liberties in Britain.[52]

Neither did the revelations end with the Cold War. During the late 1990s, two disaffected young officers in MI5 and MI6, David Shayler and Richard Tomlinson, spoke out about dubious practices, including domestic political surveillance and an alleged MI6 plot to assassinate Libyan leader Colonel Ghaddafi.[53]

This stream of revelations has resulted in a pronounced ambivalence in attitudes towards the intelligence services – attraction to the James Bond myth coexisting alongside a degree of scepticism and mistrust. Reflecting this, the distinguished historian Bernard Porter opened his 1989 history of political espionage in Britain with the observation that

> All evidence in this area is undependable. That means that even if we were able to see the official record, it might not help. It also means that we cannot rely on the evidence we are able to see. The reason for this is that all spies and secret agents are liars, trained in techniques of deception and dissimulation, who are just as likely to fake the historical record as anything else. This is why the first rule for the reader of any book about secret services, including this one, is *not to trust a word of it*. It could all be lies and disinformation; not on the part of the writer necessarily, but on the part of the sources he is gullible enough to believe.[54]

Since Porter wrote this, of course, official intelligence archives have become available at an increasing rate in Britain, and scholars have made much use of them. Nevertheless, it is important for researchers in the archives to remember that they 'have no external guarantee that what is preserved there is necessarily an analogue of reality'.[55]

Meanwhile, the emergence of highly differentiated strategic environments in different regions of the world encouraged the development of intelligence structures on markedly different lines. The national security state that arose from the early to mid-1960s in Latin America saw, with US encouragement, the principal threat to the nation as deriving from a Moscow-funded and inspired enemy within.[56] Accordingly, intelligence in these states was oriented primarily towards internal security. South Africa's international isolation during the apartheid era, combined with its perception of encirclement by pro-Moscow southern African states, contributed to the almost unique characteristics of its security services.[57] John Dziak developed the term 'counter-intelligence state' to describe how Lenin and his successors in the USSR devoted maximum effort to the destruction of domestic and foreign opponents,[58] but we can see how the term might also be applied to other states.

In a different context, Israel's perception of an acute threat to its very existence is essential to any understanding of the centrality of intelligence to the Israeli state, which ended the twentieth century spending more per head on intelligence than any other country. Indeed, Israel's success in the 1948 War of Independence was partly attributable to the role of intelligence, in part relying on structures which pre-dated the establishment of the state and were intended to facilitate the immigration of Jews in the face of restrictions applied by the British. In 1951 Mossad was added to the existing intelligence structure, modelled on the recently created CIA and designed as an arm of the executive branch that answered directly to the office of the prime minister. While the intelligence community played a role in providing intelligence that led to the pre-emptive launch of the Six Day War of 1967, it failed in 1973 to provide clear warning of the Egyptian and Syrian surprise attack. Clear evidence of war preparations existed (a movement of Egyptian troops towards the Suez Canal, Egyptian appeals for blood donors, etc.), but the intelligence community's analysis of the raw intelligence led them to conclude that this was Arab disinformation.[59] In more recent years, intelligence has had a dual focus, based on careful monitoring of the intentions of Arab states towards Israel, particularly Iraq and Syria, and dealing with the more immediate internal security problems associated with the Intifada, including the rise of an indigenous extreme religious right critical of any accommodation over the Occupied Territories, and one of whose number, Yigal Amir, assassinated prime minister Yitzhak Rabin in 1995. But the main concern has been to counter the flow of suicide bombers from the Occupied Territories. Counter-measures have included targeting Hamas, Hizbollah, PFLP, and Islamic Jihad leaders for assassination.

Israeli intelligence has been distinctive in the degree of its proactive approach to dealing with threats once identified and dealing in retribution that make it almost unique (from the capture of Adolf Eichmann in 1960, through the tracking down of the Black September terrorists responsible for the Munich massacre in 1972, the assassination of Arab scientists in Europe in the 1980s, the kidnapping of Mordechai Vanunu, etc.) and that does not require sensationalizing in any way. Unfortunately, serious study of the Israeli intelligence community has been hampered by accounts that mix reality with less reliable but more marketable accounts of derring-do, and which also suffer from failing to treat sufficiently the context in which it operates.

In the immediate post-Cold War era the collapse of the Soviet Union, the erstwhile enemy that had represented the threat against which the CIA was to guard the USA, a debate emerged as to whether there was further need for the agency, led inside the USA by national politicians such as Daniel Patrick Moynihan and public intellectuals like Theodore Draper.[60] In essence this was a combination of a coda to the Church and Pike investigations of the mid-1970s, prompted by new revelations concerning Cold War-era covert operations in the Third World, and a liberal reaction rooted in the traditional American opposition to unnecessary secrecy. Defenders of the need for a national foreign intelligence agency took refuge in metaphor, conceding that the Cold War dragon might have been slain but that, as DCI James Woolsey characterized it at his 1993 confirmation hearings, the USA was now confronted by a jungle containing 'a bewildering variety of poisonous snakes'.[61] One path that post-Cold War intelligence would take soon emerged in the form of a heightened focus on economic espionage, with tales of CIA agents attempting to bribe French officials to learn about the French position at the World Trade Organization, electronic surveillance of Japanese officials during a car import dispute, and so on. At the time, US commentators were at pains to stress that this was not a one-way street, warning that 'France possesses a well-developed intelligence service, one of the most aggressive collectors of economic intelligence in the world. Using techniques often reminiscent of the KGB or spy novels, the French in recent years have planted moles in US companies such as IBM, Texas Instruments, and Corning.'[62]

US companies have been a primary object of state-directed industrial espionage, one 1996 survey ranking China, Canada, France, India, Japan, Germany, South Korea, Russia, Taiwan, the UK, Israel and Mexico as the lead perpetrators.[63] Prior to the events of 9/11, some analysts saw a more globalized world as dictating that market intelligence would become a lead intelligence requirement. For example, Gregory F. Treverton applied the idea of the 'market state' as successor to the 'territorial state', confidently arguing that 'The era of the "territorial state" is passing away, and probably has been for a century. The change was obscured, though, by this century's preoccupation with particular, and particularly aggressive, territorial states.'[64] In this brave new world the business of intelligence, as it were, concerned 'which government's reserves are lower than it has admitted? Which respected finance minister is about to resign? Which government doesn't have the stomach for raising interest rates to defend its currency? Secrets are relevant to answering these questions, many of them puzzles. They are good targets for intelligence.'[65]

However, post 9/11 analyses would suggest that the authors of these accounts drank too freely at the well of globalization (Treverton even goes so far as to suggest that John Mearsheimer's fairly uncontroversial thesis that the nation-state and national interests were 'alive and well' was 'a provocative argument'[66]), and that while economic espionage will continue to have an important role to play, so too will more fundamental and enduring intelligence questions of state security, war and peace. Hence, while US SIGINT may well still target Japanese industrial concerns, it has also more recently been involved in the high politics of spying on the UN Security Council delegates from Angola, Cameroon, Chile, Bulgaria, Guinea and Pakistan during the period leading up to the 2003 war in Iraq.[67]

Limitations

Identifying threats, then, has been the business of intelligence agencies. Without a sufficiently serious threat, their need becomes less clear, their budgets are threatened, and hence they themselves become less secure. Sensitive to the threat to their existence that would arise from a challenge to belief in the omniscience of intelligence, agencies have both promoted the idea that they can prevent threats from crystallizing into anything more concrete, and at times exaggerated the reality of threats in order to secure their own continued existence. J. Edgar Hoover's success in establishing the FBI as an autonomous 'political police' in the USA from the 1940s through the 1960s was based on his success in asserting that the Bureau was best placed not only to understand the threat from domestic communism but also to counter it.[68]

Yet, as intelligence practitioners themselves confess, and as the Flood Report again reminded us, intelligence is not a science; rather, it is an imprecise art. This fact is not a consequence of reliance on any particular collection method, or because of a *lack* of unprocessed information. More of a particular type of input will not alter the basic fact that intelligence can deal only in probabilities, and that the range of variables that can be generated by human interaction or introduced by different, subjective analyses of a given situation will always serve to limit the utility of intelligence work and to limit its predictive power to well below 100 per cent. Hence, despite impressive budgets, the world's most high-profile intelligence agency, the CIA, has failed to anticipate a catalogue of momentous developments and acute disasters, key amongst any listing of which would have to be the construction of the Berlin Wall and the collapse of the Soviet Union. Two further fundamental intelligence failures, to anticipate the December 1979 Soviet invasion of Afghanistan or the August 1990 Iraqi invasion of Kuwait, can be attributed confidently to failures in analysis rather than failures brought about through an absence or lack of information. The case of Afghanistan additionally raises the question of intelligence agencies gearing assessments to what their customers may be thought to want to hear, or at least avoiding headlining an analysis that would be unwelcome – a subject to which we shall return in chapters 6 and 7. To illustrate the kinds of pressures involved, with regard to the case of Afghanistan in 1979, a CIA analysis concluded that

> it would be unfair not to acknowledge the pressures on intelligence either to express more certainty – justified by evidence – or to engage in safe hedging. Clearly, at a time when détente was being challenged and the SALT II treaty appeared to be in a life-threatening status with the Senate, allegations that Moscow was about to engage in yet another Third World aggression barely two years after what was regarded as its proxy intervention in Ethiopia was not something most US policy officials wanted to see casually aired.[69]

More devastatingly for the USA, while recognizing the existence of a threat, both FBI and CIA failed in a variety of ways to appreciate the *nature* and *scope* of the threat posed by al-Qaeda, the linkages between al-Qaeda and the 1993 World Trade Center bombing led by Ramzi Yousef, and failed to appreciate the significance of intelligence on a meeting in Malaysia in 2000 where al-Qaeda members and two of the 9/11 hijackers came together. Moreover, the evidence suggests that they failed to convince politicians, whose Cold War mindset determined that they saw threats as emanating from states, particularly China, rather than non-state actors.[70] With the benefit of hindsight, Senator Richard C. Shelby of Alabama, the senior Republican member of the Senate Select Committee on Intelligence, expressed a general exasperation at the scale of the failure when he complained: 'If you tie the general warnings together, and you put all of the bombings and attacks of the 90's together, then combine it with last summer's failures, it should have, in my judgment, had the bells ringing, all the way up. But it didn't.'[71]

Significance

Such cases inevitably lead us towards the question of whether the vast expenditures on, and obsession with, intelligence have actually made a difference. As Richard Aldrich has noted,[72] it remains the case that most diplomatic histories eschew detailed consideration of the role of intelligence. Key histories of the early Cold War and national security state in the USA, by such eminent historians as Michael Hogan and Melvyn Leffler, devote little space to the intelligence dimension of their subjects, all suggesting that the relative significance of intelligence is more limited than the agencies themselves profess to believe.[73] Military historian John Keegan has suggested that the importance of intelligence in warfare has been overestimated.[74] Indeed, a number of commentators – such as Phillip Knightley and Stephen Dorril – have argued that the achievements of intelligence are exaggerated or illusory, while another, Rhodri Jeffreys-Jones, has gone so far as to offer an interpretation of the operation and maintenance of the US intelligence services as amounting to little more than a highly successful confidence trick.[75] It is also worth noting in this respect that while the Soviet Union and Eastern bloc countries invested heavily in intelligence and counter-intelligence, the official Marxist line was that intelligence could not determine the course of history.[76] Neither did their heavy investment in intelligence enable them to maintain influence abroad or prevent the collapse of their parent states.[77]

How important, then, was intelligence to the course of Cold War history? As Michael Herman has noted, it was certainly extensive, constituting 'a central element of the Cold War, on both sides; never before was intelligence so extensive, institutionalized and prized in peacetime'.[78] But extent is not the same thing as influence. As Herman recognizes, it will be for subsequent generations of historians to provide answers to the more specific kinds of question that he has himself posed:

whether intelligence made a difference [?] Did it produce better knowledge and understanding, and a safer world? Or was it playing out and intensifying the Cold War as a self-serving game between opposing intelligence agencies? Did it contribute to its own *déformation professionelle*, demonizing the enemy and exaggerating threats in a destabilizing way?[79]

Alternatively, might it not be argued that the mutual interpenetration of hostile powers actually enhances security by reducing the possibility that one can surprise the other? These questions essentially build on the question set by intelligence historian Robin Winks. 'Academics generally work in an environment that respects knowledge for its own sake,' Winks argued, 'and merely knowing, rather than acting upon what one knows, is sufficient reward for many academics.' What is necessary is also to ask the 'effectiveness' question: 'So what?'[80] In turn, John Lewis Gaddis used this as a point of departure in his essay on the study of intelligence, warning of the need to go beyond the 'fascination of dealing with what was once surreptitious, sneaky, and sly'.[81] Even now, are we able to provide any firm answers to Winks's question?

One person who has offered an answer to these questions is the former head of the CIA's Soviet Counter-intelligence Division, the prize Soviet spy Aldrich Ames, himself the son of a career CIA officer. Ames has argued that:

> The espionage business, as carried out by the CIA and a few other American agencies, was and is a self-serving sham, carried out by careerist bureaucrats who have managed to deceive several generations of American policymakers and the public about both the necessity and the value of their work. There is and has been no rational need for thousands of agents working around the world, primarily in and against friendly countries. The information our vast espionage network acquires is generally insignificant or irrelevant to our policymakers' needs. . . . Frankly, these spy wars are a sideshow which have had no real impact on our significant security interests over the years.[82]

There is, of course, a significant degree of special pleading involved here, and there is far too much that remains unknown for such sweeping assertions to be accepted. Where the role of intelligence has been factored into key events of the last century, it can be seen to have affected the nature of events, if not necessarily their outcomes.[83] In particular, historians await access to SIGINT decrypts, which will add substantially to, and maybe alter, our understanding of key historical events.[84] There is also the difficulty of how to measure success or influence in the intelligence field. How, for example, is the 'security blanket' aspect of intelligence to be measured? How is the deterrent effect to be assessed? It could be argued that in a Cold War context, intelligence success or failure can best be measured by reference to the confidence that intelligence brought, and to the things that did not happen as a consequence of intelligence actions, or even its mere existence.

Moreover, there is the problem identified by Richard Betts, wherein 'particular failures are accorded disproportionate significance if they are considered in isolation rather than in terms of the general ratio of failures to successes; the record of success is less striking because observers tend not to notice disasters that do not happen'.[85] This picture is complicated a little more by Avi Shlaim's observation that if an act – for example, a terrorist act – cannot be carried out because intelligence agencies uncovered it in time to allow effective counter-measures to be put in place, then there is the possibility that the 'success of the intelligence services would have been expressed in the falsification of its predictions', raising questions about the accuracy of the initial analysis.[86] It is complicated further still by the fact that in an operational environment characterized by recent significant failure, intelligence agencies are likely to act more cautiously both in their drafting of analyses and in their subsequent presentation to the customer, more readily advocating counter-measures through identification of a threat which, for reasons of self-preservation, they dare not fail to flag up. Moreover, as we noted above, intelligence agencies are bureaucratic entities, and as such have a vested interest in continuation of threat – their budgets are umbilically linked to levels of threat – and so while at times willing to trumpet successes in ongoing campaigns, they have been more reluctant to acknowledge the successful end of campaigns. For example, in October 2002 George Tenet sought partially to explain the CIA's apparent failure to anticipate the events of 9/11 by reminding a congressional committee that in the previous decade Congress had cut the CIA's budget by 18 per cent in real terms, leading to a 16 per cent reduction of employees across the board.[87] In this wilderness of mirrors, it is tempting to conclude, therefore, that it is virtually impossible to measure success or failure.[88]

However, it is possible to suggest a number of indicators of intelligence agency success:

- Predictive success – analysis leading to timely warning, facilitating prevention (i.e. of surprise) or capitalization.
- Absence of predictive failure.
- Maintenance of customer trust.
- Maintenance of public trust.
- Maintenance of effective partnerships with allied intelligence agencies.
- Maintaining or enhancing the customer's relative advantage.

Conclusion: Towards a Theory of Intelligence?

This chapter concludes by posing key questions that will inform the discussion of theories of intelligence in chapter 2:

- What should we expect from a theory of intelligence?
- What should it be able to tell us? Is its purpose to provide a model that can be applied to direct us to the most important questions and generate answers that explain intelligence outcomes?

- Should it do so within the framework of liberal-democratic norms and expectations?
- What is the relationship between our definition of intelligence and a theory of intelligence?

As the foregoing discussion suggests, and the rest of this book goes on to demonstrate, any theory of intelligence needs to be able to do several things:

1 Be clear about just what we mean by intelligence.
2 Explain why it operates as it does.
3 Explain the circumstances under which intelligence succeeds or fails.
4 Inform us as citizens so as to help prevent intelligence doing more harm than good.
5 Facilitate comparative research into alternative intelligence structures.

In this opening chapter we have defined intelligence as a process of gathering and analysing information with a view to providing forewarning and to shaping policy so as to protect or enhance relative advantage. Conducted in secret, it has the potential for good by increasing public security, but can also do great harm by trampling on human rights. Therefore, as citizens we need to be prepared to ask questions that we will now go on to explore in greater detail in the rest of the book. Why is intelligence conducted? Who does it? How do they do it? What are its limits? How can it be controlled so that it does more good than harm?

How Do We Understand Intelligence?

Discovery consists of seeing what everybody has seen and thinking what
nobody has thought.

Albert Szent-Györgyi, 1937 Nobel Prize scientist, in Lathrop, *The Literary Spy*

Introduction

THIS chapter identifies the central conceptual and theoretical issues that we
must confront in order to enhance our ability to understand and explain
intelligence processes, including their role in contemporary governance. To
some, this may seem a rather tedious exercise – why not just get on with examining the more interesting and exciting aspects of intelligence? This is tempting
but would be ultimately futile – there is a wealth of literature that does nothing
but describe the real or imagined 'facts' of intelligence scandals, but, taken overall, it adds up to a highly coloured and distorted view of intelligence and its relation to government. Our objective here is different: we discuss some basic issues
of theory and method and suggest a framework for research into intelligence.
This goes beyond the parameters of this book, but we hope that it will prove
useful for other researchers and scholars.

In the last chapter we defined intelligence as *the umbrella term referring to the
range of activities – from planning and information collection to analysis and dissemination – conducted in secret, and aimed at maintaining or enhancing relative security by
providing forewarning of threats or potential threats in a manner that allows for the timely
implementation of a preventive policy or strategy, including, where deemed desirable, covert
activities.* We need to be concerned with concepts and theory in any field of studies, because of their indispensable role in generating and organizing knowledge.
The need is greater when studying intelligence, because, especially in Britain,[1]
historical accounts have always constituted the main literature. The memoirs of
former intelligence officers and, increasingly, the reconstruction of past episodes
from released official files are the raw material for the hitherto 'missing dimension' of historical studies.[2] The theoretical assumptions behind this work tend to
be those of the international relations school of 'realism': the 'great game' was
played out between states, threats could be objectively measured, and the 'truth'

of what happened discovered by the accumulation of oral and written evidence. More broadly, the study of intelligence within international relations has been situated mainly within realist/neo-realist analyses because the core concern of them all is security, notwithstanding national and regional variations in the ways in which security is defined.[3]

In the USA, greater efforts have been made to 'theorize' intelligence at the organizational level, especially the relationship between 'intelligence', 'secrecy' and 'policy', including covert action, but they are often too enmeshed in debates around the specific organization of the US intelligence community to move towards more generalizable findings.[4] David Kahn recently set out principles that, he argues, a theory of intelligence should offer in explaining the relationship between intelligence and policy, but they remain too narrowly focused on the issue of states and war for our purposes.[5] We need to examine theoretical issues more explicitly if we are to move beyond 'story-telling' and lay the groundwork for more systematic and comparative explanations of intelligence in different social and organizational contexts.

What kind of theory is most likely to be productive? The mainstream within Anglo-American social science since the 1950s has been behaviouralism with the following significant features: general law-like statements can be induced from empirical research and observation of social systems; political behaviour displays regularities; as in the natural sciences, appearance and reality are the same; and neutral 'value-free' research is possible. Knowledge claims are then tested by subsequent research and confirmed, modified or abandoned in the light of the findings.[6] This approach has its roots in positivism, which is based on the 'foundationalist' ontology: that is, the 'real world' exists independently of our knowledge, our knowledge of this world is developed by observation, and the aim of social science is to generate explanations of what 'is', not to be concerned with philosophical or normative questions of what 'ought' to be. Positivism incorporates a powerful preference for quantitative research, and the ultimate goal is prediction.[7]

The Critique of Positivism

Positivism and behaviouralism have been subject to numerous criticisms. Some can be reiterated *a fortiori* with respect to studying intelligence. Theory cannot be developed simply by accumulating observations of 'reality', but itself plays a part in determining what are relevant 'facts'. An approach relying solely on induction cannot suffice; to embark on research *about* the intelligence process (or analysis *within* it) without some prior conceptual framework, model or theory is to invite death by drowning or, at least, mental collapse in a deep sea of information.[8] Of course, this fate is routinely avoided, but only because of the *implicit* frameworks we employ. For the study of intelligence to become systematic, we must be more explicit about our frameworks; to do otherwise is at best naïve or, worse still, dishonest if our work is based on the presentation as 'scientific' of assumptions that are actually highly value-laden and contestable. To pursue the watery metaphor, as analysts we must remember Graham Allison's crucial point that we *select* the ponds in which we fish[9].

Behaviouralism is inadequate, because it requires 'observability' as a criterion for evidence and 'actors' who cause events (see further below on agency and structure). The intelligence literature is replete with accounts of individuals who claim to have had a great impact on events, either in the formation and operation of agencies or as agents working for some agency (and sometimes for several). Such historical accounts are a rich source of material, but of themselves can provide only part of the basis for more general statements about intelligence processes. Any attempt to devise a theory of intelligence is doomed if we can theorize only on the basis of what we can observe, whether or not it is from 'official' sources. For example, during an earlier UK inquiry into Iraq – that held by Lord Justice Scott between 1992 and 1996 into UK arms sales to Iraq – a British civil servant sought to defend the practice of providing answers to parliamentary questions that were less than complete by suggesting that, 'Of course half a picture can be accurate.'[10] Bearing in mind Porter's admonition in the last chapter that we should not 'believe a word of it', the problem for the student of intelligence is to know the extent to which the partial pictures we develop are accurate. Compared with other areas of governance, and according to our definition, secrecy being an indispensable condition of intelligence processes, we shall never be able to theorize in a way that behaviouralists would regard as methodologically credible.

The critique of positivism has been developed into a range of 'post-positivist' approaches.[11] One major strand of post-positive thinking is feminism, though this follows a number of different routes – for example, liberal, radical, Marxist. Although some feminists share a positivist approach by arguing that certain aspects of the nature and experience of women are universally 'true', others point to the different experiences of women as mediated by class, ethnicity, culture and sexuality.[12] There has been little, if any, direct feminist study of intelligence *per se*, but more critique of the state-centric definitions of 'security' deployed in traditional international relations.[13] The connection between states and sovereignty, backed up by the state's claim to the internal monopoly of legitimate violence and readiness to use force externally in pursuit of its interests, has led to national or state security becoming the central analytical concern.[14] The steady entrenchment of patriarchal norms through the process of state formation marginalizes the experience of many women, for whom (in)security means something quite different:

> A more comprehensive view of security, which begins by asking what, or who, most threatens particular groups of people, will disrupt any notion of 'national security', for the greatest threats to people's security in many cases are local state agents or military personnel, or 'home' men who are constructed as soldier-protectors of the very people they endanger.[15]

To the extent that most intelligence literature has 'spun-off' from international relations' concern with state or national security, then, it is equally vulnerable to this critique.

The Challenge of Postmodernism

Postmodernism is the most radical departure from positivism. Since intelligence is about the production of knowledge, with agencies operating at the cutting edge of deploying new information and communication technology (ICT), it seems entirely appropriate to explain it with an approach to social theory that itself emphasizes the significance of new information technologies in reshaping and subverting 'modernist' methods of generating knowledge. But postmodernism goes much further in its radical epistemological claim that there is no single rationality by which knowledge can be generated; there are no means of establishing 'truth' that transcend the location of the observer, and so there can be only competing 'discourses' or ways of representing or narrating events. For example, James Der Derian notes the relative under-theorization of intelligence, and argues that what there is is too positivistic in its attempt to 'discipline' global disorder. Rather, he suggests, what is needed is a 'meta-theory' that would take into account the fact that 'ambiguous discourse, not objective truth, is the fluctuating currency of intelligence'. The indeterminacy of what is seen or heard, aggravated by encoding, decoding and, possibly, deception, plus the gulf between what is said and what is meant, requires an approach rooted more in rhetoric than reason. This approach – intertextualism – 'aptly covers the field of intelligence, where there is no final arbiter of truth, meaning is derived from an interrelationship of texts and power is implicated by the contingent nature and ambiguity of language and other signifying practices'.[16] Further, the texts to be analysed are not just the 'factive' ones of national security studies, but also the 'fictive' literature of international intrigue that 'produce meaning and legitimate particular forms of *power* in their relation to each other'.[17]

For his part, Andrew Rathmell identifies five 'core' postmodern themes: the end of grand narratives, the end of the search for absolute 'truths', the fracturing of identities, increased blurring of boundaries between both approaches to explanation and states, cultures, etc.; and the emergence of the knowledge economy with its implications for organization shifts from hierarchies to networks.[18] He goes on to relate these to contemporary shifts in the intelligence business: first, the collapse of the 'grand narrative' of the Soviet threat and its replacement by a variety of rapidly changing and loosely organized targets such as transnational organized crime, proliferation and terrorism. Second, unlike the 'objective reality' of the Cold War, intelligence now does not even know 'if there is a single objective reality out there'.[19] Third, individual and collective identity is challenged, technologically by the development of human/machine systems, organizationally by doubts as to for whom intelligence is being produced – is it states, corporations, non-governmental organizations? – and by the collapse of old certainties about who is on whose side, and with respect to what. Fourth, the previously imper-meable boundaries within the intelligence community and between it and outside (state and private) organizations are dissolving in the face of the decline in the state's monopoly of expertise and consequently greater inter-changes of personnel and technologies. Fifth, the knowledge economy has hastened the demise of 'factories' for the production of intelligence just as much as it has elsewhere in commerce and government.[20] Rathmell suggests that the key implications of all this for intelligence organizations are that they should acknowledge their essential nature as a knowledge industry with the concomitant delayering, embrace horizontal knowledge networks, and accept change as 'dynamic, non-linear and accelerating'.[21]

Now, there is much here that can be agreed upon. Behaviouralist methods cannot readily capture the uncertainties, complexities and ambiguities of the world, and this applies to the work of intelligence as much as to those studying intelligence. Both practitioners and researchers seek 'facts' that others wish to keep secret and also make judgements about others' intentions, but the object of the exercise is not necessarily to discover 'truth'. Intelligence analysts seek knowl-edge with a degree of certainty sufficient to satisfy and inform those who wish to act upon it; academics are not seeking 'truth', but knowledge with a degree of reliability that will satisfy peer reviewers and standards of 'intersubjectivity'.[22] Thus, while a central part of the postmodern critique is that there are no objec-tive 'truths' towards which the social analyst can seek to progress, it is not at all clear that intelligence (or its scholars) assumed there were. Indeed, one of the reasons for the tension between intelligence professionals and political execu-tives is the very fact that the former deal in ambiguities and probabilities as they develop 'estimates' and recoil from the certainties that the latter wish to hear in their attempts to persuade mass publics as to the rightness of their cause. As noted in the last chapter, intelligence is more art than science, and, like art, is about nuance. Politicians distrust nuance.[23]

But there is something of the counsel of despair in Der Derian's argument: yes, making sense and explaining the world of intelligence is very difficult for all the reasons he enumerates. And any scholar who claimed to have ascer-tained the 'truth' of it would be a fool. But it is far from clear that his alterna-tive methodology would improve our understanding. The fictional literature of intelligence, some of which we referred to in chapter 1, may well serve useful purposes (aside from simple enjoyment) when it is a vehicle for the description of events that could not be recounted as 'fact',[24] and for its ability to explore and reveal aspects of life, as do art and fiction in general. But it would be highly misleading if we concluded that James Bond represented a typical SIS officer and, taken literally, might lead to the absurdity of Baudrillard's claim that the first Gulf War was not 'real'.[25] Rather, our purpose must be to seek ways of understanding and explaining intelligence, including by way of analysing texts, believing that useful knowledge (that which has some real existence beyond the text) can be ascertained and made use of by those seeking to improve the human condition. Der Derian is right when he reminds us that 'the piling up of documents does not lead to the truth',[26] but the doubts, enigmas and complex moral dilemmas that may accumulate can be tackled by the slow, steady development of critical theory and its modification in the light of research.

Although postmoderni*sm* is not helpful to us, we do need to pay attention to key elements of postmoderni*ty* as a description of the social and political conditions at the start of the twenty-first century, notably postindustrialism and globalization.[27] It is important, however, to consider just what is new here: it seems to us that there are some continuities which caution against any wholesale ditching of modernist methods. For example, the extent to which the threat emanating from the Soviet Union during the Cold War was represented as an 'objective reality' reflected not only Soviet capacities and actions, but also the success of specific organizational and political interests in institutionalizing that representation. To the extent that this actually misconstrued what the Soviet Union was seeking to achieve, then it was poor intelligence that can be blamed on a number of factors, such as politicization, 'mirror-imaging', 'groupthink', deception, or some toxic brew of all these[28]. It may well be that, in the more fluid conditions of post- or late modernity, the intelligence business has become even more complex; but it does not necessarily follow that our criteria for judging its effectiveness or otherwise have been transformed, as appears to be the postmodernist claim.

The decline of state sovereignty may well be a central feature of postmodernity, but national security remains the last refuge of the spook. Paradoxically, or perhaps not, as the greater fluidity of global change and relationships seems to demand the recognition by intelligence that it is just another knowledge industry, the concomitant increase in perceptions of insecurity since 9/11 see it acquiring yet more special powers for the penetration of privacy and maintenance of secrecy for its operations.[29] Rathmell's argument reflects a particular period when the attempt to replace the Cold War with a 'grand narrative' around transnational terrorism and organized crime failed to convince. But, the current centrality of the 'global war on terror' and overt concern with the nuclear activities of Iran and North Korea and the intelligence activities of China demonstrate the continued relevance of older themes. Competition and co-operation between states and corporations will dominate developments in intelligence for the foreseeable future. In generating our own signposts for this future and the tools with which to examine intelligence, we agree with Rathmell that postmodern perspectives capture some elements of the contemporary intelligence environment, but we do not accept that they provide a satisfactory theory for explaining it.

Critical Realism: Neither Positivist nor Postmodernist

In seeking to further the task of theorizing intelligence, it will be most fruitful to identify a path that avoids the major pitfalls of both positivism and post-modernism. Neither is able to develop knowledge that leads to understanding or is generalizable beyond the particularities of time and place. We must make our theoretical considerations explicit if for no other reason than intellectual honesty. 'Value-free' social science is impossible, because analysts are embedded within the socio-political context that is the subject of their study. Since analysts cannot claim 'value-freedom' for their findings, they must acknowledge what their value-assumptions are, in order that their arguments can be evaluated in that context. Analysts cannot claim superiority for their views simply because they occupy a privileged 'scientific' viewpoint from which to observe; but they can make their reasoning, methods and sources transparent to others, so that the validity of their arguments can be judged.

Thus, our objective is to establish some principles upon which progress can be made, rather than to argue for the necessary superiority of any particular conceptual framework; ultimately choice will be finalized on the basis of the personal beliefs and objectives of the analyst. There is some 'reality' in the world,[30] but the process of understanding it requires critical self-reflection on *how* we understand. Thus, theoretical and empirical work are inextricably linked:

> theory is a guide to empirical exploration, a means of reflecting more or less abstractly upon complex processes of institutional evolution and transformation in order to highlight key periods or phases of change which warrant closer empirical scrutiny. Theory sensitises the analyst to the causal processes being elucidated, selecting from the rich complexity of events the underlying mechanisms and processes of change.[31]

Neither deduction nor induction alone is adequate in social science: we do not 'discover' new events, but we do discover new connections and relations that are not directly observable and by which we can analyse already known occurrences in a novel way. This creative process of redescription, or 'abduction', is what investigators or doctors do as they test out different hypotheses or diagnoses.[32] By applying alternative theories and models in order to discern connections that were not evident, what intelligence scholars are doing is what good intelligence analysts do – but in doing so, neither group is merely describing reality as if through a clear pane of glass. They are seeking to make sense and thus actively 'create' the worlds of intelligence, government and international relations.[33]

This 'critical realism' seeks to avoid the hobbling effect of both positivism and its anti-foundationalist critics. It distinguishes elements of reality that are relatively unchanging and exist independently of the scientific process from those that change more frequently, being produced (socially constructed) as part of the scientific process.[34] Further, with positivism, it believes that causal statements can be made; while, against positivism, it accepts that not all social phenomena can be observed, and that research must therefore also seek out underlying mechanisms of events.[35]

Agency and Structure

This is a central methodological issue in exploring causal processes. Agency refers to action based on free will, so that 'actors' have some degree of choice or autonomy. Note that actors may be individual or collective – political analysis contains many references to groups, classes or states as actors. Analyses that emphasize the role of agency (sometimes to the exclusion of any role for structure) are referred to as 'intentionalist'. For example, Dennis Wrong argues that 'intentionality' is the indispensable defining characteristic of 'political power'.[36] By comparison, structure refers 'to the fact that political institutions, practices, routines and conventions appear to exhibit some regularity . . . over time'.[37] Sociologists are more likely to define structure in terms of class, ethnicity, gender and sexuality. While these may be 'deeper' structures than institutions and practices, the central point is that they provide the context or arena within which people do or do not act. Our object is not to explore the long-running debate between the proponents of intentionalism and structuralism as *alternatives*.[38] There is nothing 'essential' about the distinction: the (in)actions of any individual actor can be understood only within a range of structural contexts (group, organizational, social) and the constraints that these impose. For example, if our focus is on a specific organization such as the Cabinet, then we need to understand both its impact as a structure within which people and colleague groups interact – that is, within which bureaucratic politics[39] occurs – and as an agent acting within the broader context of state and society.

In a further refinement to the basic agency/structure relationship, Jessop suggests the incorporation of strategy. Thus agents are reflexive, capable of thinking strategically about their situation and reformulating their interests within the existing structural constraints. These, in turn, are not determined absolutely, but operate selectively and are always related to the situation of specific agents.[40] Thus, certain strategies will be favoured over others – the environment is not a level playing field. Outcomes are not structurally determined but, over time, certain outcomes are more likely to occur than others. This 'strategic-relational' approach can be summarized in the following way: the strategic actor makes (explicit or intuitive) choices within the strategically selective context that imposes limits on behaviour. The strategic action that results then produces some direct effect on the structural context (though it may be very slight, and not as intended) and provides some potential for the actor to learn.[41]

Thus, the analysis of intelligence proceeds best if agency and structure are viewed as existing in a dialectical relationship. Therefore the task for the analyst of intelligence becomes to develop a way to generalize about both how people understand, and are thus influenced by, their structural context and how their strategic actions (or inactions) impact upon that context. The context may be either empowering or constraining, and actions may amend or reinforce it. For example, in examining the actions of intelligence officers, one issue is how they view procedural rules and laws. Whether they view them as empowering or constraining will have some effect on their conduct – their original intention to act in a given situation may be reinforced, they may decide to act differently within the rules, act outside of the rules, or not act at all. In turn, these (in)actions may have short- or long-term implications for the rules – they may be seen as providing useful legal protection for officers, as unwieldy, or as so restrictive as to require amendment.

So, how to proceed? The social sciences (indeed, sciences in general) are characterized by increasing specialization. It is far from clear that this is entirely beneficial: as research and analysis focuses on very narrowly defined issues or problems, it sometimes feels as though we acquire ever more information about less and less. We specialize in ways that, not surprisingly, mirror the most obvious divisions in the world we study. So, for example, reflecting the dominance of the nation-state since the seventeenth century, political science is dominated by national studies, sub-national studies, international relations and comparative politics (as between nations).[42] While intelligence studies have clearly not escaped this dominance, for the purposes of seeking a greater generalizability, a more helpful way of characterizing the field of interest may well be to talk in terms of 'levels' of intelligence.[43]

Specifically, we suggest that five distinct levels may be deployed in order to organize our thinking about the key issues and appropriate analytic strategies. They are

- individual,
- small group,
- organizational,
- societal, and
- inter-societal.

These are convenient because they are commonly used categories that require distinct study. But we must not forget that this is an analytical device; these social 'levels' actually coexist within great complexity.[44] Yet they enable us to establish a framework for the analysis of intelligence that alerts us to factors or processes that characterize intelligence at each of these levels (thus assisting the goal of generalizability). Before examining the utility of this approach in more detail, however, we need to discuss the central concept of surveillance.

Surveillance: Knowledge and Power

We shall adopt *surveillance* as the core concept because of its importance in explaining modern governance, including the behaviour of agents and development of structures at each of the five levels identified above. Though discussed in different ways by social theorists such as Dandeker, Giddens and Foucault, there is a core of similarity in their definitions of surveillance as constituted by two components: first, the gathering and storing of information, and second, the supervision of people's behaviour. In other words, it is concerned with knowledge and power: 'Much of the study of intelligence concerns the relationship between power and knowledge, or rather the relationship between certain kinds of power and certain kinds of knowledge.'[45] Arguably, all the non-trivial study of intelligence is concerned with this relationship.

In contemporary Western social theory, surveillance is seen as the central aspect both of the establishment of modern 'sovereign' state forms[46] and of the more recent decline of sovereignty as it is replaced by 'governance' (or, for Foucault, 'governmentality'[47]), including the concomitant recognition of the significance of private forms of governance. Furthermore, studies of non-Western societies show that surveillance is similarly central there: its philosophical basis may be crucially different – for example, rooted in the rejection of individualism, but its core goals – understanding and control – are constants.[48] So, not surprisingly, global surveillance is argued to be an intrinsic part of the general economic restructuring of capitalism that is referred to as globalization,[49] and post-9/11 developments have served only to accelerate this already existing trend.[50] We defined our interest in chapter 1 as the generation of knowledge in conditions of secrecy that can inform the formation and implementation of security policy; this is essentially a subset of the more general surveillance that constitutes contemporary governance.

Levels of surveillance

States clearly depend as much on internal as external security for their well-being, but most writing on intelligence at the national or 'macro' level has concerned external intelligence within the context of international relations.[51] This was established half a century ago when Sherman Kent reflected on the agenda for post-1945 US 'strategic intelligence', and excluded from his discussion internal or police intelligence.[52] We suggest that this is no longer tenable, if it ever were. The blurring of boundaries between intelligence disciplines and attempts to 'join the dots' invalidates the analytical isolation of foreign or military intelligence from domestic. Also, there are discussions as to the possibility of organizing intelligence at a transnational level.[53] Initially, this was limited to the discussion of transnational sharing agreements[54] – a much enhanced concern since 9/11 – but now includes consideration of how intelligence can support multilateral peacekeeping.[55]

Surveillance is equally central to the 'meso'-level body of literature that has sought to explain, more specifically, how intelligence 'works' (or not) in organizations. All organizations spend some resources on seeking information about the environment within which they operate, though in many this will not be specifically organized or even referred to as 'intelligence'. Even the most humble organizations will engage in information gathering regarding their strengths, weaknesses, opportunities and threats (SWOT analysis) and those of their competitors, and will then seek to translate the findings into action aimed at better achieving their goals. But the concern here is with a more specific subset of the literature that is concerned with the examination of various 'INTS' – foreign, military, security, criminal, environmental, economic, business – and how they contribute to the goal of increasing *security*.

At the 'micro' level of individuals (cognitive psychology) and small groups (social psychology), there are extensive literatures on the processes involved in information gathering, problem solving and decision making. For example, cognitive psychology is characterized by an 'information processing' approach that makes much of the computer metaphor. The means by which information acquired *via* the senses is transformed into experience is described as 'perception', which, according to some, is direct, or 'bottom-up', while for others – constructivists – it is indirect, or 'top-down'; it 'occurs as the end product of the interactive influences of the presented stimulus and internal hypotheses, expectations, and knowledge, as well as motivational and emotional factors'.[56] 'Attention' is the term used to refer to the selectivity involved in processing; again, this may be 'top-down', when determined by the individual's goals rather than directly in response to the external stimulus. Memory involves both structure and the processes operating within the structure: encoding, storing and retrieval. This 'knowledge' has to be organized or categorized in a way that is both economical yet sufficiently detailed to be informative, and may be 'represented' internally or mentally as well as externally through language – for example, speaking, writing or drawing. The object of this thinking and reflection is to plan and solve problems by creativity, discovery, reasoning, judgement and decision making.[57] In terms of our overall argument, it is significant to note that, even in this self-proclaimed 'hardest' of the social sciences, processes of selectivity and 'construction' demonstrate the limits of behaviouralism.

Thus, we might safely assume that the desire for information is ubiquitous among individuals, groups, organizations, states and societies. Faced with uncertainty, risk, feelings of insecurity, or in search of some other goal, all human entities face a 'knowledge problem'[58] and seek information that (they hope) will reduce uncertainty, enable them to address their vulnerabilities, and advance their interests. This search is necessarily selective: complete scanning is unrealistic (which, as discussed below, is why rational actor theories can exist only as ideal-types), and therefore the criteria guiding the search are crucial. How do agents define problems in order to render them 'thinkable' for the purposes of governance – doing something about them?[59] We shall return to this later.

Producing knowledge

Information gathered can be classified as one of two main types: defensive and offensive. The object of the former is to identify one's own (personal, organizational or societal) vulnerabilities or weaknesses and the threats emanating from either external or internal sources in order to maintain the existing state of affairs by defending oneself. Risk analysis provides much of the contemporary language used to discuss threats and normally seeks to calculate two main dimensions: the magnitude of the risk and the likelihood of its occurrence. The object of 'offensive' information is to bring about change. An individual may take either intentional or habitual action to bring about some improvement in personal prospects or feelings of security; an organization may perceive the need to develop new markets (in the private sector) or improve its performance (in the public sector), while states may seek information with a view to the maintenance of public order or the acquisition of new territory. There are also significant 'grey areas' of intelligence: for example, in economic intelligence the efforts of states to gather information on competitors within the context of market economies may be defined as offensive (in terms of increasing market share) or defensive (in terms of domestic jobs).

Information is gathered in two broad ways (discussed in more detail in chapter 4): either openly through the collation of already published material and relatively passive 'environmental scanning' ('overt'), or through more aggressive techniques of penetrating the secrecy and privacy of others ('covert'). The first of these may be conducted more or less self-consciously, and the amounts of potentially relevant material available on any issue are prodigious and, thanks to the internet, readily available. Covert information gathering requires the commitment of greater resources. Expertise in the gathering of information held covertly by others is significant within 'intelligence', but covert information should not be privileged, because it is not *necessarily* more useful than open source information.

What is to be done with the information gathered? It is useful to draw the common distinction between 'information' and 'intelligence': the latter is produced by a process of analysis or evaluation of the former. Again, this process may be more or less conscious: in the case of individuals, the act of obtaining some information is often accompanied immediately by an intuitive evaluation of its meaning and significance based on the credibility or otherwise of its source and substance. On other occasions a more explicit process is undertaken in which we are forced to confront information from various sources that does not apparently 'make sense'. This is where the process of abduction identified earlier is so important. Analysis can never be reduced to induction, the simple accumulation of data; it also requires creative reasoning to compare the utility of different frames of interpretation – what is sometimes called alternative analysis.[60] Even in organizational settings, those involved in collecting information will often evaluate its meaning immediately, if only to decide whether further information needs to be sought. Thus collection and analysis often occur in a rapid cycle; indeed, there is a danger that 'process' and 'cycle' both present an image of linear neatness that rarely occurs in practice.[61] However, it remains helpful for research purposes to view stages of the process such as gathering and analysis as distinct activities. 'Facts' do not 'speak for themselves'; if they seem to, there is the danger that they will mislead. Analysis is the crucial process through which appearances are subjected to critical scrutiny.

Memory plays a key role in this collection/analysis cycle: again, this is a feature that exists at all levels. What is or is not consigned to an individual's conscious memory is itself a highly complex process involving not just the significance of the information but also the will to remember. Evaluation is carried out with respect to, for example, the veracity of sources and the consistency or otherwise of fresh information with what is already in the 'store'. One of the characteristics of the bureaucracies that came to signify the emergence of modern state forms was the maintenance of records that could provide the basis for greater consistency of decisions over time. In specialized intelligence agencies 'the files' represent the formal organizational memory that provides the structural context for current analysis. Yet organizational memories also have an informal dimension, and, to the regular frustration of those who would reform and reorganize bureaucracies, intelligence or otherwise, organizational subcultures persist, fuelled by employees' memories, preferred ways of working, and reluctance to entrust everything known to the files.

Exercising power

Collection and analysis processes may or may not be followed by 'action'; the crucial connection between 'knowledge' and 'power' (or 'intelligence' and 'policy') being provided by the dissemination of intelligence. If the 'knowledge problem' is believed to have been solved, then what can be done about the threat, the vulnerability or the ambition? Can the 'power problem' be solved? In considering this, it is useful to identify two broad theoretical streams with respect to power. The first, sometimes referred to as the 'sovereign' view of power, is principally concerned with the power that one agent may exercise over another in a 'zero' or 'constant sum' relationship. The second stream is more concerned with agents' ability to facilitate things – that is, with the 'techniques' of power – and sees power as more widely dispersed in society, rather than concentrated in 'sovereign' states or individuals. As such, power may facilitate as well as repress, and therefore is 'non-zero' or 'variable sum'.[62] Again, the point is not that one of these streams is superior to the other; it is that the analyst needs to be aware that power is contingent and may be manifested as either constant or variable sum.

Dissemination may take several forms, but what they all have in common is the link with power. Even the simple decision to pass 'intelligence' on to another person or organization will have consequences for power. We must distinguish between situations in which the intelligence disseminated is believed to be true, and thus may persuade because it is accepted on trust, and those in which the intelligence is believed to be misleading, in which case deception or manipulation are more appropriate terms.[63] But whether believed to be true or not, intelligence is itself a *form* of power: 'knowledge *is* power'. Indeed, dissemination may not be necessary in order for knowledge to have an impact: by the 'law of anticipated reactions', someone may act in a particular way as a consequence of anticipating how other participants would react were he or she to behave otherwise.[64] More generally, the same idea is at the core of the argument that surveillance breeds self-regulating subjects: the principle of the panopticon is that those surveilled base their behaviour on their understanding that they *may be* under surveillance. Thus they regulate their own behaviour despite their ignorance as to whether they actually *are* under surveillance at any particular time. This creates difficulties for analysis, since no observable behaviour on the part of those wielding power may be necessary – another illustration of the fact that understanding based entirely on empirical work will only ever be partial, if not actually misleading.

Otherwise, information is not so much a form of power in itself as a resource which can support the exercise of other forms of power – for example, material or coercive. This is the more common view, that intelligence provides the basis for policy or decisions: that people, organizations and states, if they are to act 'rationally', will do so after canvassing fully the alternative courses of action open to them and their costs and benefits. Of course, as the voluminous decision-making literature indicates, rational action is really only useful as an 'ideal-type' against which practice might be measured. Various phrases have been used to describe the messier realities of the relationship between information and action: for example, 'bounded rationality', 'garbage can' model, and incrementalism.[65] Key to these is 'selectivity', whereby a combination of prior assumptions and limited resources mean that we are very rarely willing or able to conduct a full canvass of potentially relevant information.

Indeed, as noted earlier, there can be significant tension between the conditional conclusions in intelligence and politicians' craving for certain answers. Policy tends to be formulated deductively from first principles or grounded in ideology. Intelligence is produced abductively, by evaluating the information gathered against alternative hypotheses. When they meet, the contest is uneven: 'When intelligence clashes with policy preference, intelligence loses; when information runs up against power, information is the casualty. Indeed, when information is countered by perception or, more accurately, conception, evidence is discounted.'[66] In practice, therefore, the 'normal' knowledge/power connection will be reversed, so that the urge to act pre-exists the search for information, and the significance of what is collected will be judged in terms of its ability to support a chosen course of action rather than to inform it. Here, the relation between knowledge and power is like that of lamppost and drunk, to

provide support, not illumination. As we shall see in chapter 7, just such a relationship characterized the use of intelligence by US and UK administrations in
the lead-up the invasion of Iraq in 2003.

Secrecy and resistance

There are two additional variables permeating the knowledge/power relation at
the centre of security intelligence. The first is secrecy, as we explained in chapter 1. Apart from the sheer complexity of modern society, another reason why
'knowledge problems' exist lies in the conscious effort that individuals, organizations and states make to keep their affairs secret. Individuals' privacy rights
are contained in human rights declarations and conventions because privacy is
seen as indispensable to people's dignity and autonomy. Corporations seek the
same privilege via notions of commercial confidentiality that are written into
contracts with employees and also present a significant bulwark to the work of
outside regulators. At the level of states, current ideas of 'official secrets' developed alongside modern state bureaucracies, but may be traced back further to
the notion of *arcana* in pre-modern religious states.[67] Thus, once open sources
are exhausted, the privacy of subjects presents an obstacle to surveillance that
provokes a whole panoply of covert gathering techniques. But secrecy is
significant not just as a barrier to surveillance; it permeates aspects of the
process itself. Security requires the protection of information gathered, methods and the identity of sources by means of elaborate internal procedures,
including the restricted circulation of documents on a 'need-to-know' basis. But
the consequent limitation on the availability of information can, in turn,
hinder the free flow of ideas and the quality of analysis. Secrecy may also apply
to power: some actions make no sense unless carried out with an element of
'surprise', such as arrests. But there are other, more controversial examples
where actions are taken secretly in the hope that responsibility can be disguised
or 'plausibly denied'.

   The second variable is resistance. Secrecy is one form of resistance: attempts to
maintain personal privacy or business confidentiality are forms of resistance to
the efforts of others to collect information. But if privacy fails, then lying and
deception are other forms of resistance. Evaluation or analysis is, in turn, an
attempt to resist the attempt of others to mislead. Resistance to other forms of
power such as coercion may well take on a more physical aspect, but often these
will be intertwined with the use of information. The central point here is that the
relation between surveillance and its subjects is dialectical: efforts at gathering
information and wielding power (in whatever form) will provoke greater or lesser
attempts to resist. 'Blowback' – when the unintended consequences of information and other covert operations damage the initiator of the operations – is a
particular example of 'resistance'.[68] If resistance succeeds, then fresh approaches
to surveillance may be deployed, and so on.[69]

Conclusion:
A Map for Theorizing and Researching Intelligence

Any community of scholars and researchers shares certain assumptions about the way in which knowledge claims in their field are generated. As a result of academic specialization and/or personal taste, some people choose to spend more time concerned with conceptual and theoretical issues, while others prefer to 'get their hands dirty' with empirical work. The democratization of intelligence in many countries over the past quarter-century and the accompanying avalanche of released files and papers, not to mention the increased tendency of former officers to write their memoirs, has given an extraordinary boost to scholarship in the field. However, this has been based more on an urge to provide some historical accounting for the past – the 'missing dimension' – than to reflect on how we study and write about intelligence. This is entirely understandable – in former authoritarian regimes the unearthing of intelligence secrets has been a painful but necessary part of making political progress, and even in liberal democracies it has contributed to reforms intended to reduce the likelihood of future abuses of state power.

So the production of detailed historical accounts is a necessary part of intelligence scholarship, but we need to move beyond this if we are to develop understandings and explanations of intelligence that transcend particular times and places. The theoretical assumptions that precede research are too often implicit, and thus disagreements between scholars and practitioners may be generated as much by different assumptions as by different empirical findings. Therefore, we must be explicit about the conceptual frameworks and theoretical assumptions we use. We have argued that the behaviouralist paradigm that has dominated Anglo-American social science for fifty years is inadequate because, if for no other reason, the insistence on 'observability' is entirely disabling to the study of intelligence. Yet we argue against switching wholesale to an interpretist approach. This can seem very tempting when trying to make sense of the 'wilderness of mirrors' that is intelligence. Indeed, the dichotomies of appearance and reality are precisely what the intelligence business is about. Hence any approach to theory must include an important place for the social construction of knowledge. We have emphasized issues of security and secrecy, and identify the central significance of the unknown (and possibly unknowable) in analysing intelligence. But to deny that there are any 'realities' independent of our research efforts is to disable ourselves in a different way, leaving us enmeshed in endless debates as to how we might describe the world, with no chance of proceeding further. We should heed the cautionary tale that is postmodernism, but must not allow this 'modish apparition'[70] to immobilize us.

We suggest that understanding and explanation can best be furthered by the self-conscious development of a reflexive critical theory. This proceeds by the interplay of theoretical approaches and empirical studies. The object is to produce 'knowledge' that is applicable beyond particular time/space dimensions and that can serve the purposes of all those concerned with intelligence. Whether what we produce counts as 'knowledge' will be determined by the judgements of the scholarly and professional communities. In practice, their concerns are different, but there is no necessary incompatibility between 'theory' and 'practice' in intelligence; laws, techniques, policies and practices are all informed by theoretical assumptions, and better that they be explicit and generally accepted than implicit and highly debatable once exposed. The point is that we seek to ensure that intelligence is conducted in proper and efficacious ways. Reflexive consideration of the role of intelligence in society is required: intelligence is the handmaid of public and private political power, with potentially great consequences for people's lives. Theory must be developed in such a way that it does not become a simple apologist for that power.

Of course, work of different degrees of abstraction interests people in different positions and with varying interests, but this makes it all the more important that there is some core understanding that is acknowledged as establishing basic principles of knowledge upon which more specific studies, reconstructions, policies and explanations can be built. We have suggested that the core concept be *surveillance*, understood in terms of the two components of *knowledge* and *power*. This is the best place to start because there is already considerable work regarding its significance at all levels of society from the micro to the macro, and it includes everything in which we might be interested. Yet it needs narrowing down to our field of interest, namely, *intelligence*. This can be distinguished from the generality of surveillance by the characteristics of *security, secrecy and resistance*.

Table 2.1 summarizes the argument so far. Our **research focus** is the **intelligence process** (see chapter 1). The left- and far right-hand columns indicate that intelligence needs to be studied in the light of differences between times (**historical dimension**) and places (**spatial dimension**). Studies of single agencies and countries at particular times are important, both in their own right and as potential building blocks for broader, comparative work. The **research elements** correspond to the 'levels' of analysis identified earlier in the chapter: each provides the context for, and is influenced by, the actions and dispositions of those 'below'. Put another way, each element acts as an 'agent' with respect to the level above it and as a 'structure' for the level below. Note also the concept of 'emergence': phenomena or actions at any one level cannot be explained simply by analysing processes or properties at lower 'levels'. New causal factors and mechanisms emerge at each level – the whole is greater than the sum of the parts.[71] The **theoretical approaches** identified in table 2.1 illustrate the range that already exists within social science that can be deployed by scholars and researchers. Our choice of theoretical approach will depend largely on the 'level' of our analysis, but, in order to develop our discipline, analysts must test out alternative approaches with a view to identifying those that are most fruitful. Theory performs a number of tasks;[72] here it can be used to generate propositions that can then be researched.[73] Analysts will use various **research**

Table 2.1 A map for theorizing and researching intelligence[a]

Historical dimension	Research element	Research focus: intelligence process	Theoretical approaches	Spatial dimension
↑ nature of regimes through history and of transition between regimes ↓	context a) (trans-societal)	international relations; transnational corporations; international co-operation and sharing agreements; peacekeeping	*macro a)* realism, international political economy, constructivism	↑
	context b) (societal)	macro social organization: values, traditions, forms of organization and power relations, e.g. types of regime, property ownership, governance.	*macro b)* hierarchies, markets, networks; realism, idealism, constructivism; social divisions	i) study of intelligence at different 'levels': transnational national local/regional
	setting (organizational)	**sectors of intermediate social organization:** *state*: departments, agencies *corporate*: profit-making corporations *community*: neighbourhood, community associations, non-governmental organizations (NGOs)	*meso:* incrementalism; rational action; bureaucratic politics; cybernetic systems; profit-maximization; risk-minimization; organizational cultures	ii) comparative studies
	situated activity (small group)	Face-to-face activity in small work groups, associations, etc.	*micro a)* social psychology; 'groupthink'	
	self (individual)	self-identity and individual's social experience	*micro b)* cognitive psychology	↓
Research techniques	Taking 'slices' across levels and sectors, applying theoretical approaches to case studies, for example, comparisons between states, regime transitions, intelligence 'successes' and 'failures', modifying those approaches in the light of research findings and so on . . .			

[a] The headings 'historical dimension', 'research element' and 'research focus' are derived from Layder's 'research map' in *New Strategies in Social Research*, p. 72. The headings 'sectors' and 'spatial dimension' are derived from Gill, 'Not just joining the dots', and are discussed further in chapter 3. The heading 'research techniques' is derived from Danermark et al., *Explaining Society*, pp. 101–5.

techniques as they focus on different levels of intelligence processes in order to produce the detailed empirical work we need, but individual case-studies must be conducted with an awareness of the larger picture. We know already how important are the mutual interactions between these 'levels': for example, how the organization of intelligence agencies reflects broader issues of political culture and regime type,[74] how the formal bureaucratic organization of agencies clashes with the working preferences of officers working in specialized groups. The specific need to examine organized intelligence **sectors** beyond the state is discussed in detail in chapter 3.

The consequences of the use and abuse of intelligence are clearly profound, even more so now that post-9/11 security concerns threaten to escalate into paranoia (see discussion in chapter 8). The last few years have seen unprecedented levels of public controversy regarding intelligence. If academics are to make a serious contribution to better explanation, understanding and public education on the key relationships of intelligence to law, politics, security and governance, their work must be based on an appreciation of central theoretical issues. Then they will be able to speak truth unto power and not simply find themselves conscripted as and when power finds it convenient.[75]

Who Does Intelligence?

> As presently configured, the national security institutions of the U.S.
> Government are still the institutions constructed to win the Cold War.
>
> *9/11 Commission Report*

CHAPTER 3

Introduction: Security Networks

MOST writing on intelligence has been concerned with state agencies. As we noted in the last chapter, this is hardly surprising given the state-centrism of international relations and, with respect to internal security, the central concern with the impact of state surveillance on citizens' rights and liberties. While states remain the central actors with respect to security intelligence, we must now include an analysis of corporate and other non-state security agents as part of the general shift towards 'security governance'. This has been in progress for some time: as the Cold War ended, Fry and Hochstein noted that in future, 'Intelligence activities would involve formally a network of units where sovereignty is dispersed among non-governmental actors, international organizations and corporations, and pay due attention to the worm's eye view of the world, i.e., the view from the streets.'[1]

Noting the current 'pluralization' of security governance, partly through privatization but also because of the role for private concerns enabled by property law, Johnston and Shearing argue for the adoption of a nodal (network-based) rather than a state-centred conception of governance. They identify four sets of governmental nodes: state, corporate, non-governmental organizations (NGOs) and the informal or voluntary sector.[2] This represents a development from Buzan et al.'s notion of 'security complexes' of regionally based clusters of states.[3] Yet, although security *intelligence* is central to security *governance*, Johnston and Shearing say very little explicitly about the role of intelligence. This needs to be corrected, lest it remain the 'missing dimension' of historical and government studies.[4]

At root, the idea of networks is 'of informal relationships between essentially equal social agents and agencies'.[5] Both informality and 'essential equality' are, indeed, significant in security networks: informality, because this is how they have developed in the first place – as links made between security agents for the sharing of information – and 'essential equality' because, in contrast to the ranks of formal super- and sub-ordination in police and other security organizations, what matters in a network is that you are trusted and have information with which to trade. However, neither of these tells the whole story: on the one hand, we see the slow but steady development of *formal* networks between security agencies via treaties and formal legal agreements, and on the other, some agencies and some agents are clearly more equal than others in their ability to structure networks and operate within them. Security does not depart from the general rule that networks 'link up different places and assign to each one of them a role and a weight in the hierarchy of wealth generation, information processing and power making that ultimately conditions the fate of each locale'.[6] For example, national wealth is a key factor in understanding different intelligence systems,[7] in terms not only of their independent capacities to conduct surveillance but also of their ability to trade intelligence with other states.

One reason why networks are potentially most useful for the study of developments in security intelligence is that they provide an umbrella concept for comparative study. In what has become a commonly deployed device, it has been suggested that markets, hierarchies and networks represent the three dominant modes in which social life is co-ordinated.[8] Applying this idea to security, we can see how *markets* are the organizational logic for corporate providers of private security, and *hierarchies* for traditional state policing. What, however, is the underlying model for the provision of security by NGOs and voluntary groups of citizens? The answer can be found in what Leishman[9] describes as the *communitarian* orientation in policing that has been most pervasive in Asia, although aspects have been 'borrowed' by police elsewhere. To be sure, this is a very wide category, which can incorporate neighbourhood watch schemes, victim support, Guardian Angels and, at the extreme, vigilantism. No particular position is taken here as between these; the term is used simply to describe security provision that is neither commercial nor statist, and thus in effect combines the third and fourth nodes identified by Johnston and Shearing above.

But where do *networks* fit in? Although *individual* security providers are likely to be located quite clearly within a market, state or community model, we may well find *elements* of two or all three different models within any single provider – for example, a public police force whose dominant strategy is 'community policing' and which charges citizens for services such as policing sporting events. The strength of networks is that they can map the multifarious connections *between* security agencies, whatever the precise mix of market, hierarchy and community they embody. Further, it can be suggested that networks are the most general category of co-ordination: the market resembles a security network of firms in price competition and their customers; hierarchy is a network of bureaucratically organized public police and intelligence agencies; and community is constituted by a network of voluntary and non-governmental residents and victims' groups.[10] The actual mix of these forms sets up tensions:

for example, informal intelligence sharing between security officers may develop out of frustration with the rule-bound and time-consuming formal procedures required within bureaucracies.[11]

Mapping Intelligence Networks

It has been suggested that

> Network analysis, by emphasizing relations that connect the social positions within a system, offers a powerful brush for painting a systematic picture of global social structures and their components. The organization of social relations thus becomes a central concept in analysing the structural properties of the networks within which individual actors are embedded, and for detecting emergent social phenomena that have no existence at the level of the individual actor.[12]

Figure 3.1 is an attempt to draw a picture or map of the 'territory' within which police and security intelligence networks develop. This territory is as much symbolic as physical now – while much greater use is made of information and intelligence in order to support traditional policing of people and spaces, so there have been major developments in the policing of information flows themselves.[13] Drawing a map is the relatively easy part of deploying network analysis; what is much harder is moving beyond metaphor to analyse the extent to which the network structure is an independent variable distinct from simply the actions of individual actors.[14] Ironically, perhaps, our endeavours to understand security networks mirror those facing intelligence analysts when they map criminal or terrorist networks. For all of us, providing structural maps is a complex but essential prerequisite to attempts to explain how networks operate and why.

Globalization – the process that has brought about the current territory for policing and security intelligence – manifests itself along three dimensions: a 'deepening' of levels so that there is increased interaction between local and transnational developments; a 'broadening' of sectors that are involved in governance; and spatial 'stretching', so that developments in one part of the globe can have immediate and world-wide impact.[15] All three account for contemporary security networks, but it is the second of these on which we concentrate here. We already noted in chapter 2 the utility of using appropriate theoretical approaches for the empirical study of different spatial 'levels'. Here we examine the development not only of state intelligence agencies, but also 'intelligence beyond the state' in order to pave the way for a consideration of the networks that now govern global security.

The three main sectors identified in figure 3.1 coincide with the organizational models discussed above: the state (organized in bureaucratic hierarchies), corporate security (competing in markets) and non-governmental organizations

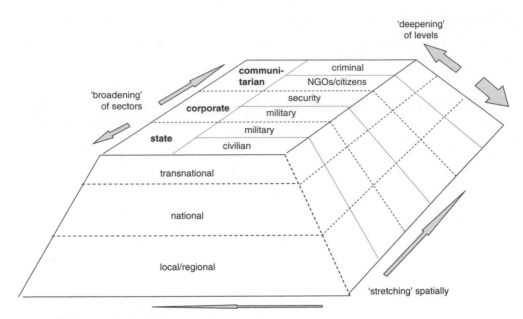

Source: Gill, 'Not just joining the dots', p. 29

Figure 3.1 Security intelligence networks

and voluntary associations (communitarian). There are, of course, many subdivisions within each of these sectors.

State sector

The most obvious division within the state sector is between civilian and military agencies, the former usually divided into 'police' and 'security', and the latter into the separate services. Various patterns for organizing civilian security intelligence exist: the main question is how separate domestic intelligence should be from mainstream policing. In the USA and Canada it developed as part of policing at the national or federal level, with both the FBI and the Royal Canadian Mounted Police (RCMP) having special sections devoted to counter-intelligence, counter-subversion and so on. UK police also developed 'special branches' with similar functions, but the main internal security agency since 1909 has been MI5. However, the police/security distinction has become more blurred recently because of the police's own embrace of 'intelligence-led policing' and deployment of techniques of surveillance long used by security intelligence.

Police intelligence

Police intelligence developed only slowly in the UK: specific criminal intelligence squads were established first in London after World War II, and by the mid-1970s all forces and their constituent divisions had some criminal intelligence capacity, though it was often poorly developed. Regional criminal intelligence offices were created in 1978 to complement the work of the regional crime squads, and in the 1990s the National Criminal Intelligence Service (NCIS) was formed from the merger of the regional offices but also incorporated Customs personnel and civilian analysts. Also in the early 1990s, arguably in the face of the discrediting of then current crime control policies, the notion of 'intelligence-led policing' was promulgated with the intention of intelligence techniques being applied not just to organized but also to volume crime. To reinforce this, a National Intelligence Model was published in 2000.[16] In the USA it is not always easy to disentangle the development of police intelligence aimed at 'political subversion' from that aimed at 'rackets' or organized crime: in the main urban centres anti-radical 'Red Squads' were established in the wake of the 'red scare' of 1919–20 and during the 1950s squads targeting 'organized crime' were established. The similarities derived from the common ideological pedigree, that is, threats of subversion, corruption and organized crime were believed to emanate from ethnic and foreign conspiracies that required special powers for covert investigation.[17]

Police intelligence with a more specifically political and security emphasis started earlier in the UK, with the establishment of Special Branch in the London Metropolitan Police in 1883 in response to Irish Republican bombings, but it was the 1960s before all forces formed their own branches. The key feature of police special branches in the UK is that, while they are part of their parent police force in terms of budget, recruitment and direction, their day-to-day activities are determined largely independently of other policing objectives and mainly by current MI5 priorities. Branches vary widely in size: in general they are largest in those forces with significant ports (especially those serving Ireland, since the Port Units were responsible for the surveillance of travellers to and from Britain), while in many forces they are quite small. Their official functions are summarized in guidelines issued by the Home Office, first published in 1984 when controversies around the activities of special branch officers at the time of the miners' strike and the peace movement prompted the House of Commons Home Affairs Committee to conduct the first parliamentary inquiry. Updated since, these identify the role of the branches generally 'to acquire intelligence' both to meet local policing needs and to assist MI5 in their role of protecting national security.[18] The mandate is detailed by reference to terrorism, including personal protection, firearms and explosives offences where there is a security connection, animal rights extremism, public order and immigration. Controversies surrounding the role of special branch officers have followed as night follows day, because their roles require them to monitor what is normally entirely peaceful political and campaigning activity. For example, anyone organizing a protest meeting or march may find themselves under surveillance, because the police 'need accurate assessments of the public order implications',[19] and in the post-9/11 security panic their role in assisting with 'immigration enquiries'[20] may be highly tendentious if undertaken aggressively in a climate of anti-Islamism.

In the wake of the 1992 decision that MI5 would take over from the Metropolitan Police the lead role in countering Irish Republican terrorism in Britain and the Provisional Irish Republican Army (PIRA) cease-fires later in the 1990s, it appeared that there would be a move to integrate special branches more thoroughly into criminal investigation divisions, but any moves in this direction have not survived 9/11. A review of special branches conducted by Her Majesty's Inspectorate of Constabulary (HMIC) in 2002 confirmed the semi-detached status of special branches in terms of the security requirements of their work, and the continuing significance of MI5 in providing training and co-ordination.[21] Following publication of this report, the government announced, as part of a broader paper on counter-terrorism powers, that it was establishing a specific post to oversee national co-ordination of special branches and regional special branch intelligence cells.[22] Partly as a result of the 7 July 2005 bombings in London, the Metropolitan Police has announced that its special branch will merge with the Anti-terrorist Squad to create a new Counter Terrorism Command that will eventually include 2,000 officers.[23]

Domestic security intelligence

After 1909 the size of MI5 fluctuated, increasing significantly during the two World Wars and dropping back between them. The onset of the Cold War meant that it remained nearer the wartime level, and from the 1970s onwards the number of personnel was around 2,000, of whom about one in six were case officers and analysts, with the rest as technical, administrative and other staff. It was not until 1989 that a statutory mandate was passed. What prompted this was the realization in Whitehall that a case pending before the European Court of Human Rights (ECtHR) concerning the surveillance of people working at the (then) NCCL was almost certain to succeed in the light of developing jurisprudence that intrusive surveillance must be authorized by legislation and that citizens must have a mechanism for the redress of grievances against security agencies.[24]

In the 1989 Security Service Act, the function of MI5 is described as

> the protection of national security and, in particular, its protection against threats from espionage, terrorism and sabotage, from the activities of agents of foreign powers and from actions intended to undermine parliamentary democracy by political, industrial or violent means. It shall also be the function of the Service to safeguard the economic well-being of the United Kingdom against threats posed by the actions or intentions of persons outside the British Islands.[25]

In 1996, 'support of the prevention and detection of serious crime' was added.

As a consequence of the greater openness regarding security intelligence matters in the 1990s, we now have more official information than before regarding the allocation of resources to different areas of the mandate: in 1993 the first public announcement and press conference of a new director general of MI5 – Stella Rimington – was accompanied by the publication of a corporate brochure that was updated in 1996 and 1998. Now, the information is updated

Table 3.1	Security Service resources in main intelligence areas (per cent)				
	1990/1[a]	1995/6[a]	1998/9[b]	2002/3[c]	2004/5[d]
Counter-espionage	50.0	–	24.4	14.6	11.5
Counter-proliferation	–	25.0	4.2	4.5	2.3
Counter-terrorism	37.5	72.0	63.1	68.5	77.0
– international	*20.0*	*33.0*	*26.8*	*37.1*	*50.6*
– Irish & other domestic	*17.5*	*39.0*	*36.3*	*31.5*	*26.4*
Counter-subversion	12.5	3.0	–	–	–
Serious crime	–	–	8.3	9.0	4.6
Emerging threats and international assistance	–	–	–	3.4	4.6

Source: [a] MI5, *The Security Service* 2nd ed (London: HMSO, 1996), p. 17.

Source: [b] <www.mi5.gov.uk>, accessed 22 May, 2001.

Source: [c] <www.mi5.gov.uk>, accessed 19 June, 2003.

Source: [d] <www.mi5.gov.uk>, accessed 25 June, 2005.

from time to time on the website: <www.mi5.gov.uk>. While reading table 3.1, it needs to be remembered that 12–13 per cent of MI5's budget is consumed by protective security advice to government and private firms who are either engaged in security and defence contracting and/or perceived to be otherwise vulnerable. The figures in the table have been adapted to take that into account.

Even as the Cold War drew to a close, in 1990/1, counter-espionage was still the main target, and counter-subversion – historically the most controversial part of the mandate, since, as with special branches, the definition required the surveillance of a range of lawful political activity – was still a significant activity. In 1995/6, counter-espionage had disappeared entirely, though it seems to have been partly replaced by counter-proliferation as a result of the then new discourse of post-Cold War threats. Counter-subversion had almost disappeared, while counter-terrorism had doubled. This reflected not just the new world disorder, but also that MI5 had taken over lead responsibility for Irish Republican terrorism in 1992. In 1998/9, counter-espionage was back on the official agenda, and counter-terrorism work had declined somewhat, reflecting the cease-fire in Northern Ireland. Work supporting NCIS and the police with respect to organized crime featured for the first time after the 1996 addition to the mandate. Since 9/11 there has been a significant increase in resources allocated to international terrorism, and in 2004 the Home Secretary announced that MI5 was to increase by 50 per cent over the next three years.[26] This would be rapid growth for any organization to absorb in such a time, but for one in which recruitment procedures are particularly lengthy because of vetting requirements, it is a major challenge. Furthermore, there is clear tension between the need for rapid recruitment of, say, linguists, on the one hand, and the risk of the organization being infiltrated by those it is targeting, on the other.

In the USA, as a police agency, the FBI has always struggled to face in several different directions. Hoover's development of domestic political intelligence programmes from the 1930s onwards led to a massive scandal after his death, and the Bureau was reoriented towards white-collar and organized crime in the 1970s, though it retained responsibility for counter-intelligence.[27] In May 2001, despite some rhetoric about the importance of counter-terrorism, FBI budget allocations reflected concerns with gun crime, drugs trafficking and civil rights.[28] In the wake of 9/11, fundamental criticisms were made of the Bureau; mainly that, as a 'law enforcement' agency that saw its primary goal as making cases against people who might then be prosecuted, the agency was simply unsuited to intelligence work aimed at the prevention of terrorist attacks. Other criticisms made of the Bureau were of its chronically inadequate ICT and its inability to conduct all source analysis.[29]

The Bureau was apparently in the grip of sclerosis, in which following agreed procedures took priority over imaginative investigative work, to the extent that, it was argued, possible chances to prevent the 9/11 attacks were lost. For example, Zacarias Moussaoui, possibly the '20th hijacker', was detained in Minneapolis in August 2001 for having overstayed his visa after suspicions arose as to his behaviour at a flight school. FBI agents wanted to search his laptop computer, but FBI headquarters ruled that there was insufficient 'probable cause' to apply to the US Attorney's office in Minneapolis for a warrant. In order to obtain a warrant under the Foreign Intelligence Surveillance Act, the FBI would have needed to show that Moussaoui was an 'agent of a foreign power'. Relevant information was sought in London and Paris, but substantial disagree-ment remained between Minneapolis agents and FBI headquarters: accusations from the latter that the former were exaggerating the threat reportedly brought the comment from a Minneapolis agent that he was 'trying to keep someone from taking a plane and crashing into the World Trade Center'. George Tenet was briefed on Moussaoui in August, but drew no connection between him and the other increased threat reporting during the summer of 2001.[30] This and other examples have been used as a reason for dismantling the so-called wall erected between law enforcement and intelligence gathering after the abuses under Hoover exposed in the 1970s, but, arguably, the problem was less an issue of the inappropriateness of legal standards to counter-terrorism and more one of over-bureaucratization of decision-making procedures. Rapidly dismantling these protections in the wake of 9/11 runs the risk that history repeats itself – the FBI concentrates surveillance on people whose politics may be in opposition to US policy and/or specific Middle Eastern regimes but who pose no *security* threat.

Interestingly, similar criticisms that police agencies are unsuited to security intelligence work were made by the McDonald Commission in Canada when it investigated wrongdoing by the RCMP and provided the basis on which the civil-ian CSIS was created.[31] The issue of whether the USA should follow the same path has certainly been on the agenda, but the 9/11 Commission recommended against it.[32] Rather, strenuous efforts are under way to re-focus the Bureau away from 'law enforcement' and towards counter-terrorism; indeed, CIA personnel were deployed to advise the Bureau on establishing its new Office of Intelligence.[33]

The FBI is formally located within the Justice Department, which includes also the Drug Enforcement Administration (DEA) – another agency much involved in intelligence. The other five national civilian intelligence agencies are located in the Energy Department (covering, for example, nuclear proliferation), the Bureau of Intelligence and Research (INR) in the State Department, which draws on classified diplomatic reporting, the Treasury Department (covering *inter alia* taxation and money laundering) and the CIA. The newest kid on the US domestic intelligence block is the Information Analysis and Infrastructure Protection (IAIP) division of the Department of Homeland Security established in the wake of 9/11. It was not intended that IAIP conduct its own intelligence operations, but rather that it should conduct assessments of the information from its own personnel such as border guards and secret service plus whatever is shared by CIA and FBI.[34] However, three years later, it appeared that IAIP had been trying to develop its own sources, albeit with little success. Therefore it seemed likely that the original intention would be resurrected and that it would concentrate on co-ordinating the intelligence efforts of its own constituent agencies and disseminating intelligence to state and local governments and the private sector.[35]

Foreign intelligence

As we showed in chapter 1, in the popular imagination, intelligence work centres on foreign intelligence agencies conducting espionage and covert operations against real or imagined enemies. Academic work, too, has concentrated on this aspect, as intelligence has been seen as part of the international relations story, and therefore it is hardly surprising that probably the best-known intelligence agencies in the world are the US's CIA,[36] MI6 in the UK,[37] and the Soviet KGB.[38] The main difference between these agencies is that the KGB conducted both foreign and domestic intelligence and was the central element of what John Dziak called the Soviet 'counter-intelligence' state.[39] Although both the CIA and MI6 have on occasion become involved in their respective domestic politics, this was of an entirely different order to the ubiquity of the KGB in Soviet life and, perhaps, the role of its Russian successor, the FSB.

The CIA was established by the National Security Act 1947 as the successor to the wartime Office of Strategic Services (OSS). Originally intended as primarily an agency for the collection and analysis of foreign intelligence, it quickly developed two main functions, one for analysis and the other for covert operations. It is the latter that is primarily responsible for the agency's reputation – for good or ill – as the agency was in the forefront of US postwar policy to contain communism behind the Iron Curtain. The agency was therefore embroiled in all the accompanying political controversies in Central and

South America – including the abortive invasion of Cuba in 1961 at the Bay of Pigs, subsequent attempts to assassinate Fidel Castro with Mafia assistance,[40] and the successful attempt to destabilize the elected government of Chile in 1973 that led to the killing of President Salvador Allende and the installation of the Pinochet dictatorship.

With regard to this latter case, in 2000 the CIA released 16,000 documents covering the Pinochet era and its role in the *coup* that ushered it in.[41] President Nixon personally ordered the CIA intervention in Chile as soon as Allende was elected and before he had assumed office. DCI Richard Helms's handwritten note of a September 1970[42] White House meeting outlined the framework dictated by Nixon:

- 1 in 10 chance perhaps, but save Chile!
- Worth spending
- Not concerned risks involved
- No involvement of embassy
- $10,000,000 available, more if necessary
- full-time job – best men we have
- game plan
- make economy scream
- 48 hours for plan of action

After the US Ambassador to Chile pointed out that constitutionalist commander-in-chief of the Chilean armed forces, General René Schneider, represented an obstacle to plans to either prevent Allende from assuming office or remove him thereafter by means of a *coup*, the CIA became involved in a plan to kidnap Schneider.[43] During the kidnap attempt, Schneider was killed. The following day a telegram from the director of the CIA Chile Task Force in Langley congratulated those involved: 'The Station has done excellent job of guiding Chileans to point today where a military solution is at least an option for them. COS [and others involved] are commended for accomplishing this under extremely difficult and delicate circumstances.'[44] The destabilization programme was antithetical to notions of democracy[45] and culminated in the 11 September 1973 *coup* in which Allende died.

More recently, it was the analytical side of the agency that fell into disrepute as its estimates of Iraqi WMD turned out to be entirely inaccurate (as discussed in chapter 7). By comparison, MI6 managed to remain within the shadows, at least until 2003. Indeed, until 1992 its existence outside wartime was not even officially acknowledged by the government. In a more relaxed government environment after the fall of Margaret Thatcher, the end of the Cold War, and, encouraged by the fact that the sky had not fallen in when the Security Service Act 1989 was passed, the Major Government passed the Intelligence Services Act 1994 (ISA) that provided statutory mandates for both SIS and its SIGINT partner, Government Communications Headquarters (GCHQ – see further below) and also established the Intelligence and Security Committee (ISC) to oversee the agencies (the ISC is discussed in chapter 8). However, the ISA presaged no heady rush into the sunlight by MI6 – it was October 2005 before it launched its own website, available in French, Spanish, Russian, Chinese and Arabic, as well as English, incorporating brief information on the agency's role, relevant legislation, available careers and a potted history.[46] Compare this with the CIA website with a run-down on official history, organization, recruitment, a 'virtual tour' and a special section for children![47] Up to a point, CIA and MI6 self-descriptions are analogous: they both gather information with respect to threats to national interest and conduct operations to pre-empt or disrupt these threats. Where they differ is in the role of analysis: the CIA describes this as one of its three missions, whereas MI6 says it does not recruit specialist analysts. This reflects the different US and UK systems for the production of national-level assessments that we discuss below.

Signals intelligence

Complementing the domestic and foreign intelligence agencies in those countries wealthy enough to afford the major investment involved are what are usually referred to as SIGINT (signals intelligence) agencies. The US National Security Agency (NSA)[48] and GCHQ[49] both have offensive and defensive functions: the first is the interception of the communications of others (states, armies, companies, etc.), and the second is 'information assurance' – protecting the state's own communications from interception and disruption by others. Historically, they have developed out of code-breaking efforts in wartime, and during the Cold War they represented the cutting edge of technological developments in cryptography. Currently they face major problems as a result of the ICT revolution: for example, the sheer increase in volume of communications overloads the ability of the agencies to process information despite developing sophisticated tools for selecting messages of interest, while digitization, fibre optics and commercial encryption make interception harder. Whereas during the Cold War the agencies had one central target – Soviet military capabilities – they have now been enlisted in the surveillance of the other more mobile security threats: terrorism, proliferation and organized crime. For example, the former UN weapons inspector in Iraq, Scott Ritter, has provided a fascinating account of how SIGINT was deployed to counter Iraqi deception in the mid-1990s.[50]

Military intelligence

Formally, military intelligence is concerned with the conduct of tactical and strategic intelligence in support of military operations. The more broadly these are defined, the more likely it is that military intelligence will spill over into the surveillance of civil society and political life. Military agencies have the broadest functions in regimes that could be characterized as 'national security states' (see chapter 1), and have been involved in the surveillance of their own civilians as much as, if not more than, potential foreign enemies. Twenty years ago, internal security surveillance was still the main task of military intelligence agencies in a number of Latin America and Eastern European regimes, but has also been carried out in democratic regimes – for example, illegal operations carried out in the USA by the army under the guise of counter-intelligence.[51] In the last quarter-century, one aspect of the democratization of intelligence in former authoritarian regimes has been to replace military with civilian agencies – for example, in Brazil.[52] Currently, there is concern that, to the extent that fears of terrorism are defined as a 'War on Terror', there is a risk of military agencies again becoming too significant in civil society – to get a sense of this, look no further than Northern Ireland since 1969.[53]

In the UK and the USA, state military intelligence is basically organized within each service, plus some mechanism for joint assessments; in the UK, for example, the Defence Intelligence Staff (DIS) provides a central assessment process for military intelligence. In the USA the parameters of organization are similar, but complicated by the sheer size and extreme fragmentation of the military and intelligence establishment. There are nine national intelligence organizations within the Defense Department: one for each of the four Services; the Defense Intelligence Agency (DIA) that both runs military espionage agents and provides assessments similar to the DIS in the UK; the National Reconnaissance Office (NRO) with responsibility for spy satellites; and the National Geospatial Agency (NGA), which interprets satellite imagery and prepares world maps.

Central intelligence assessments and security co-ordination

One of the paradoxes facing those countries wealthy enough to maintain a variety of different intelligence agencies collecting information by different technical and human methods is how to make sense of the masses of information and possible competing analyses that result. For example, in the USA the CIA is just one of a number of agencies seeking to collect and analyse intelligence, and the Agency also housed the National Intelligence Council that sought to produce National Intelligence Estimates (NIEs) from the combined efforts of all the agencies. This would often result in fierce bargaining, and dissent from majority views might be reflected in footnotes, as in the infamous October 2003 NIE on Iraq that we discuss in chapter 7.

In the UK the system is far less fragmented: the collection agencies send their product both directly to customers (if they believe it important enough) and to the Joint Intelligence Committee (JIC) structure in the Cabinet Office.[54] JIC, located within the Cabinet Office, represents the main instrument for determining collection priorities and providing a national assessment of what is gathered. JIC consists of the heads of the three intelligence agencies (MI5, MI6 and GCHQ), the head of defence and intelligence at the Foreign Office, the Chair of DIS, and senior representatives from the Ministries of Defence, Trade and Industry, Treasury and the Home Office. Other departments attend the weekly meetings when necessary. The Butler Report described the JIC's main function as to provide ministers and senior officials with co-ordinated intelligence assessments on a range of issues of immediate and long-term importance to national interests, primarily in the field of security, defence and foreign affairs.[55]

Further insight into the actual workings of the JIC and its assessments staff was provided by witnesses to the Hutton Inquiry. The then Chair of the JIC, John Scarlett, described the basic JIC process to Lord Hutton: 'raw intelligence' is issued by the collection agencies together with their evaluation to customers in the policy departments and to relevant JIC assessment staff. The actual work programme for staff is set by an interdepartmental group chaired by the chief of the assessment staff responding to requests from policy departments. An initial draft of an assessment would be prepared by the relevant staff officer based on her own expertise and contacts in Whitehall. This would be circulated to interested parties for comments and then go before a formal meeting of an interdepartmental Current Intelligence Group (CIG). Chaired by one of the deputy heads of assessment staff, this would agree a new draft for recirculation and, after any further changes, presentation to a full meeting of the JIC. After any further changes that JIC 'almost always' makes, the approved assessment would be circulated.[56] As well as the text of the assessment that seeks to answer the questions raised by the sponsors, it includes a section of 'key judgements' in which the JIC states its formal view on the central questions posed within the broader context of other JIC assessments, open sources and so on.[57]

The split between assessment for 'intelligence' and 'security' purposes was indicated in the UK by the relative autonomy of MI5 from JIC targeting decisions and the separate committee structure for protective security advice. The post of Intelligence Co-ordinator was established in 1968 to attempt to overcome interdepartmental rivalries. In its first published summary of the *Central Intelligence Machinery*, the government said:

> The Intelligence Co-ordinator advises the Secretary of the Cabinet on the co-ordination of the intelligence machinery and its resources and programmes. He chairs various formal and informal groups charged with intelligence management. He has particular responsibility for reviewing the UK's intelligence requirements and for advising on the allocation of resources to enable the Agencies to meet them.[58]

The description of the role remained essentially unchanged until 2001, since when the post reflects a greater concern with 'security'. When Sir David Omand was appointed as Security and Intelligence Co-ordinator in the summer of 2003, the status was increased to that of a Permanent Secretary, and he replaced the Cabinet Secretary as the senior security adviser to the Prime Minister.

Immediately after 9/11, a Counter-Terrorist Analysis Centre (CTAC) was established, staffed mainly by MI5.[59] Review of these arrangements was still under way when the Bali bombing occurred in October 2002 and provided further rationale for a Joint Terrorism Analysis Centre (JTAC) that started operating in

June 2003. This had more staff from agencies other than MI5: mainly from MI6, GCHQ and DIS, but with others from the Foreign and Commonwealth Office, Home Office, Police, Cabinet Office, Office of Nuclear Safety and Department of Transport Security Division (TRANSEC). JTAC sought to overcome the problems of information sharing in the normal fashion of 'task forces' by ensuring that each representative had access to their home database.[60] A year later, the ISC was complimentary about the early performance of JTAC as it developed all-source 'security' assessments to parallel those of the JIC regarding 'intelligence'.[61]

There have been problems with the co-ordination of both intelligence and security assessments in the UK, but, compared with those in the USA, they are nothing. The National Counter Terrorism Center (NCTC) started work in May 2003, providing all-source analysis of terrorist threats. It was initially located at CIA headquarters, but will eventually be located elsewhere, together with the Counterterrorist Center (CTC) and the FBI's Counterterrorism Division. The NCTC will develop its own database and be able to task collection and analysis by other intelligence community agencies and networks. It is difficult to see how these changes have reduced the possibilities for confusion. The NCTC, CIA and CTC now all have analytical responsibilities regarding international terrorism, while FBI's Counterterrorism Division and IAIP share analytical work for domestic terrorism.[62] On top of this, of course, is the myriad of inter-agency groups seeking to co-ordinate across the broader and highly fragmented law enforcement community at federal, state and local levels.[63]

Another structural flaw at the heart of the US intelligence structure has been the designation of the CIA director also as the Director of Central Intelligence (DCI) with the role of co-ordinating intelligence. But the DCI has never been able to 'co-ordinate' the Department of Defense, which controls the lion's share – about 80 per cent – of the intelligence budget, and is institutionally bound to see the main function of intelligence as support for the military. This flaw has been exposed repeatedly: for example, by both the 9/11 and Silberman–Robb commissions (see further discussion in chapter 7), and, following their recommendations,[64] the Intelligence Reform and Terrorist Prevention Act 2004 established a new Director of National Intelligence (DNI) with greater formal authority over the fifteen intelligence agencies. Initial signs are that, while the DNI's appointment reflects a loss of prestige and autonomy for the CIA, the Pentagon has retained its essential autonomy, and the problem of 'co-ordinating' the fragmented US system will remain.[65]

Corporate sector

In the corporate sector there is a wide range of security providers. These are divided into civilian (or security) and military in figure 3.1, since some companies are fairly clearly one or the other, but others operate within both sectors. Distinguishing between private security (PSCs) and private military companies

(PMCs) is useful, since they are likely, respectively, to be deployed defensively or offensively, though they are likely to merge in conflict zones.[66] Not only does private sector security provision have a very long history, but, more importantly, it has been for the direct benefit of states as well as corporate clients. Pinkerton, for example, did not just provide 'low policing' functions of guarding and watching for corporate clients, but 'high policing' surveillance of labour activists and intelligence activities on behalf of the US government during the Civil War.[67] There is now an extensive literature on private security in general,[68] but less on the extent to which 'intelligence' is a specific part of these activities.[69]

Corporate security tends to be either organized in specialist departments or provided by outside contractors. The security sector has seen a wave of mergers and acquisitions in recent years; for example, in July 2004 Securicor and Group 4 merged into a group whose joint turnover in 2002–3 had been £3.8 billion. Both groups are best known for their provision of technical security systems and guarding and patrolling services, but they still offer 'consultancy and risk audit services' that incorporate elements of security intelligence.[70] The group's US-based division is Wackenhut, whose Consulting and Investigation Services offer forensic accounting, fraud detection, litigation support (including case and document analysis), investigative due diligence (when dealing with new customers and potential partners), surveillance (for example, videotaping suspected incidents), and undercover services, where 'a skilled investigator, posing as an employee, is placed into an unsuspecting workforce to gather information on workplace problems'.[71] Acknowledging the problems of providing a wide diversity of expertise around the globe, Wackenhut has sought to develop its own network of 'Strategic Alliance Partners'. Securitas, founded in Sweden in 1934, embarked on an aggressive acquisition policy in the 1990s, taking over well-known firms such as Burns International and Pinkerton. The latter acquisition in 1999 made Securitas the world's largest security company. Offering a range of security systems, security services and cash handling, the company strategy is continued expansion from its current position of having 8 per cent of the global security market.[72] Pinkerton, in turn, has outsourced its Global Intelligence Services to iJET Travel Intelligence Link, which provides clients with travel-related intelligence relating to security, financial, legal and other factors for more than 460 destinations. Clients may also obtain daily intelligence briefings, monthly intelligence reviews, country security assessment services and other 'travel risk management solutions'.[73]

Military Professional Resources Inc. (MPRI) was founded in 1987 by eight retired military officers, and is engaged primarily in military contracting, but with law enforcement expertise also. It is not large in terms of number of employees – 1,500 – but draws its workforce on a contracting basis from a database of more than 12,500 former military and other personnel. It was involved in South-East Europe in training both the Bosnian and the Croatian armies, and is generally credited with having carried out, at one remove, the US policy of neutralizing the Serb military in the mid-1990s.[74] Control Risks Group, founded in 1975, appears to bridge the civilian and military sectors, offering government and corporate clients a range of services, including political and security risk analysis, investigations, pre-employment screening, crisis management and information security. Political risk analysis includes due diligence investigations into potential partners, especially in countries where risks and uncertainties exist, including 'where single-issue action groups are active'.[75] Thus these risks extend beyond the normal concerns with violence or kidnap into criminal and environmental areas, and are examined through a Total Risk Assessment Methodology (TRAM) that identifies, evaluates, assesses and offers management advice on the handling of risk.[76] The current occupation of Iraq has seen the involvement of unprecedented numbers of private military personnel and contractors,[77] and Control Risks has established a project office there that is, so they claim, providing security management services for government departments, companies and NGOs.[78] Concerns have been aired both about the risks run by security personnel as they carry out the work of the regular military and the lack of regulation or accountability of these private firms.[79]

Communitarian sector

NGOs are an element of civil society that need to be included, since they have a crucial presence in areas of insecurity and carry out their work in conjunction with state agencies. Personnel involved in aid, migration or peacekeeping functions may well find themselves, knowingly or unknowingly, part of security intelligence networks. Individuals and voluntary groups are involved in local security networks in various ways: for example, 'gated' communities – either horizontal on private estates or vertical in apartment blocks – or other neighbourhoods which may buy in the services of a private contractor or establish watch schemes to mobilize collective community resources. From a different perspective, Deibert identifies the development of citizen intelligence networks from the merging of NGOs, activists and computer hackers.[80] Communities based on shared cultural beliefs and practices may also organize their own security, and individuals have always provided for their own security via the right of self-defence, though some have always been able to afford a great deal more than others.[81]

The issue of citizens deploying self-defence can be quite controversial – witness the recent debate in the UK as to just how much violence householders should be permitted to use on intruders – but there is less ambiguity when it comes to individuals involving themselves in information gathering. For example, *Crimestoppers* is an innovation whereby individuals who provide information anonymously leading to an arrest or a conviction may be paid a reward, funded by the private sector.[82] After 9/11, US Attorney General John Ashcroft sought to introduce a programme called TIPS whereby millions of American workers would involve themselves in reporting suspicious behaviour or people, but the scheme foundered on a wave of opposition. Yet some still envisage a much wider role for citizens than merely that of self-defence. Robert Steele argues vigorously for a 'citizen-centred intelligence' on the grounds that the public – the 'intelligence minutemen of the twenty-first century' – can rely only on themselves, not on elites, to protect their interests.[83] Some people apparently need little encouragement: it is estimated that about forty citizen militias voluntarily patrol US borders with Mexico and Canada.[84]

Finally, we need to acknowledge the place of illegal organizations. First, they are themselves most likely to resemble networks: the idea of criminal networks provides a common discourse among investigators and analysts, and they use social network analysis (SNA) in order to map the networks specifically to identify their strengths and weaknesses, in order to formulate strategies of disruption.[85] But, crucially, they may, on occasion, be involved in networks with legal organizations – for example, if state agencies wish to 'subcontract' illegal operations because of the risks they run if exposed. This may involve just information gathering, but, far more controversially, state agencies may subcontract *covert action* – for example, the use by the CIA of organized crime to attempt to assassinate Castro in the 1960s, the deployment of 'death squads' by authoritarian regimes in several Latin American countries,[86] and the 'collusion' between British intelligence and loyalist paramilitaries in the assassination of Republicans in Northern Ireland (see chapter 5). There is a wide variety of groups that might be involved: some might amount to 'para-states'[87] that challenge the state's legitimate monopoly on the use of force; others will be criminal enterprises; and yet others will be national liberation movements. At different times any of these may be agents of state intelligence, and therefore be part of a broader network of security governance.[88] More broadly still, the very social and insurgent movements against which state agencies deploy resources may actually be created by the actions and inactions of state and corporate powers – if not directly, then in the sense that those movements are reacting to the impact of the conditions created or sustained by the powerful.[89]

Cross-sectoral networks

Networks may develop within and/or between any of these three dimensions. States or corporations will often appear to be the 'dominant node' or partner in a security network; but Johnston suggests that, in general, the most productive view to take is of 'a changing morphology of governance in which partly fragmented states interact with commercial, civil and voluntary bodies both within and across national jurisdictional boundaries'.[90] Similarly, Deibert identifies 'transnational networks of citizen activists weaving in and around the traditional structures of state interaction'.[91] Security companies and NGOs themselves maintain intelligence capacities in network form as they operate globally and within specific nations and localities – that is, as a form of multi-level governance. The development of 'local security networks' between agencies both public and private[92] and citizen groups provide clear examples of cross-sectoral networks, and other examples can be found at regional, national and transnational level. Some 'networks' may be little more than a euphemism for state police and security officials who act also as 'corporate' or 'citizen' vigilantes. For example, up to 200 Italian police and former intelligence officials were under investigation in 2005 for having set up a private security firm called the Department for Anti-terrorist Strategic Studies, specializing in counter-terrorism. Allegedly, they maintained their own weaponry and accessed Ministry of Interior databases.[93]

Clearly there must be some shared interest in order to bring the actors into the network in the first place. It is not difficult to identify the interest shared by many Western states and corporate security providers, summed up as it is by the neo-liberal preference for market provision of security (along with all other services) subject to steering by states. But the actual nature of relationships must be subject to empirical validation, and conflicts may occur between nodes within networks. These will arise for a variety of reasons; within the state sector, for example, agencies have different mandates and objectives that sometimes overlap but sometimes do not; corporations may agree to some joint project, but they are also in a competitive relationship. Conflicts will be resolved depending on the relative power of the actors; in some cases they may lead to some restructuring of the network. In all of this we must not forget the impact on security networks of those who are their objects; as we have seen, groups who are the primary targets of security may, under certain conditions, become part of the network. Similarly, the way in which targets react to attempts at information gathering and repressive action may have an impact not just on specific operations but also on the form of the network as it has to adjust further.[94] This is a particular manifestation of the point we made in chapter 2 – that resistance is an integral part of intelligence.

But conflict within networks is not the only reason that they are far from 'seamless' – to the great frustration of authorities and practitioners. The organizational boundaries between intelligence agencies (represented in figure 3.1 as dotted or broken lines between sectors and levels) interrupt the flow of information; although borders may be transformed or blurred, they will remain, even if redefined. Also, the traditional 'border-maintenance' conducted by hierarchies ensures the ubiquity of 'bureaucratic politics', and will remain a structural barrier to network flexibility. But as well as being blocked at the borders, information may just locate in voids where no agency has an immediate interest or adequate resources to analyse or otherwise deal with it.[95] The sheer quantity of security data within information systems far outstretches their capacity to analyse it. Therefore a more accurate image of figure 3.1 would be as an 'exploded' diagram that incorporates both the borders between agencies operating in whatever sector, level or space and the voids into which information 'disappears' (see figure 3.2)

Source: Gill, 'Not just joining the dots', p.35

Figure 3.2   Borders and voids

Making Security Networks Work

There are many issues raised by the rapid development of security networks, both formal and informal; the final section of this chapter concentrates on their management. Within state hierarchies, management is essentially by means of implementing rules and procedures appropriate to the level of responsibility. While this has never been entirely adequate to explain policing and security organizations where discretion is a highly significant feature of the work, networks are even more fluid – that is precisely their strength. Kickert and Koppenjaan suggest that network management has two main features: 'game management' and 'network structuring'.[96] Game management includes

- activating networks in order to address a particular problem and arranging for the interaction of those actors who can help (activation);
- bringing together otherwise disparate actors, problems and solutions (brokerage);
- creating the conditions for favourable developments (facilitation).

We can identify a number of recent developments in security intelligence that illustrate these activities – all of them present to some degree before 9/11, but accelerated thereafter. Although the budgets and personnel of state agencies have been significantly increased since 9/11, a combination of neo-liberal governance and perception of a range of asymmetrical threats across a wide variety of locations has brought into play increased public–private-community co-operation.

However, barriers to information sharing and operational co-operation are an inevitable by-product of specialization within state hierarchies, and are aggravated in intelligence work by the high premium placed on source protection and general reluctance to pool 'sensitive' information.[97] For example, Eliza

Manningham-Buller, MI5 director general, speaking after the July 2005 bomb-ings in London, said:

> we have a very strong interest in international co-operation, in all similar services having both the full legal powers to collect intelligence and the skill and experi-ence to handle it carefully but if we splash it around carelessly we shall soon have none of it. So I could never agree to a compulsory exchange of intelligence as that would risk compromising valuable sources of intelligence. There would soon be little to exchange.[98]

Thus it is no surprise that European and US officials all complain of the reluc-tance of the other to share,[99] though we should note that the UK has always considered herself to be more of a transatlantic intelligence partner than a European one.

The main form of 'brokerage' to be found in the intelligence community – before and since 9/11 – has been 'fusion centres' or 'task forces'. Representatives from several agencies are brought together, each with access to their home data-base, so that they can combine the analytical resources of otherwise separate agencies on a targeted problem or person by overcoming the incompatibility of different databases or privacy restrictions on the sharing of information. Examples include the US NCTC and the UK JTAC referred to above and discussed further in the next chapter. In terms of figure 3.2, these centres act as 'bridges' across voids and may provide partial solutions.[100] Liaison officers between agen-cies represent another development that transcends borders.[101]

Apart from breaking down the borders between agencies,[102] post-9/11 attempts at facilitating networks have addressed technological and political issues regarding access to and combining information – in both public and private sectors.[103] Not only have extra powers for technical collection been sought, but also, throughout the USA and Europe, agencies are seeking improved access to electronic data collected by others. However, access to specific databases is one thing, bringing together multiple databases is another. The 'big idea' since 9/11 is the 'mining' of 'data warehouses' constructed by linking public and private databases. This has been made technically possible by XML (Extended Markup Language) software that enables previously separate databases to be 'merged' via a universal language, and mining 'involves the use of sophisticated data analysis tools to discover previously unknown, valid patterns and relationships in large data sets'.[104]

Some of the examples being considered in the security field are truly awesome: inspired by the conclusion that in the period before 9/11 there was a failure within the intelligence and law enforcement communities to 'join the dots' between items of information already in the system, major efforts are under way to seek solutions. For example, in a report commended by the 9/11 Commission, the Markle Foundation proposes a Systemwide Homeland Analysis and Resource Exchange (SHARE) network that will enable information sharing by federal, state, local government and private sector users.[105] Progress is being made on the technical issues, but what can be said without doubt is that it reflects an enormous faith in the possibility of a technological fix to a highly complex problem – human security – and that nothing in the history of the extraordinarily fragmented American intelligence and law enforcement communities suggests that it has the slightest chance of being achieved. Even in the nationally organized military, where there has been enormous investment in the ideas and technology for network warfare, major issues remain with respect to security and sharing.[106]

A number of factors condition the ability to manage networks: for example, first, diversity – the higher this is, the more likely that management will be possible only at a distance (and the diversity of the US intelligence network is extremely high). Second, intelligence networks are self-referential systems. As a consequence of secrecy, the networks are harder to manage except to the extent that their self-regulatory capacity can be utilized. Self-regulation is a characteristic of 'professions', and, as recent controversies around intelligence assessments of Iraqi WMD show, professionalism among analysts is much needed as an essential (but not necessarily successful) counterweight to 'politicization' (see chapter 7). But such 'self-regulation' can also operate negatively: for example, it might sustain 'groupthink' (see discussion in chapter 5). Third, how extensive are the conflicts or convergence of interest? Beyond the simplistic rhetoric of 'all being on the same side', different agencies have varied legal mandates and, given their extensive discretion to identify priorities, may well have even more varied short- to medium-term organizational goals.

Fourth, what is the political and social context within which the network operates, and is there the political will and skill to manage in the desired direction? A high profile for the 'problem' in politics and the media will increase the pressure on organizations to commit the resources required for collaboration and, where different legal frameworks are in existence, action might be taken by the agency operating within the most permissive legal context. Fifth, management is facilitated if previous contacts have produced a desire to reciprocate. Eliza Manningham-Buller's comments above show why people do not like passing on information obtained possibly at high cost because of the unpredictable consequences of losing control over it, or they may just fear someone else getting the credit for an operation. Security concerns may be real or exaggerated, but they will increase, the more extensive the network over which the information will be dispersed. Sixth, given broad mandates and limited budgets, the costs of an operation (whether aimed at 'intelligence' or an investigation) will be a prime consideration. The more specific and credible information is, the more likely it is to lead to commitment of additional resources. The greater the complexity of a case in terms of jurisdictions and agencies involved, the more likely it is that a formal agreement will need to be negotiated between the contributing agencies, identifying who will do what.

If problems cannot be 'managed' within existing organizational frameworks, then it may be necessary to restructure networks, and we have already discussed some examples of this. The 'misfit' between the structure of the US intelligence network and the task of preventing terrorist attack was clear to many well before 9/11.[107] Now, some institutional restructuring has become a political imperative for the Bush Administration, and the Department of Homeland Security is one result. It is hard to see how this will succeed beyond the level of symbolic politics; for example, the constituent agencies will keep their varying mandates, which will prevent them from becoming simply the counter-terrorist intelligence clearing-house that some desire. The enterprise appears to be driven by a belief in the possibilities for hierarchical co-ordination, rather than the creative possibilities of networks. But even this restructuring affects only the national level; by comparison, the regional and local law enforcement community is positively atomistic. Quite how are the approximately 18,000 law enforcement agencies at federal, state, local and tribal levels to get their act together? [108] The task is immense: bearing in mind that a significant number of these agencies are one- or two-person strong, it defies comprehension.

There have been fewer demands for restructuring in the already unitary governmental structure of the UK, but one relevant innovation is the creation of a Serious Organised Crime Agency (SOCA). This is less a reaction to 9/11, however, than unfinished business, as it, in effect, merges NCIS and the National Crime Squad. The function of SOCA is to be 'gathering, storing, analysing and disseminating information relevant to – a) the prevention, detection, investigation or prosecution of offences, or b) the reduction of crime in other ways or the mitigation of its consequences' (s.3[1]).[109] Thus the Agency is clearly in the intelligence business.

Network structuring also takes place transnationally: in Europe, for example, the Berne Group was formed in 1971 by six European internal security agencies, and now includes seventeen, the newest member being Greece. Following 9/11, the Berne Group created a new organization called the Counterterrorist Group (CTG), with a wider membership of EU intelligence and security services plus the USA, Switzerland and Norway. CTG is mainly concerned with threat assessments regarding Islamic terrorism, and since the Madrid bombings has been playing a major role in implementing intelligence-related aspects of the European Council's Declaration on Combating Terrorism. In 1994 the Middle Europe Conference was set up at the suggestion of the Dutch and assisted the preparation for accession of the ten new countries in 2004.[110] Part of the reason for the rapid growth of the corporate sector is that large private security companies are themselves transnational networks, and thus provide a degree of flexibility unavailable to state agencies still operating within the confines of national sovereignty.[111]

Conclusion

We have shown that there is a wide range of 'actors' now involved in the intelligence business, and that not all of these are in the state sector that has been the traditional focus of intelligence studies, as we discussed in chapter 1. However, although state agencies remain very important, a combination of the neo-liberal desire of US and UK governments to control the size of the public sector and the post-9/11 security panic have provided much space that is being occupied readily by private security companies. Citizens too have been mobilized. Security intelligence networks develop partly organically, as security officials and agents make relationships with people who can help them with information, and partly by design, as states in particular acknowledge their information dependence on others. In both cases, however, key issues of oversight and accountability arise: just as, in the last twenty-five years, we have started to tackle the problem of controlling state intelligence agencies, so the explosion of security networks poses the even more difficult problem of controlling networks – not unlike nailing jelly to a wall. We return to this in chapter 8.

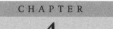

How Do They Gather Information?

Data! Data! Data! I can't make bricks without clay.

Sherlock Holmes, in Arthur Conan Doyle, *The Adventure of the Copper Beeches,*
1892, in Lathrop, *The Literary Spy*

Introduction

IN this chapter we look at the different methods that agencies use to acquire
the information that forms the basis of intelligence, and at the issues that
arise from developing the knowledge component of surveillance – the first stage
of the process outlined in chapter 2. This stage – collection – is by far the most
expensive of the intelligence cycle. The methods used to acquire information
can be placed in four broad categories. First, agencies mine open source material via the collection of publicly available data, speeches, official documents,
newspapers, magazines and so on. The other three categories involve information that targets seek to keep secret. HUMINT is human intelligence obtained by
a range of methods, including the use of agents or informers, deception,
kidnapping and torture. SIGINT is signals intelligence: that is derived from
communications and electronic sources. Finally, imagery intelligence, IMINT, is
derived from spy planes and satellite photography.

Planning and Direction

In figures 1.1 and 1.2 we identified the first stage of the intelligence process as
'planning and direction', sometimes referred to as 'targeting'. Whatever the
precise terminology used in different countries and agencies, the point is the
same: while there are unimaginable quantities of information potentially
available about all manner of threats to the well-being of states, corporations
and communities, only limited resources are available to intelligence agencies. Therefore some organizational process is required to allocate priorities
for information gathering and analysis. In the UK, for example, the JIC determines the intelligence 'requirements' that define the priorities for MI6 and

GCHQ, while MI5 has determined its own domestic security priorities. Thus, in general, priorities for targeting may be determined by the agencies themselves or be provided for them by governments. Historically, many agencies determined their own targets, in part because ministers preferred not to know what they were doing, though often there were close informal relationships between agencies and governments. It is now acknowledged that this posed several dangers, for example, that agencies might become 'states within a state' or act as 'rogue elephants'. In response, the new wave of democratization has seen a general shift toward more ministerial control.[1] Of course, this also involves dangers: specifically, that ministers may try to use agencies for the surveillance of political opponents rather than genuine security threats. Hence, in Canada, for example, the 1984 reforms that established the civilian CSIS provided for ministerial directions to the Service, but also provided for independent oversight of those directions to safeguard against political abuse.

Targeting can be seen to take place at different levels: ministers and government committees may lay down broad requirements, but the details of intelligence operations are determined at agency level or, in the case of networks, by some joint mechanism. For example, in Northern Ireland from the late 1970s onwards, greater efforts were made to co-ordinate the activities of military, police and MI5 operations in an environment that had been characterized as an 'intelligence war' between different agencies. Tasking and Co-ordinating Groups (TCGs) were established, a practice that has subsequently spread into mainstream police intelligence in the UK.[2]

Open Sources

Traditionally, a large proportion of intelligence material has been derived from open sources. Writing in 1970, Harry Howe Ransom estimated that '80 per cent or more of intelligence material in peacetime is overtly collected from nonsecret sources such as newspapers, libraries, radio broadcasts, business and industrial reports, or from accredited foreign service officers'.[3] In the post-Cold War period, this figure may well have risen to over 90 per cent.[4] It is worth noting that the Flood Report into Australia's intelligence agencies emphasized the role played by open source material in the Australian intelligence process, advising that

> Information from open and diplomatic sources is significantly less expensive to collect than is covert intelligence. Public sources also contain much of the key information required by government analysts. For reasons of principle and practicality, open and diplomatic sources should be exploited fully before information is sought from secret intelligence. Intelligence agencies are therefore the information collectors of last resort. But some information cannot be obtained from open sources or diplomatic reporting.[5]

Box 4.1   Open versus secret sources: the case of Burundi

During its investigation into US intelligence activities in 1995, the Aspin–Brown Commission explored the relative value of open and clandestine reporting by looking at both sources with respect to events unfolding in Burundi. The Commission asked the firm Open Source Solutions to explore the open side, drawing on the resources of such private information companies as Jane's Information Group, Lexis-Nexis, and Oxford Analytica. The open sources performed well, providing a brief, accurate history of the tribal conflict between the Hutu and Tutsi factions, and detailed order-of-battle statistics and descriptions of weapons in the Burundian inventory. However, contrary to some reports, the US intelligence community shined as well. The CIA generated up-to-date information on the growing political polarization in the country and the high likelihood that violence would soon erupt. The CIA also presented comprehensive data on regional ethnic population patterns, illustrated with impressive four-color maps, along with facts on Burundi's acquisition of arms in the international marketplace. The information provided by Jane's Information Group on the characteristics of weapons in Burundi proved richer than the CIA's profiles, but the CIA offered better insights into the evolving humanitarian crisis in Burundi, the attitudes of leaders in surrounding nations, and the need for the United States to begin preparing for the evacuation of US and European nationals. The open and clandestine sources each revealed pieces of the Burundian jigsaw puzzle; when joined together, the picture became much clearer.

Source: L. K. Johnson, 'Spies', pp. 22–3

However, volume should not necessarily be equated with significance. With regard to the USA, while 'overt collection provides the bulk of information gathered by the CIA, covert HUMINT and technical collection often unearth the most important knowledge for decision making'.[6] Nevertheless, as the concept of 'all-source intelligence' suggests, it would be wrong to see the debate over the relative significance of open versus secret sources as being based on some kind of zero-sum equation. The reality is that both sources can be combined to produce the most effective analyses, as the example in box 4.1 indicates.

Domestic security intelligence also makes extensive use of open source materials – for example, monitoring newspapers and websites produced by target groups and attending their public meetings. Information held by government agencies for health, insurance and tax purposes is also potentially valuable to security officials; in the past they often depended on informal contacts in the departments that were in breach of data protection rules, but now governments develop data networks that are intended to make such information readily available. Of course, the privacy implications of this are significant.

Secret Sources

HUMINT: human intelligence

HUMINT comes in a variety of forms. Defectors and 'walk-ins' provided some of the most important sources of intelligence during the Cold War contest, and their stories and contributions are well documented.[7] Recruiting members from, and undercover infiltration of, target groups has been a staple of domestic surveillance operations. Political opponents and exiles are another source of information, although a significant degree of risk attaches to these sources because of their vested interests and questionable motivation. A range of agents can be co-opted or bought. For example, businessmen who frequently travel to target countries and/or work in fields of particular interest, such as the arms trade, can be recruited to provide what are termed 'holiday snaps'.[8]

These approaches typically appeal to the patriotism of the businessman.[9] In the UK the Matrix Churchill affair and subsequent Scott Inquiry provided an important window on the extent of this activity. Matrix Churchill's Managing Director, Paul Henderson, had reported back to MI5 on his dealings in Eastern Europe in the 1970s. Initially, export sales manager Mark Gutteridge had supplied information on Iraq to MI5. When he left the company, Henderson was approached by MI6 and agreed to resume his reporting role. Conveniently, the value of the intelligence he provided generated governmental support for continued trade with Iraq when it might well otherwise have been prohibited. Supergun project manager Chris Cowley told of the debriefing of engineers on return from working in China and Iraq.[10] Such revelations were clearly damaging to the intelligence services, making future recruitment all the more difficult by heightening the risk that businessmen would henceforward be under suspicion. As the MI6 officer in heading UK intelligence collection on Iraq at the time told the Scott Inquiry:

> In speaking to an intelligence officer agents do so in confidence. They are given the undertaking that their *identities* will be protected. In extreme cases this means that their lives are at risk. In the vast majority of cases, and especially with British nationals, it is to protect their identity from being revealed to their work colleagues, family, friends, the press or Whitehall officials. If agents wanted their identity revealed, then the information they provided would be overt and in the public domain. In these circumstances the case officer should recommend contacting the relevant Whitehall department directly. If agents of any nationality did not trust SIS to deal with their information in confidence we would not have many agents.[11]

Where recruiting agents involves an initial approach from an overseas intelligence agency, patriotism is less likely to be a factor, although ethnic or religious identity can play a strong role, as with Israel's Mossad.[12] During the Cold War, of course, ideology played a significant role, although agent-runners tended to dislike working with ideologically motivated agents and preferred those, like Aldrich Ames, who were motivated by money and a sense that they 'don't see any harm' in what they are doing.[13] Such relationships are inherently corrupt and corrupting, because they are based on a combination of deception and financial inducement. Former CIA officer Miles Copeland offered the following advice in relation to agent running:

1 Buy the man, not his information.
2 It's the regularity and dependability of the pay that matters, not the amount.

3 Supplement the agent's income from regular sources enough to ease his financial worries, but not enough to cause him to make basic alterations in his life-style.
4 Pay no bonuses in connection with specific acts. Give the agent only rewards that will make him think in terms of consistent performance rather than individual 'coups'.[14]

As a former CIA station chief in Jordan put it:

> You have to understand what makes a guy tick and how to manipulate him. . . . What are his problems – his wife, girlfriend, boss, money? You become the friend he doesn't have. You feed his ego. You agree that his boss is unfair. Then you plant a seed. Perhaps he needs money for private school for his kids. You say, 'I can help.' The process of recruitment can take years. It's not overly complicated. It's all about manipulating people, gaining their trust, finding out what makes them tick, and using them to get the information we want.[15]

A different approach was that most associated with the East German Stasi, of utilizing a 'romeo' network to exploit vulnerable women, usually secretaries, in a position to pass on useful information. 'Romeo' agents would research their target thoroughly before making contact, identifying the area of vulnerability:

> Perhaps she had been left by her boyfriend, or her mother had recently died, or she didn't have many friends. When the romeo approached her, he already knew everything about her – her likes and dislikes, her history. One woman told me that the agent who approached her knew that she was interested in the environment, and after two days he was calling her his 'little herb witch'. So they got to the point pretty quickly.[16]

Having been subjected to this form of espionage for years, the West German state also adopted it. In 1990 a Bundesnachrichtendienst (BND) officer, Karl Heinrich Stohlze, formed a relationship with a secretary in a US company in Boston in an attempt to acquire information on gene-splicing technology. Having agreed to spy for West Germany, the secretary reconsidered, only to be blackmailed by Stohlze.[17]

When working overseas, intelligence officers adopt 'cover' to conceal their true identity and allow them to penetrate an organization or use it as an entrée into target groups. This kind of cover is termed 'non-official cover' (NOC) – for example, working within multinational companies that allow for routine travel and a range of opportunities to recruit agents or gather information.[18] Another form of cover is 'official cover', where intelligence officers act as diplomats attached to an overseas embassy. A third kind is 'notional cover', which can involve the establishment of false identities, cover stories, front companies, etc. that are mission-specific and unlikely to withstand sustained scrutiny.[19]

The case of the UNSCOM weapons inspection teams in Iraq during the 1990s represents a classic example of intelligence infiltration. Given the problems associated with generating reliable intelligence about Iraq after the 1991 war, this should come as no surprise. Former MI6 officer Richard Tomlinson has recounted how he was offered 'an undercover slot with the UN weapon inspection teams in Iraq' while working for MI6.[20] US intelligence agents spied on Iraq under UNSCOM cover for three years.[21] The context in which they did so was one of divergent agendas – UNSCOM focused on disarming Iraq, the CIA seeing disarmament as part of a wider strategy of removing Saddam. As UNSCOM inspector Rod Godfrey recalled: 'It did become clear to me throughout 1997 and 1998 that there were people associated with the mission who had functions which were not explained to the rest of us. . . . People would travel in with us and travel out with us but nobody ever explained quite what they were doing with the mission.'[22] According to Scott Ritter, US intelligence did not share all of the information collected under the cover of, and ostensibly to aid, UNSCOM:

> In the end the United States took over the whole programme, UNSCOM wasn't in control of anything. We didn't know what was being collected, we didn't know how much was being collected, when it was being collected. We had no control over the process. That shows the corruption of the operation. It became a United States operation, not a United Nations operation.[23]

As one aide put it, Kofi Annan had 'become aware of the fact that UNSCOM directly facilitated the creation of an intelligence collection system for the United States in violation of its mandate. The United Nations cannot be party to an operation to overthrow one of its member states.'[24] Iraqi diplomats, who in private had admitted that they had little or no evidence to justify their repeated claims that UNSCOM was a front for US spying, were reportedly delighted at this public relations disaster for UNSCOM.[25]

The volume and quality of HUMINT on any given target can be limited by a number of factors. Where there is limited bilateral contact with the target state, the cover provided for collecting intelligence via or under cover of government contacts, diplomatic missions, cultural and educational exchange programmes, etc., is also limited. During the Cold War and in the context of the post-9/11 security environment, the most highly prioritized targets have also been the ones that have presented the greatest problems of physical access, meaning that the CIA 'traditionally performed poorly in human operations against the United States's most ardent adversaries'.[26] For relatively isolated target states whose nationals were not as free to travel overseas, sporting exchanges have offered important opportunities. Whenever East German football teams, usually containing a significant number of Stasi informants, played games elsewhere in Europe, it offered an opportunity to gather information.[27] Olympic games could provide cover for a range of espionage activities.[28]

Where the target state is a relatively closed society, and internal travel opportunities are limited, even if defectors appear, their useful knowledge may be severely limited. As noted above, where defectors appear to have knowledge in areas of particular interest, the intelligence they provide may be inaccurate and motivated by a desire to further a particular agenda, by the prospect of financial gain, or both. Unfamiliarity with the language(s) of the target state can represent a further barrier, as with post-2003 Iraq. In March 2005, the *Economist* claimed that 'About half of all the CIA's case-officers are in Baghdad. But with only a handful of them fluent in Arabic, they are mostly confined to the green zone, condemned to interview Iraqi interpreters and watch endless episodes of *Sex and the City* on DVD.'[29] (However, reversing a language deficit by rapid recruitment heightens a risk of infiltration.[30]) A history of mutual antipathy between the states in question may serve to hamper recruitment of local informants, while the ethnic composition of target groups may create barriers to infiltration. As a former CIA operative explained with regard to infiltrating Islamic fundamentalist groups:

> The CIA probably doesn't have a single truly qualified Arabic-speaking officer of Middle Eastern background who can play a believable Muslim fundamentalist who would volunteer to spend years of his life with shitty food and no women in the mountains of Afghanistan. For Christ's sake, most case officers live in the suburbs of Virginia. We don't do that kind of thing.[31]

In situations where HUMINT is either sparse or unobtainable, there may also be a heightened dependence on second-hand intelligence from allies (intelligence sharing), in whose estimates the home agency may have only limited confidence, or in which they may have a high degree of confidence which turns out to have been misplaced.[32] In addition, co-operation with geographically important states may result in the imposition of restrictions on the scope of operations, as with the US experience of seeking approval to fly the Predator surveillance drone over Pakistani airspace in the hunt for the al-Qaeda leadership.[33] The search for the al-Qaeda leadership has also thrown up the problem of intelligence operatives working undetected in a friendly country, 'a country that we're not at war with, if you will, a country that maybe has ungoverned spaces, or a country that is tacitly allowing some kind of threatening activity to go on'.[34]

Undercover infiltration is also commonly associated with domestic surveillance. The definition of subversion used in the UK and enshrined in the 1989 Security Services Act (actions 'intended to overthrow or undermine parliamentary democracy by political, industrial or violent means') meant that the domestic surveillance net was cast wide, encompassing far left and far right groups, trade unions, civil liberties groups and student leaders. Growing concern about the potential for disorder from left-wing groups in the wake of the 1968 anti-Vietnam war demonstrations in London led Special Branch to set up the Special Demonstration Squad. Otherwise known as the 'hairies', this was a group of officers who would grow long hair and beards, cut themselves off from family and close friends, assume new identities in the manner of the *Day of the Jackal* graveyard search, 'go native' by studying and mastering the necessary Marxist (or other appropriate) language and positions on key issues, infiltrate left-wing groups on behalf of the state, and report back to MI5. As with the above examples, such infiltration was based on a deception deemed necessary, and therefore legitimated by the state, leaving former colleagues feeling betrayed when the true identity of the informer was exposed. As one of those involved, Special Branch officer Tony Robinson reflected: 'I suppose the whole business of being a Special Branch Officer in many instances is based on lies, on deception or you can't do your job.'[35] The business of infiltration also took a toll on the agents involved. Former MI5 officer David Shayler recalls a debriefing with a Special Branch officer who had infiltrated the anarchist group Class War:

> When I met M2589 in February 1992, at a safe house in London, it was quite obvious that this peculiar arrangement had affected the agent psychologically. After around four years of pretending to be an anarchist, he had clearly become one. To use the service jargon, he had gone native. He drank about six cans of Special Brew during the debrief, and regaled us with stories about beating up uniformed officers as part of his 'cover'. Partly as a result, he was 'terminated' after the 1992 General Election.[36]

The question of agent-running was brought powerfully to the fore in the context of Irish Republican terrorism with the 2003 unmasking of the long-rumoured British agent at the heart of the PIRA, code-named Stakeknife, run by military intelligence's Force Research Unit (FRU). Coming just one month after the death of Brian Nelson, himself a FRU agent who operated within the Protestant paramilitary UDA,[37] the identification of the deputy head of PIRA internal security (the 'nutting squad'), Alfredo Scappaticci, as a British agent raised a number of ethical questions. As one of the PIRA's chief 'molehunters', his recruitment was similar to the Soviet recruitment of Aldrich Ames, and was even likened to a situation where British intelligence had been able to run Reinhard Heydrich during his time as head of the Reich security service.[38] Nevertheless, Stakeknife's PIRA role involved the regular torture and disposal of suspected informers. The dilemma, as outlined by former FRU handler Martin Ingram, was that 'Stakeknife produced high-grade intelligence, much of it read at the highest levels of the political and security establishments. He was, without doubt, the jewel in the Crown. The problem was, Stakeknife could only shine if he immersed himself in the activities of those he was reporting upon, including murder and other illegal acts.'[39] Could any of these lives have been saved? How many of these were actually informers – that is, agents operating for other British intelligence agencies? Did the FRU let these other intelligence agencies know of Scappaticci's recruitment? How many were innocent? These questions themselves raised even more fundamental ones. How much is intelligence worth? What price should the state pay to secure it? This ethical dilemma is heightened by the suspicion that, according to Ingram, Scappaticci may have killed another FRU agent in his internal security role,[40] and that Brian Nelson was tasked by the FRU to identify an innocent man – Francis Notarantonio – to be murdered by the UDA in 1987, in order to divert loyalist attention from Scappaticci as a possible 'double agent', thereby protecting the FRU's informer at the innocent man's expense. In ethical terms, it is difficult to see any justification, and certainly the principle of double effect – used to govern the morality of endangering or killing non-combatants in times of war – does not apply here.[41]

One by-product of the unmasking of Scappaticci was to create a mood of uncertainty and mutual suspicion within and around the Provisional IRA.[42] Indeed, with reports of a number of further, unmasked agents still within its ranks,[43] the situation being described seemed at times not too far removed from that of the Central Anarchist Council in G. K. Chesterton's *The Man Who was Thursday*.[44] In this, Scappaticci's exposure had an effect that former MI6 officer Baroness Daphne Parks had talked of as being an MI5 tactic, 'to set people very discreetly against one another. They destroy each other. You don't destroy them.'[45]

SIGINT: signals intelligence

The role of SIGINT in the twentieth-century history is increasingly coming to be recognized as one of the biggest remaining gaps in our historical understanding.[46] While in this chapter we refer to the US experience with SIGINT primarily as a means of illustrating its potential and limitations, it is important to bear in mind that a wide range of countries maintain SIGINT capabilities, including Russia, France, the UK, Germany, Canada, China, Israel, India and Pakistan, and a number of other Asian and Middle Eastern states. In recent times it has been the richer cousin of HUMINT, eating up a far higher proportion of leading national intelligence budgets as new technologies are developed, launched, maintained and perfected. It has also been the principal source of intelligence, in the UK, for example, accounting for around 80 per cent of incoming information.[47] As outlined in chapter 3, within the US intelligence community, the NSA is responsible for SIGINT, derived from a combination of SIGINT satellites, listening posts, including some covertly operated from within US embassies abroad, and airborne, ship and submarine-based listening platforms. In a variation of the idea of the intelligence cycle, the NSA represents the signals intelligence process as shown in figure 4.1.

While there has been a perennial debate over the relative merit (and appropriate relative funding) of HUMINT and SIGINT, except in the aftermath of serious intelligence failures (for example, the fall of the Shah, 9/11, and the failure over Iraqi WMD), SIGINT has been viewed as an essentially superior source, as discussed below.[48] SIGINT has represented the fastest-growing source of current intelligence, as reflected in the view that the NSA gives decision-makers the present, while the CIA and other intelligence bodies provide contextualizing history. It also claims a flexibility that is absent from HUMINT, connected to the ability to re-target SIGINT as long as the platforms and operating expertise are available. In contrast, the capacity of HUMINT to rapidly and effectively redirect its focus is hampered by the fact that sudden shifts in emphasis could require

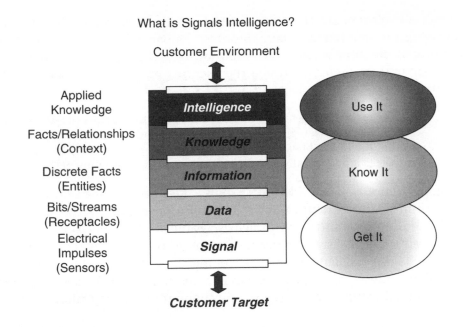

Source: <http://www.nsa.gov/sight/index.cfm>.

Figure 4.1 The SIGINT Process

the time-consuming infiltration of new structures and the creation of new networks of informers, although cross-national intelligence co-operation can provide help in such situations.

HUMINT has simply not enjoyed the same reputation for reliability. It is true that SIGINT can provide decision-makers with a sense of reliability that HUMINT cannot always match. As former DCI Stansfield Turner put it, 'electronic intercepts may be even more useful [than agents] in discerning intentions. For instance, if a foreign official writes about plans in a message and the United States intercepts it, if he discusses it and we record it with a listening device, those verbatim intercepts are likely to be more reliable than second-hand reports from an agent.'[49] It is certainly important to apply the appropriate caveats to human intelligence, to bear in mind when considering information from human sources that they are not intelligence agents. Where they are defectors, dissidents or exiles, they are also political actors and have an interest both in the situation on which they report and in the reaction of the agency with which they share their (dis)information. Nevertheless, it would be equally erroneous for agencies to assume that SIGINT can not also mislead, if for no other reason than as a consequence of the 'two idiots' dilemma. Simply stated, this is that 'Electronic intercepts are great, but you don't know if you've got two idiots talking on the phone.'[50]

A further potential problem involves misinterpretation of SIGINT. Potentially, the most costly example of this occurred in November 1983, during 'Able

Archer 83', NATO's secret exercise to test release plans for nuclear warheads involving the simulation of launch orders. As part of the exercise, US SIGINT monitored the Warsaw Pact's own monitoring of the test, only to discover that they had misinterpreted the test as representing preparation for a genuine pre-emptive strike:

> Instead of the normal monitoring to be expected from across the Iron Curtain, a sharp increase was registered in both volume and urgency of the Eastern bloc traffic. The incredible seemed to be happening, namely that the Warsaw Pact suspected it might really be facing nuclear attack at any moment.[51]

Perhaps ironically, it was a HUMINT source, KGB officer Oleg Gordievsky, who first confirmed the extent of Soviet fears of a pre-emptive strike during Able Archer.[52] However, SIGINT was immediately able to inform decision-makers that 'Soviet air units in East Germany and Poland were placed on alert and routine training flights suddenly stopped; Soviet nuclear-capable fighter bombers were placed on runway alert on airfields in East Germany; and the Soviets suddenly ceased broadcasting weather reports throughout the Soviet Union and Eastern Europe.'[53]

A final problem is that the volume of information generated by SIGINT can create an information glut whereby a significant volume of information is never analysed. Indeed, one of the 'seven sins of strategic intelligence' identified by Loch Johnson was indiscriminate collection of intelligence, resulting in information being warehoused until resources allowed for its processing.[54] However, the rapid expansion of communications technologies in recent years (a greater range of modes of communication, both faster and more affordable, together with access to commercial encryption systems), has vastly complicated the task of SIGINT in two respects. One is the technical question of collection being made more difficult by encryption and other denial techniques. The second is a consequence of the increased volume of traffic, meaning that more sifting is required to find targeted information concealed within the ever-expanding mass, a problem to which the Echelon system was one response.[55] While the NSA responded to these developments by investing most of its budget in improved collection systems with dazzling capacities,[56] analytical capacities lagged some way behind, as there was no equivalent investment in analytical staff. As a result, the NSA was collecting more information, but producing less intelligence. The debate about where to invest within the SIGINT community – systems or personnel – anticipated the wider debate about the relative merits of SIGINT and HUMINT that would erupt post-9/11.

Bugging represented the basic level of electronic surveillance during the Cold War. The CIA employed hundreds of engineers and craftsmen to secrete bugs in a wide range of items, 'from kitchen cutting boards to felt-tip pens. Oil filters, videotape cassettes, tool boxes, toy trains, batteries, cigarette lighters, basket covers, teddy bears, chess sets, paintings, wallets, statues, hot plates, and toilet kits' were all utilized.[57] At one point experiments were even carried out to implant a bugging device in a cat's ear and train it to listen to target conversations.[58] Targets were equally broad, as Ronald Kessler recounts, and bugging was routine with regard to

> Ambassadors' offices, the homes of foreign intelligence officers, the hotel rooms of treaty negotiators and United Nations delegates, the meeting room where OPEC held its deliberations, and the cars of possible terrorists. Trade meetings were usually bugged as well. When foreign countries built new embassies overseas, the CIA obtained the plans and planted bugs in the offices most likely to be used by top officials.[59]

Ethical questions around bugging resurfaced in the run-up to war with Iraq in 2003 and the controversy over the need for a second UN Security Council resolution explicitly authorizing the use of force. GCHQ translator Katharine Gun leaked a memo from the NSA's Defence Chief of Staff (Regional Targets), Frank Koza, asking for UK help in bugging six target delegates to the UN Security Council (Angola, Cameroon, Chile, Bulgaria, Guinea and Pakistan) in order to gather 'the whole gamut of information that could give US policymakers an edge in obtaining results favourable to US goals or to head off surprises'.[60] Gun was prosecuted under Section 1 of the Official Secrets Act. When, in February 2004, the charges were dropped, former Cabinet minister Clare Short publicly revealed that the UK had also spied on the office of the Secretary-General of the UN, Kofi Annan:

> This had been going on since we came into government and probably before. It may well have been a hangover from the Cold War. It had seemed odd, but basically harmless during the time that we were working closely and very supportively with him; but it became positively insidious when we were engaged with the US in manoeuvring and bullying to try to get Security Council approval for war at a pre-ordained date. I knew the transcripts of phone conversations were closely monitored because a senior intelligence official once came to see me and asked if we could speak alone. He pointed out that after I talked to Kofi from Kigali I had referred to something I could only know because I had read previous transcripts of calls to the Secretary-General. . . . This meant of course that my calls, like all others, had been carefully monitored and analysed.[61]

A variety of technical methods for gathering information are used by police and security agencies – for example, tax and welfare departments. These can be summarized as electronic surveillance ('bugging') and interception of communications ('tapping') and the ability to enter private property in order to place bugs, steal records, or for some other purpose (officially referred to in the UK as 'interference with property'). We can get some sense of the extent of these practices from the annual reports of the various commissioners set up to oversee the agencies (see further in chapter 8). For example, it is reported that for the year 2004–5 UK law enforcement agencies received 2,210 property interference authorizations and 461 intrusive surveillance authorizations. The latter are defined so as to include people or devices *in* private dwellings or cars or the use of devices to access what is happening therein.[62] Both of these figures were slightly lower than they had been two years earlier.[63] Equivalent figures for the three security intelligence agencies, MI5, MI6 and GCHQ, are not published.[64] Interception of communications incorporates two basic areas, one being the actual interception and transcription of calls, and the other 'metering', that is, the record of calls between different numbers that provides the basis for item-ized billing. The latter, being much cheaper, is used extensively by police, secu-rity and many other public bodies, in order to develop maps of communications networks between targeted individuals.[65] Unlike bugging, where agencies can normally authorize themselves subject to subsequent judicial check, telephone and mail intercepts require a ministerial warrant, and in 2004 1,849 new warrants were issued by ministers in England and Wales, and 124 by the Scottish Executive. Figures for warrants issued by Foreign Office and Northern Ireland ministers remain secret.[66]

Currently, the problem of accessing electronic communications via e-mail and the internet have added to the challenge facing security officials. Throughout the USA and Europe, executives are seeking improved access to electronic data. For example, the European Union has amended its 1997 Directive on Privacy so that the obligation of communications service providers to erase traffic data is deleted and they can retain data for 12–24 months.[67] Documents obtained through the Freedom of Information Act (FOIA) in the USA show that under the PATRIOT Act there is increased use of 'national security' letters under which banks, ISPs, tele-phone and credit companies, etc. can be compelled to hand over customers' records. Prior to the Act, the government had to show 'probable cause' (compara-ble with 'reasonable suspicion' in the case of the UK), but now they do not, and companies are prohibited from telling anyone of the disclosure.[68]

IMINT: imagery intelligence

The use of photographic surveillance to monitor targets became public knowl-edge in the wake of the Soviet downing of a US U-2 spy plane in May 1960, the same year that the CIA's CORONA satellite made its first successful flight, three years after the Soviet Sputnik had become the world's first. At this time, photoin-terpretation was undertaken in the CIA's National Photographic Interpretation Center by photointerpreters using stereoscopic magnifying instruments. Its founder recalled the process: 'You look at a place and then what it was like last year or yesterday. It's like looking at a movie. The frames are farther apart, but you can infer much more of the intentions by seeing the changes on the ground than by doing it one frame at a time.'[69] By the mid-1990s, KH-11 satellites were routinely supplying high-level imagery across a range of sensitive targets, includ-ing the sites of a massacre in Bosnia, a North Korean missile test, Chinese mili-tary deployments, and a Libyan chemical weapons facility.[70] Nevertheless, reliance on satellite imagery was not without its drawbacks.

For instance, employing satellite reconnaissance to compensate for an absence or lack of HUMINT can induce a false sense of confidence. There is a limit to what satellite reconnaissance can reveal, particularly with respect to intent.[71] Indeed, since the events of 9/11, there has been a widespread acceptance that excessive faith in the promise of SIGINT left the USA exposed. As one leading proponent of this view, former CIA field officer Robert Baer, puts it thus: 'Like the rest of Washington, the CIA had fallen in love with technology. The theory was that satellites, the internet, electronic intercepts, even academic publications would tell us all we needed to know about what went on beyond our borders.'[72] But, as former DCI Richard Helms put it:

> This idea that photographic satellites, satellites that pick up electronic emissions, satellites that provide communications, and all the rest of it – all those technical things – they're Jim-dandy when it comes to photographing missile installations, listening to missile firings, checking on telemetry, looking at the number of tanks being produced in certain factories – in other words, bean-counting mostly. Great. But once you eliminate the issue of bean-counting, what good do those pictures do you?[73]

Second, effective concealment from satellites is far from impossible, due largely to the orbital predictability of satellites in their current form. While technological advances in satellites are likely to allow the USA to at least lessen this predictability, there does not appear to be any insurmountable barrier to concealment technologies keeping pace with these. States involved in non-conventional weapons proliferation have learnt the lesson of the 1981 Israeli attack on Iraq's Osirak reactor, and are developing production, storage and possibly even delivery capabilities underground. The use of readily available tunnelling equipment in place of reliance on blasting with explosives has made these complexes very difficult to detect whilst under construction.[74]

For the USA, there is also the uncomfortable fact that the huge relative advantage it gained from being a world leader in satellite technology is diminishing. The dispersal of technology and the advent of commercial satellites mean that the USA's relative immunity to surveillance by satellite will be compromised as time goes on.

US and coalition forces relied heavily on SIGINT and satellite imagery during the 1991 Gulf War via a combination of high- and low-altitude systems.[75] Indeed, satellite surveillance had played a vital role in capturing the buildup of Iraqi forces on the Kuwaiti border prior to the 1990 invasion, but did not offer a definitive guide as to how to interpret these troop movements. Crucially, the satellite photos did not show *intent* – only human intelligence could provide hard information on this. On their own, the satellite photos created uncertainty about Iraqi intent. As Bob Woodward recorded: '[Colin] Powell realized . . . that in a totalitarian regime, the only way to be sure of intent was to know what was in the leader's mind, and neither the CIA nor DIA had good human sources in the Iraqi government.'[76] Neither was Powell alone in not knowing what Saddam would do next:

> Giving a status report on the location of the 100,000 Iraqi forces, [Norman Schwarzkopf] said they were positioned in a way to give Saddam lots of options – not just an attack. He did not predict an invasion or border crossing.

> [Dick] Cheney agreed that everything Saddam had to do to prepare for an inva-
> sion was exactly what he also had to do if his intention was simply to scare
> the Kuwaitis. There was no way to distinguish between the two. The bluff was
> only credible if Saddam did all the things he had done. . . . No one, certainly
> not Powell, could say for sure what Saddam was going to do. Absent any indi-
> cation, it seemed there was no immediate response for the US military to
> take.[77]

Having failed to provide a solid basis from which to predict and possibly prevent
the invasion, by October 1990 a number of SIGINT sources, including AWACS,
intelligence ships and ground stations were monitoring Iraqi military communications, but with limited success, as the Iraqis used secure underground
cables to communicate between Baghdad and Kuwait, a step taken years previously after a US newspaper disclosed details of an electronic eavesdropping
operation aimed at Iraq. Nevertheless, intelligence systems were able to provide
information on Iraqi troop deployments in Iraq and Kuwait, assess the degree
of damage inflicted by attacks, and provide warning of Iraqi Scud missile
launches, although here again with limited success, as Iraq adopted counter-
measures such as electronically shielding communications from eavesdropping, broadcasting false messages, and maintaining silence on prime military
channels. As one former NSA official put it, the Iraqis were 'quite sophisticated
in matters of electronic deception . . . what Iraq learned from us is having
consequences for both SIGINT and imagery'.[78]

   Indeed, there was some irony in that less than a decade before, the USA was
sharing SIGINT and satellite intelligence with Iraq to help it stave off defeat in
the Iran–Iraq war. As early as June 1982, the USA had offered Iraq satellite intelligence of its vulnerabilities, and had even dispatched an intelligence officer to
Baghdad to ensure that the images were fully understood. This had been the
prelude to President Reagan's 1984 signing of a National Security Directive that
formally authorized a 'limited intelligence-sharing program with Iraq'. The
information which the USA supplied thereafter included satellite reconnaissance photographs of strategic Iranian sites for targeting bombing raids, data
on Iranian air force and troop positions gathered from US-manned AWACS
based in Saudi Arabia, and communications intercepts. Journalist John
Simpson was one observer who felt that Iraq's new-found success at the front in
early 1988 was facilitated by US intelligence:

> On 17 April 1988, having spent most of the war on the defensive and refusing to
> attack even when the opportunity arose, the Iraqi army stormed the Faw
> Peninsula which two years previously had been captured by Iran. The Iranian posi-
> tions were thinly manned by old men and reservists; it seemed remarkable at the
> time that the Iraqis, whose intelligence had never been very good, should have
> chosen their moment so well. In May the Iraqis recaptured land around Basra
> which had cost Iran 70,000 casualties during three weeks' bitter fighting the
> previous year. Again the Iraqis chose their moment with extraordinary percep-
> tion and the battle lasted only seven hours.[79]

HUMINT versus SIGINT: The Post-9/11 Debate

As noted above, while investment in satellite and SIGINT technologies was seen as representing the future during the 1990s, post-9/11 this investment has been criticized as being at the expense of investment in HUMINT. Perhaps the classic expression of this belief that HUMINT had been neglected is contained in Robert Baer's book *See No Evil*.[80] Baer's central argument was implicitly recognized by the 9/11 Commission which highlighted the relative neglect of HUMINT capabilities (see box 4.2), and then by the White House, which asked the CIA to provide a plan and timetable for a 50 per cent expansion in its clandestine service.

Nevertheless, a renewed emphasis on HUMINT in the context of the 'War on Terror' raises serious ethical issues, as it suggests a loosening of the moral code that intelligence agents can be expected to follow – a loosening consistent with the wider context of detentions and abuse at Guantánamo Bay and Abu Ghraib,[81] and the signing of an executive order by President Bush effectively overturning the post-Church Committee ban on targeted assassinations.[82] Post-9/11 there was little support for the kind of restraint introduced by the Clinton Administration. Under Clinton, Baer complained, 'Running our own agents had become too messy. Agents sometimes misbehaved; they caused ugly diplomatic incidents. Worse, they didn't fit America's moral view of the way the world should run.'[83] Now the climate was very different. In this new climate former General Counsel to the CIA, Jeffrey Smith, argued that

> The CIA must be able to recruit individuals with terrible human rights records and with criminal records. There is no way that the CIA can penetrate terrorist groups . . . without dealing with people who are part of the groups. A judgement is to be made as to whether the value of the intelligence to be acquired outweighs the cost to the United States of dealing with some very bad people.[84]

More emphatically still, other US commentators argued that to 'obtain the information required to protect the lives of US citizens, dealing with people who have blood on their hands is necessary . . . by not recruiting people who lower themselves to the level of terrorists, the IC [intelligence community] loses everything'.[85]

Box 4.2　Human intelligence

Recommendation: The CIA Director should emphasize (a) rebuilding the CIA's analytic capabilities; (b) transforming the clandestine service by building its human intelligence capabilities; (c) developing a stronger language program, with high standards and sufficient financial incentives; (d) renewing emphasis on recruiting diversity among operations officers so they can blend more easily in foreign cities; (e) ensuring a seamless relationship between human source collection and signals collection at the operational level; and (f) stressing a better balance between unilateral and liaison operations.

Source: 9/11 Commission Report, p. 415

For its part, the *9/11 Commission Report* recommended that in future the US Defense Department, rather than the CIA, should take the lead in paramilitary operations, recognizing that in conducting past paramilitary operations the CIA 'relied on proxies . . . organized by CIA operatives without the requisite military training'. The results of this, the 9/11 Commission concluded, were 'unsatisfactory':

> Whether the price is measured in either money or people, the United States cannot afford to build two separate capabilities for carrying out secret military operations, secretly operating standoff missiles, and secretly training foreign military or paramilitary forces. The United States should concentrate responsibility and necessary legal authorities in one entity.[86]

A further expression of concern at the neglect of HUMINT relative to SIGINT came in late 2004 when it emerged that, over the previous two years, Republican and Democrat members of the Senate Select Committee on Intelligence had been voting to block a new US $9.5 billion stealth satellite system, which would be able to take photographs only during the daytime and in clear weather. One former government official observed that the proposed satellites 'would be irrelevant to current threats, and this money could be much better spent on the kind of human intelligence needed to penetrate closed regimes and terrorist networks. There are already so many satellites in orbit that our adversaries already assume that just about anything done in plain sight is watched, so it's hard to believe a new satellite, even a stealthy one, could make much of a difference.'[87]

Gathering and Hunting: An Erosion of Boundaries?

Before we move on from looking at how intelligence agencies gather the information they need to looking at what they do with it, it is worth asking whether, post-9/11, the boundaries between the two functions are breaking down. This is essentially the argument of former CIA officer Charles Cogan, for whom intelligence has come to be in part characterized by an 'offensive hunt' strategy, as a result of which intelligence operatives have become 'hunters' as well as (Cogan prefers 'rather than') 'gatherers'.[88]

The shift from gathering to gathering and hunting can be traced back to President Ronald Reagan's January 1986 presidential finding that allowed the CIA to identify terrorists suspected of committing crimes against US citizens abroad and to participate in their capture, a provision extended to killing them by President George W. Bush in the aftermath of the events of 9/11. Reagan's finding led to the creation of the CIA's Counterterrorism Center. Robert Gates felt that its creation 'represented a huge cultural change. . . . Before, we issued analyses to policymakers about terrorist organizations. Now we were operational.'[89]

The present situation represents a qualitative advance on this position. As outlined by Cogan, in the future, intelligence operatives 'will not simply sit back and gather information that comes in, analyse it and then decide what to do about it. Rather they will have to go and hunt out intelligence that will enable them to track down or kill terrorists.'[90] Two examples well illustrate this trend in practice.

The Predator: a vision of the future?

In the months following 9/11, the CIA's investment in unmanned reconnaissance aircraft came to be viewed in the US intelligence community and military circles as being money well spent. Having previously been deployed in Bosnia (from 1995) and Kosovo (in 1999), the Predator, a 27-foot-long aircraft that can relay images in real time, and the Gnat, a 24-foot-long unmanned reconnaissance aircraft, both featured in the hunt for leaders of al-Qaeda in the latter months of 2001. In addition, the Predator was equipped with Hellfire anti-tank missiles, vastly narrowing the gap separating information collection from policy response. In November 2002, a Predator attacked and killed six suspected al-Qaeda terrorists in Yemen, marking the first time it had been used offensively outside a war zone. This practice of what amounts to high tech–low risk state-targeted assassination has been heavily criticized. For example, Amnesty International argued that the Yemen case demonstrated the 'relatively low value that appears to have been placed by the US administration on the lives of Afghanistan and Iraq citizens killed by US forces', and that instead of 'killing them by remote control, lethal force should have been used only as a last resort. To the extent that the US authorities deliberately decided to kill, rather than attempt to arrest these men, their killing would amount to extrajudicial executions.'[91]

Extraordinary rendition

Extraordinary rendition is the practice of seizing terrorist suspects from foreign countries and removing them to third country destinations for interrogation, raising the spectre of the effective outsourcing of torture.[92] Prior to 9/11, it was used by the USA in the case of alleged drug traffickers, but it has been much more widespread since – it is estimated that approximately 150 people have been 'rendered' since 9/11, mainly to Egypt but also to Jordan, Morocco, Afghanistan, Uzbekistan and Syria, with UK airports emerging as key transit points alongside airports in Spain, Portugal, Norway, Sweden, Denmark and Iceland.[93] One example cited by Amnesty International involved two Egyptians seized in Sweden by CIA officers and flown to Egypt where they were subsequently tortured. The report notes how

> The two Egyptians were seized by Swedish security police in Stockholm on 18 December 2001, handed to CIA agents at Bromma airport and flown to Egypt on board a US-registered Gulfstream jet. According to a Swedish police officer who was present at the deportations, 'the Americans they were running the whole

situation'. The detainees had their clothes cut from them by the masked US agents, were reportedly drugged, made to wear diapers and overalls, and were handcuffed, shackled, hooded, and strapped to mattresses on the plane. The alleged torture they subsequently faced in Egypt included electric shocks.[94]

In March 2005, the Swedish Parliamentary Ombudsman ruled that their treatment by the CIA agents 'must be considered to have been inhuman and thus unacceptable', and that 'the Swedish Security Police lost control of the situation at the airport and during the transport to Egypt. The American security personnel took charge. . . . Such total surrender of power to exercise public authority on Swedish territory is clearly contrary to Swedish law.' However, this was becoming routine. A man seized from Gambia by US agents late in 2002 and transported to Guantánamo told his Combatant Status Review Tribunal in September 2004, 'in Gambia, the Americans were running the show. . . . The US was there and in charge from day one. They were not very respectful to the Gambians.'[95]

While French officials were happy to confirm their role in the June 2003 abduction of Christian Ganczarki and in other operations,[96] in the summer of 2005 relations between the USA and Italy were affected by a case involving the kidnapping by CIA officers of an Egyptian cleric, Hassan Osama Nasr, in Milan, of which the Berlusconi Government denied any knowledge. He was taken by Learjet from a joint US airbase at Aviano to the US airbase at Ramstein in Germany, and then via a chartered Gulfstream jet to Cairo, where the Egyptian claimed he almost died under torture.[97] In June a judge in Milan issued arrest warrants for thirteen US intelligence agents on kidnapping charges after identifying names via mobile phone contracts signed while they were in Italy. One of the phones was being used from Egypt at the same time that Nasr claimed to have been tortured there.[98] By the end of September 2005, warrants for the arrest of twenty-two people had been issued by the Italian authorities.[99]

By this time the scale of the operation was becoming more apparent, alongside reports of captives being held in Soviet-era compounds, so-called 'black sites', in Poland and Romania.[100] While Republican congressmen reacted angrily to the disclosure, it was to the fact of disclosure, not to the subject being disclosed.[101] The focus of human rights groups was rather different. Human Rights Watch warned that

> Arbitrary incommunicado detention is illegal under international law. It often acts as a foundation for torture and mistreatment of detainees. U.S. government officials, speaking anonymously to journalists in the past, have admitted that some secretly held detainees have been subjected to torture and other mistreatment, including waterboarding (immersing or smothering a detainee with water until he believes he is about to drown). Countries that allow secret detention programs to operate on their territory are complicit in the human rights abuses committed against detainees.[102]

Conclusion

It is now clear that the 1990s insistence on the inherent superiority of SIGINT and IMINT encouraged an undervaluing of the importance of HUMINT and, assisted by the renewed caution and disdain arising from various revelations during the decade, led to its relative neglect. The view, expounded by Robert Baer and others, that this neglect was a contributory factor in the events of 9/11, found a receptive audience in Washington, and led to a renewed emphasis on the operational aspects of human intelligence gathering. However, the pendulum has swung rapidly and too far. While there may well be a domestic constituency supporting the core elements of this pre-emptive approach and allies who feel too weak to resist US requests for co-operation, the practices it embodies are corrosive of the very norms it purports to protect. In particular, the post-9/11 practice of extraordinary rendition is constructed so as to side-step the need for accountability and conformity with human rights norms. However, while kidnapping and torture must now be considered as central to any review of how, in the post-9/11 world, intelligence agencies collect information, there is no certainty that the information thus yielded is either useful or reliable.[103]

What Do They Do with the Information Gathered?

Most of our intelligence came from good old-fashioned intellectual sweat.

William Donovan, in Lathrop, *The Literary Spy*

Introduction

WE have already made the distinction between 'information' and 'intelligence', identifying the former with material (documents, maps, photos, taped conversations, computer files) that may be donated, found or collected, and the latter with what is produced after analysis – the process of evaluation of the information. While attempting to ascribe meaning to or interpret information is something we all do in everyday life, being a social science student is similar to being an analyst, and in state and corporate organizations the position of analyst is increasingly specialized. Sometimes referred to as assessment, this process is one of the three main foci of this chapter.

The second focus is dissemination: what, if anything, is done with the intelligence that is produced? Is it passed on to other people or agencies? Is it passed on to executives for some action to be taken? Much of the information gathered by agencies – whether analysed or not – goes no further than the files, or 'store' of information in the organization itself. If intelligence is disseminated, it may take various forms – oral briefings, short or longer papers addressing immediate or longer-term issues. Whatever the form or substance of the intelligence, analysts frequently complain that they find it difficult to make their executives listen. In the short term, one of the main problems is the dissemination of 'warnings': how certain does an agency want to be before it will tell its 'customer' of a threat of attack? Executives are people of action, they crave certainty whereas analysts occupy a world of uncertainties – very rarely will analysts be able to provide warnings with the degree of certainty that executives demand, and therefore they may exaggerate or mislead. If they get it wrong, then it is going to be even harder to convince the executive of the accuracy of their analysis in future, like the boy who 'cried wolf'. On the other hand, if an analyst errs on the side of caution and there is an attack without warning, then executives will demand explanations and, possibly, resignations. Fear of this may lead to an inbuilt tendency to adopt worst-case scenarios with the consequent distortion of the policy process.

Although much military and security policy is based to a greater or lesser extent on intelligence, public policy pronouncements do not normally state this explicitly. Yet in the recent and controversial case of Iraqi WMD, intelligence was used explicitly as part of an attempt by governments to justify and gain support for their policies. During 2003, in those countries of the 'coalition of the willing' that invaded Iraq, unprecedented public controversies regarding intelligence and policy developed because of the failure to find the WMD that had been the primary justification for the invasion. The deeper sources of the controversy lay in the redefinition of the circumstances under which 'defensive' war might be waged: specifically, a doctrine of *prevention* was embraced on the grounds that nations could, after 9/11, no longer risk catastrophic attack from states or non-state groups, possibly by non-conventional means of chemical, biological, radiological or nuclear attack (CBRN).

As we have discussed, intelligence has always been central to states' efforts to protect themselves, but the new doctrine embraced by both the Bush and the Blair administrations gave it, crucially, more public significance. Governments of states finding themselves under military attack from outside did not need intelligence to tell them (if they had had no forewarning, then they would certainly regard this as a catastrophic intelligence 'failure' – but that is another issue), and their publics would need no persuasion that defence was required. However, intelligence is much more crucial if states are to prevent anticipated attacks. It is both central to the process by which the seriousness of the threat is assessed and will have to provide the basis for some process of convincing sceptical publics that preventive war is required. In the case of Iraq, this has caused enormous controversy, as we discuss in chapter 7.

Third, intelligence is not just the basis for state or organization policies that are openly announced, debated and implemented. It has always had a crucial role to play in informing and implementing actions that are not openly avowed and, indeed, may actually infringe domestic or international law. Such strategies go by different names, varying between countries and the area of intelligence involved. For example, most discussed in the literature and most controversial is 'covert action' as practised by the CIA. Indeed, the very organization of the CIA enshrines the two disciplines of 'analysis' and 'operations' in different directorates. Another example, though less well attested in the literature, is what law enforcement agencies describe as 'disruption'. In one sense this is not new – police have always aimed to prevent crime – but the recent application of intelligence techniques against criminal organizations engaged in drugs, arms or people trafficking has involved an increase in the disruption of particular crimes or crime series or crime markets, rather than necessarily arresting, charging and prosecuting with a view to conviction.[1] Since 9/11, further impetus has been given to this development by the convergence of security, police and military intelligence with respect to perceived terrorist threats and the enhancement of the prevention doctrine for internal security also.

Analysis

As we saw in chapter 4, large sums of money have been poured into the development of ever more sophisticated technical systems for the collection of information. By comparison, the funds expended on analysis are miniscule; the 9/11 Commission reported that

> the FBI's information systems were woefully inadequate. The FBI lacked the ability to know what it knew: there was no effective mechanism for capturing or sharing its institutional knowledge. FBI agents did create records of interviews and other investigative efforts, but there were no reports officers to condense the information into meaningful intelligence that could be retrieved and disseminated.[2]

Arguably, failures of intelligence are as likely to result from incorrect or inadequate analysis as from a failure to gather, access and process information. The modern transformation of intelligence by the application of highly sophisticated surveillance and information technology has overshadowed the fact that, at its core, it remains an intellectual process. Technology can contribute to analysis; for example, since 9/11 there has been great emphasis on developing relational software to provide links between disparate data sets in order to develop 'data warehouses',[3] but the 'attribution of meaning' to items of information or linked networks of items requires the application of thought and judgement. However many 'facts' are compiled or integrated, they still do *not* 'speak for themselves', and analysis requires the testing of different possible explanations against the evidence – what we called 'abduction' in chapter 2.

Intelligence analysts seek knowledge with a degree of certainty sufficient to satisfy and inform those who wish to act upon it. 'Assessment is the search for truth. How do you arrange it so that you have the maximum chance of coming near to that elusive ideal, and how do you ensure that if you come near to it you are listened to?'[4] This ideal is certainly elusive, even in principle. The objects of intelligence are often divided into mysteries and secrets – the latter being those things that are, with sufficient access, knowable, while the former are those things – for example, the intentions of a foreign leader – that may be unknown even to the leader herself. In practice, examining the realities of the intelligence process demonstrates just how far short of 'the truth' its product may be.

The processing of information never takes place in a vacuum – there is always a personal or organizational context,[5] but there are factors intrinsic to information processing that may be problematic whatever the context. Fundamental are the problems of overload and complexity. In order to deal with the former, all systems must *select* information as being relevant to the purpose for which it is required; but if the methodology for selection is misguided or outdated, then relevant information may be missed. The less an agency or analyst knows about a problem, the greater the danger of overload; on the other hand, experts in their fields may be the most likely to cling to long-standing interpretations in the face of anomalous information – the 'paradox of expertise'.[6] One way of reducing complexity is to narrow the focus of analysis. However, the more this is done, the more there is a risk of error as a result of over-simplification. A frequent reaction to the difficulties of analysing other societies and cultures is 'mirror-imaging': assuming, simplistically, that they operate much like one's own.[7]

The very sophistication of the modern information-gathering systems discussed in chapter 4 produces the problem of overload. Intelligence systems may demand ever more data in the empirical illusion that more data will solve the mysteries and secrets – whereas, rather, they are likely to suffer the fate of the thirsty individual who tries to drink from a fire hose.[8] As the 9/11 Report noted:

> one can see how hard it is for the intelligence community to assemble enough of the puzzle pieces gathered by different agencies to make some sense of them. . . . Accomplishing all this is especially difficult in a transnational case. We sympathize with the working-level officers, drowning in information and trying to decide what is important.[9]

Overload manifests itself also in the concept of 'noise', wherein the glut of extraneous material inhibits the analyst from focusing on the information that is central to the analytical problem or even prevents the analyst from spotting it.[10] Despite the problems of overload, of course, it may well be that the information system just does not contain the information that is needed in order to develop the required 'intelligence.'

Broadly speaking, analysts are deployed to produce two main types of analysis: tactical (short term or limited in area) and strategic (long term or more extensive in area). Ideally, agencies will achieve some balance of effort toward both, but in the security field there is enormous pressure dragging the agencies towards the tactical at the expense of the strategic. Certainly law enforcement is dominated by tactical intelligence with respect both to investigations of past offences and to disrupting ongoing illegal markets, and pressure from investigators and managers tends to ensure that little strategic intelligence is carried out. Since 9/11, similarly, most intelligence effort has been put into the investigation and prevention of terrorist attacks. Many analytical techniques deploy sophisticated software facilitating the analysis of relational data. However, the cleverness of the software cannot provide a 'technological fix': analysis remains at heart an intellectual exercise based on reasoning.

One basic technique is risk assessment, deployed in the corporate world for many purposes in addition to security, but basically involving 'the estimation of the likelihood of an adverse event balanced against the possible harm caused by the event'.[11] Other examples of techniques used extensively in both crime and security intelligence include network analysis – basically used to 'map' networks of target individuals, organizations and locations. This is relatively easy to do in terms of measuring quantities of contacts between 'nodes' in the network – for example, by the metering of telephone calls – but is much harder if it is to examine the quality or nature of those contacts. Here, techniques derived from social network analysis will be used, but they are time-consuming and expensive.[12] Another analytical technique based on the large data warehouses now under construction (see chapter 3) is profiling – a technique based on the examination of large data sets for unusual or suspicious patterns of behaviour that are used as the basis for targeting decisions for stops, searches and additional checks at airports.

Agencies may tend to recruit people from similar backgrounds, and then to indoctrinate them thoroughly into the traditions and ways of the agency. This may well produce (more or less) subtle pressures towards conformity of thinking that is not receptive to contrary ideas.[13] This is assuming, of course, that they do actually recruit people with appropriate education, experience and skills. The 9/11 Commission shows that this was not always the case in the CIA:

> Security concerns also increased the difficulty of recruiting officers qualified for counterterrorism. Very few American colleges or universities offered programs in Middle Eastern languages or Islamic studies. . . . Many who had travelled much outside the United States could expect a very long wait for initial clearance. Anyone who was foreign-born or had numerous relatives abroad was well-advised not even to apply.[14]

The issue of training is linked directly to the way in which analysis is conducted and can contribute to well-attested problems such as groupthink and mirror-imaging. The former was initially developed as a concept to show how independent critical thinking could be driven out from groups of policymakers as *esprit de corps* developed,[15] but is now used more widely.

Within organizations there are numerous possible obstacles to the 'search for truth'; some result from formal, others from informal aspects of organizations. Specialization is a key feature of the Weberian bureaucracy and serves many useful purposes, but maximizing the efficiency of information flows and encouraging imagination are not prominent among them. In intelligence bureaucracies there are additional hurdles that, again, may be soundly based, but further hinder the flow – notably, secrecy and compartmentalization of information.[16] This may occur within and between organizations: because they are perceived not to be need-to-know aspects of specific operations, analysts may be in complete ignorance of information that would be important for their work – for example, the degree of confidence in sources. This may be compounded by the existence of different databases; if they cannot be linked, the information is effectively hidden from analysts.[17] The 9/11 Commission showed how, given the poor state of the FBI's information systems, analysts' ability to access information depended largely on whether they had a personal relationship with anyone in the squad where the information resided. These problems were further aggravated in the Bureau when procedures intended to manage carefully the flow of information from investigators to *prosecutors* became misunderstood as inhibiting sharing of information between different groups of investigators. Over time, these procedures became known as 'the wall', and in the eyes of many officials became a serious constraint on intelligence sharing.[18]

Organizational mandates vary, and officials may well judge the priorities of another organization to be less important than their own. Of course, good management, training and supervision can alleviate these factors, but they cannot be eliminated entirely. Research into how organizations work and what they actually produce indicates the great importance of organizational or bureaucratic subcultures. In part because they are made up of people with varying attitudes and beliefs, and in part because bureaucratic formality creates obstacles to 'getting the job done', the way in which information processes actually work (or not) may depart significantly from the images presented by organization charts and mission statements. Within agencies, typical differences exist between the 'doers' and the 'thinkers': in the CIA this difference is institutionalized in the split between the Directorate of Operations and the Directorate of Intelligence; in UK police forces there is evidence of the divide between detectives (usually sworn, male police) and analysts (usually younger, civilian, better-educated and female).[19] The low status of analysts may mean that they are reduced to not much more than in-putting endless streams of information[20] or are diverted to immediate investigative tasks rather than actually doing analysis.

Mandel argued that bureaucratic obstacles to information processing are at their greatest when co-ordination is required within and between many organizational units, and personal obstacles can be seen at their worst when rapidly changing political circumstances expose the rigidity fostered by groupthink and cognitive consistency. Within the information process itself he identified crisis, the failure of past policies, and need for quick decision as the conditions most likely to provoke serious problems. These may accumulate: 'From the vantage point of national security, many of the circumstances when there is the greatest need for sound intelligence are precisely those when these distortions are worst.'[21] As we shall see in chapter 7, the period after 9/11, including the decision to invade Iraq, illustrate the accuracy of Mandel's argument. We can see how a combination of 'groupthink' *within* agencies or sections and turf wars over access and sharing information *between* agencies produced a cocktail of dysfunctions that were fatal to states' efforts to develop security intelligence. But there are plenty of examples prior to 9/11.

Linguistic barriers may limit the number of analysts not susceptible to basic mistakes of translation or interpretation. The more difficult, accurate, first-hand understanding of the target becomes, the easier it becomes for politicians to apply their own ideologically informed explanations to specific behaviour and to see these explanations carry the day. There will simply be few qualified dissenting voices. Elsewhere, in certain contexts, members of the analytical community may consciously or subconsciously engage in groupthink that acts as a barrier to the application of intuition and to taking imaginative approaches to the study of problems. Analysts may well be taught techniques involving the testing of competing hypotheses[22] (a process similar to that of abduction discussed in chapter 2), but the short time-scales they are required to work to serve to reinforce tendencies to seek support for what is organizationally dominant instead.[23]

The 9/11 Commission concluded that failure of imagination was one of the main factors causing that intelligence failure, and in its report it considered the enormous (if not entirely contradictory) task of building imagination into the national security bureaucracy. It pointed out that, with respect to terrorism, the agencies simply had not developed the sort of warning indicators and had not performed the kind of competitive analysis that was done with respect to more traditional forms of military attack.[24] In the UK the Butler Report made a number of recommendations aimed to improve analysis and JIC assessments, and the Government responded by increasing the size of the assessments staff, appointing a head of analysis to advise on careers structures, common training and methodologies.[25]

'No good will come of this': Problems with Dissemination

In the same way that analysis has been ignored relative to collection in the intelligence literature, so has dissemination.[26] This is very odd, since it represents the crux of the intelligence process – the very link between knowledge and power; between intelligence and policy. Dissemination matters – the adequacy or otherwise of agencies' performance will be judged on the utility and timeliness of what they produce.[27] If intelligence is to amount to more than a self-serving cycle of endlessly collecting and storing information and is actually to inform ministers, governments and executives, then it must be communicated to them but, in fact, 'Dissemination tends to be intelligence's Achilles' heel'.[28] The central questions to be asked about this process are 'what, how much, when, how and to whom?'

What is produced and when

Sherman Kent's work on US intelligence is generally regarded as providing the basis for much subsequent intelligence scholarship, even though he concentrated on strategic foreign intelligence and was not concerned with police, security, counter-intelligence or tactical intelligence. He argued that there were three main forms in which strategic intelligence was produced: basic descriptive, current reportorial and speculative-evaluative.[29] Taking this classification as a starting point, the basic intelligence report will be a standard product of any state or corporate intelligence system in which analysts will provide an overall assessment of the state of play in some other government, military, market or company, usually based on open sources but including available covert information to 'add value'. Current intelligence seeks to provide executives with the latest information on current events: in the USA the best-known examples of this kind of product are the President's Daily Brief (PDB) and the more widely circulated Senior Executive Intelligence Brief (SEIB). During the 1990s the growth of continuous news channels reinforced the pressure on analysts to disseminate their reports at an ever faster pace. These are intended not simply to repeat what has been dominating the 24-hour news, but to analyse them within a broader context and with the benefit of covert information. However, they are not always successful. Daily briefings may amount to no more – or in some cases even less – than journalism, thus failing to add any value to what ministers may have seen on TV.[30]

Taking a broader view of intelligence than Kent's, and moving from the immediate past to the immediate future, another form of current intelligence that is particularly important for policing and security intelligence is warnings. In the broadest sense, all intelligence provides warnings, but states and corporations alike view warnings of nasty surprises as the central intelligence function. During the Cold War sophisticated systems were developed for the surveillance of indicators that an attack might be pending; for example, during 1950–75 the USA had a Watch Committee and National Indications Center, and Soviet military intelligence (GRU) and the KGB maintained similar systems for indications of Western attacks.[31] Now that the fear of attacks from non-state actors has replaced these, the process of providing appropriate indicators is much more difficult, and the judgements to be made in issuing warnings are acute. The 9/11 Commission noted that, with the exception of the analysis of al-Qaeda attempts to obtain WMD, the US intelligence community failed to apply warning methodologies to the potential threat of a terrorist attack on the USA.[32]

Generalized warnings, such as increasing the level of threat on the US 'traffic light' system, are highly unsatisfactory, since they may just increase a general level of anxiety without enabling anyone to actually do anything to minimize their vulnerability. Over time such warnings fall foul of the 'cry wolf' problem. Alternatively, if an attack takes place, failure to provide a warning will lead to much negative evaluation of the agencies, as we have seen with the continual criticism of the US agencies since 9/11 (see box 5.1) Timeliness is an issue for all intelligence dissemination: the recipients of intelligence will value its delivery only if it is in time for actions to be prepared – for warnings, this is especially vital.

The third main form of intelligence attempts to 'estimate' or 'assess' possible futures: in other words, to provide the forewarning that we included in our definition in chapter 1. These are the most ambitious and problematic of intelligence products. In the USA a specialist staff builds on the work of analysts throughout the intelligence community to produce NIEs. These may be self-generated from within the community or requested from elsewhere in

> **Box 5.1   The problem of warning**
>
> 'Most of the intelligence community recognized in the summer of 2001 that the number and severity of threat reports were unprecedented. Many officials told us that they knew something terrible was planned, and they were desperate to stop it. Despite their large number, the threats received contained few specifics regarding time, place, method, or target. Most suggested that attacks were planned against targets overseas; others indicated threats against unspecified "U.S. interests." We cannot say for certain whether these reports, as dramatic as they were, related to the 9/11 attacks.'
>
> *Source: 9/11 Commission Report*, pp. 262–3

government, including Congress. More urgent requirements may be met by special NIEs (or SNIEs).[33] A NIE was distributed in July 1995 predicting future terrorist attacks against and in the USA, and it specified particularly vulnerable symbolic targets such as the White House, the Capitol and civil aviation, and was described by the 9/11 Commission as 'an excellent summary of the emerging danger, based on what was then known'.[34] Thereafter, there was an updated NIE on terrorism in 1997 and a series of 'very good analytical papers' on specific topics, but no further NIE prior to 9/11.[35]

To whom is it disseminated, and how?

There is nothing automatic about the process of delivering intelligence to customers. As with all communications, as much attention needs to be paid to how it will be received as to how it is sent. The language of the marketplace (if not all its practices) has crept into the vocabulary of intelligence – policymakers are 'consumers' or 'customers' for intelligence, and so, for the agencies, 'Salesmanship is part of the game.'[36] So, the means of disseminating intelligence has shifted in line with the general advance of ICT; for example, the US intelligence community has its own intranet, Intelink, enabling agencies to trade publications, photographs, reports and so on.[37] But for customers outside the community, the emphasis may well be upon brevity and snappy presentation, electronic or otherwise including 'death by powerpoint', as agencies compete for the scarce time of policymakers. Briefings will often be distilled to one or two pages for no other reason than that the recipient will not read anything longer. Indeed, it is reported that, being aware of Ronald Reagan's dislike of reading and love of movies, Bill Casey, then CIA director, encouraged colleagues to present intelligence pictorially so that the President could watch it on a cinema screen.[38]

Traditional hierarchical organization of state intelligence production is not conducive to the free flow of information, but is especially inimical to the rapid production of intelligence about fast-moving events in non-traditional threat areas. Michael Herman noted that 'security reinforces formal organization against loose structures and easy information flows'.[39] 'Task forces' are recommended to deal with new problems, because they avoid established boundaries and divisions within intelligence and provide policymakers with the specific intelligence that they want – now.[40] More radical proposals have been made to 'marketize' intelligence, on the grounds that the greater flexibility of markets will better serve customers and prevent the politicization of intelligence.[41] Essentially, this applies to intelligence arguments based on new public management (NPM), as it has been introduced throughout the public sector in many Western states since the 1980s. But a number of its claims cannot be sustained. For example, the proposal that requests for intelligence could be posted on the internet (like the FBI's 'Ten most wanted') might certainly attract more information from a myriad of open sources and expertises beyond the capacity of any agency, but ignores the fact that the information generated would then need to be evaluated – police appeals for public information can be very helpful, but also generate enormous amounts of work to sort the wheat from the chaff. It may well be that a decentralized network of analysts will make it easier for dissenting views to survive, but markets are not apolitical; indeed, they provide the fora within which the most affluent and powerful interests prosper. While there may well be a need for intelligence to provide more 'customized' products for their policymakers, the more control that customers have over what analysts produce, the more likely it is that the product will represent what the customers *want*, which may be far from what they *need* in terms of 'truth'. The market model may simply increase the propensity for analysts to tell policymakers what they want to hear.

How intelligence is presented will depend on to whom it is addressed. Some reports prepared within agencies may simply stay within the agency, entering the 'store' of knowledge. It is by no means certain that they will be shared even within an agency. This may be based on short-sighted criteria; for example, analysts need to know the credibility of the sources of the information with which they are dealing, but handlers may be reluctant to admit their own doubts or, as we saw above, may fail to share because of misunderstandings about the rules. Obstacles to sharing information with other agencies are even more extensive: this may reflect the choice of the agency not to share the information outside or simply a lack of awareness that anyone outside would be interested. Much criticism in the USA since 9/11 concentrated on the failure of intelligence agencies to share information with others – in some cases this rightly aimed at failures to share based on nothing more than ignorance, poor understandings and so on, but there are also understandable and defensible reasons that may apply. For example, all agencies jealously guard their sources and methods, not just because they are short-sighted but also because they fear their compromise if information they provide is used unwisely, as expressed by the MI5 director general in chapter 3. Recipients outside the community may not appreciate that the publication of an item of intelligence can enable a target to identify and eliminate its source – in some cases a person. Nevertheless, the 9/11 Commission recommends that the Cold War assumption that intelligence can be shared only with those who 'need to know' be replaced by a 'need-to-share' culture of integration.[42]

Whether or not an agency will share with another will depend partly on the nature and location of that agency, its mandate and the framework of rules. On the face of it, agencies will be most willing to share with those within their own national community, but this cannot be assumed; to the extent that different national agencies believe that they are competing for resources, they may use their intelligence to maintain their 'comparative advantage' over others. For example, there is anecdotal evidence that agencies operating with similar techniques, say SIGINT, but in different countries, would be more willing to share with each other than with their national agencies involved in a different intelligence discipline, say counter-intelligence. Indeed, the whole point of the transnational intelligence networks identified earlier is that they provide a vehicle for intelligence sharing and co-operation across borders.[43] Yet the 9/11 Commission described clearly the failures of national agencies to share information prior to the attacks.[44]

Dissemination within the community is an important factor in the quality of final products, but it is dissemination outside of the community that establishes the credibility and utility of intelligence. The primary consumers of intelligence are the 'doers' – political or corporate. How intelligence conclusions are presented is important: specifically, how does intelligence present degrees of uncertainty? The use of language is crucial; indeed, it is determinative of what, in the end, is considered to be 'knowledge' upon which policy may be based or by which it is rationalized. Intelligence seeks to improve knowledge by reducing uncertainty, but, by widely varying degrees in different conditions, is ever only partially successful. The way in which different national systems seek to convey this uncertainty varies. For example, US NIEs incorporate footnotes recording the dissent of particular agencies from the main conclusions, and the CIA provides percentage probabilities of success in possible future operations.[45] An excellent example of the significance of language is provided by the 9/11 Commission in their account of the discussions in the Clinton Administration as to how to respond to the attack on the *USS Cole* in August 1998 (see box 5.2).

In the UK, the JIC eschewed dissenting footnotes, and the Butler Report described how the JIC accommodated uncertainty as of 2004. When the intelligence was unclear or inadequate, the JIC reported different interpretations as long as the membership agreed that they were viable alternatives,[46] but alternative or minority hypotheses were not stated. So it normally attempted to reach a consensus in the assessment, and the section of 'Key Judgements' would often include warnings as to any thinness of the evidence. Inevitably this search for consensus

> may result in nuanced language. Subtleties such as 'the intelligence indicates' rather than 'the intelligence shows' may escape the untutored or busy reader. We also came across instances where Key Judgements unhelpfully omitted qualifications about the limitations of the intelligence which were elsewhere in the text.[47]

Box 5.2 Language, certainty and knowledge

'President Clinton told us that before he could launch further attacks on al Qaeda in Afghanistan, to deliver an ultimatum to the Taliban threatening strikes if they did not immediately expel Bin Ladin, the CIA or the FBI had to be sure enough that they would "be willing to stand up in public and say, we believe that he did this." He said he was very frustrated that he could not get a definitive enough answer to do something about the *Cole* attack . . . .

. . . on December 21 [2000], the CIA made another presentation to the Small Group of principals on the investigative team's findings. The CIA's briefing slides said that their "preliminary judgment" was that Bin Ladin's al Qaeda group "supported the attack" on the *Cole*, based on strong circumstantial evidence tying key perpetrators of the attack to al Qaeda. . . .

. . . A CIA official told us that the CIA's analysts chose the term "preliminary judgment" because of their notion of how an intelligence standard of proof differed from a legal standard. Because the attack was the subject of a criminal investigation, they told us, the term *preliminary* was used to avoid locking the government in with statements that might later be obtained by defense lawyers in a future court case . . . .'

Source: Extracted from the *9/11 Commission Report*, pp. 193, 195, 196

But if language was nuanced in order to satisfy those who were producing it, the subtleties of what they meant might well escape those who received it. If, as Butler noted, not even the producers were clear as to the significance of the language:

> We have been told that some readers believe that important distinctions are intended between such phrases as 'intelligence indicates . . . ', 'intelligence demonstrates . . . ' and 'intelligence shows . . . ', or between 'we assess that . . . ', 'we judge that . . .' and 'we believe that . . . '. We have also been told that there is in reality no established glossary, and that drafters and JIC members actually employ their natural language.[48]

Then what hope was there for the reader? Butler did not suggest any particular way of trying to deal with this problem – it is indeed inherent in any process involving language – but did recommend that the intelligence community review its conventions.[49] The government's response was that the guidance to staff on use of language had been reviewed and reissued (we might also hope that politicians are inducted into them!), and that JIC minutes were now to include 'alternative and minority hypotheses or uncertainties'.[50]

The other main consumer of intelligence, albeit in rather more sporadic circumstances, is the media and, through them, the public. Until relatively recently, all intelligence agencies made efforts to minimize their contact with the media (and some still do) apart from planting stories with friendly journalists.[51] It is now more likely that agencies will have press liaison officers with whom journalists will make contact; some will themselves deal openly with the media through press statements – for example, the CIA – while others will still deal at one remove through their sponsoring departments. For example, the UK Home Office deals with the press on behalf of MI5. There has always been an unofficial and symbiotic aspect to relationships between the media and intelligence agencies – all agencies have tended to cultivate those working in the media both as potential outlets for information that the agency wants to see in the public domain and as potential sources. Journalists, for example, have often acted (with or without payment) as sources for agencies (after all, the job of a journalist is indistinguishable from that of other information collectors). This relationship has sometimes given rise to great controversy and danger. For example, in the wake of revelations about the CIA's use of journalists, it was forbidden from recruiting them. On other occasions, the suspicion that journalists were working for a foreign intelligence agency – whether correct or not – have led to their murder, as in the case of Farzad Bazoft in Iraq in 1990.[52]

Also, a less noted aspect of the row between the British government and the BBC in 2003 regarding the accuracy of the Iraq arms dossier was that the fateful meeting between BBC journalist Andrew Gilligan and weapons inspector David Kelly on 22 May was their second – the first was when Gilligan sought Kelly's advice on what to look out for on an upcoming trip to Iraq earlier in 2003. So, for Kelly, the object of the 22 May meeting was mainly to find out what Gilligan had seen.[53] Also, agencies may well use media as outlets for information as exercises in disinformation. For example, giving evidence to the ISC, David Kelly explained in answer to a question from the Chair, Ann Taylor, that within the DIS he liaised with the 'Rockingham cell' that serviced the weapons inspectors in Iraq.[54] This DIS group had the role, according to Scott Ritter, the former weapons inspector, of using intelligence from the UNSCOM inspectors in order to sustain in public the claims that Iraq was not in compliance with UN resolutions, while ignoring ambiguous or contrary findings.[55] The Butler Review gave a more anodyne account of Rockingham as the means whereby UK intelligence assessments were provided *to* UNSCOM,[56] but did not address the issue of what was done with the material received *from* UNSCOM via post-inspection briefings, and therefore did not deal with the question of whether Rockingham was part of a propaganda operation.

Agencies may now make some of their analyses directly available to the public; by definition, these will be unclassified, and they are likely to be in the category of basic intelligence, but they are a welcome element of the more general democratization of intelligence in recent decades. Many agencies now have their own websites on which reports are available. Typically, they include descriptions of the agency mission, information about applying for jobs with the agency, lists of previous publications (in some cases, such as the Australian Security Intelligence Organisation (ASIO) and CSIS these include corporate-style annual reports) and, especially since 9/11, special reports and assessments of terrorist threats and invitations to contact the agency with information. Some include an archive of press releases; NCIS publishes a non-classified version of its annual threat assessment for serious and organized crime in the UK, and CSIS publishes *Commentary*, which provides single-issue reports, some by CSIS personnel and others written by outsiders.[57]

Where Intelligence Turns into Action: The Intensification of Surveillance

Even if intelligence is disseminated, it may not be 'heard': ministers and other executives may not receive it; they may not believe it; they may pay attention only to those parts that tell them what they want to hear; they may lack the resources to do anything with it; or they may simply not know what to do with it. The 9/11 Commission examined the response of US security agencies to the increased threat information during the summer of 2001:

> In sum, the domestic agencies never mobilized in response to the threat. They did not have the direction, and did not have a plan to institute. The borders were not hardened. Transportation systems were not fortified. Electronic surveillance was not targeted against a domestic threat. State and local law enforcement were not marshaled to augment the FBI's efforts. The public was not warned.[58]

Recalling our definition of 'surveillance', which includes both the monitoring of behaviour and attempts to 'discipline' it (or the development of knowledge, in order to deploy power), then we must acknowledge that, in practice, the two may be indistinguishable. For example, while the use of informers may be intended primarily to acquire information about their target, they may also (knowingly or unknowingly) have some impact on the activities of the target. Similarly, technical surveillance may be used overtly, so that it simultaneously gathers information and acts as a 'scarecrow' to deviant behaviours. Yet it is still important to consider separately how intelligence affects policy, whether the latter is pursued overtly or covertly and bearing in mind that the policy's impact may not be as intended, perhaps because of the resistance of others.

Figures 5.1 and 5.2 seek to summarize and classify the major forms of action that might be deployed as a result of intelligence. This needs to be grounded at the most general level in the literature on power. We saw in chapter 2 that there are two broad theoretical streams with respect to power: the constant sum or 'sovereign' view that power is exercised *over* people and a second, variable sum view of power as 'facilitative'. Using ideas from these two streams of power, Scott argues that two complementary modes of power can be identified: corrective influence and persuasive influence.[59] The former operates through two main sub-types of force and manipulation. Force is the use of *physical* sanctions to compel or prevent some action on the part of others, while manipulation involves the use of positive or negative *material* sanctions such as money, credit and food. Persuasive influence operates by offering reasons for acting in some way, and the success or otherwise of the offer depends on factors such as the reputation or expertise of the offerer and the extent to which there are shared

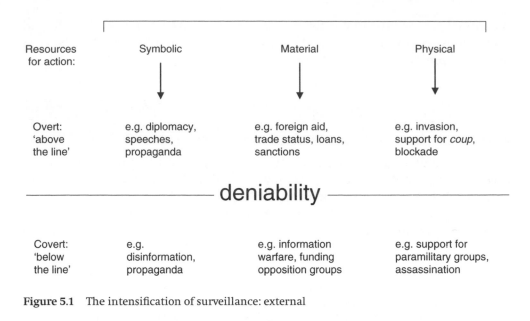

Resources for action:	Symbolic	Material	Physical

| Overt: 'above the line' | e.g. diplomacy, speeches, propaganda | e.g. foreign aid, trade status, loans, sanctions | e.g. invasion, support for *coup*, blockade |

deniability

| Covert: 'below the line' | e.g. disinformation, propaganda | e.g. information warfare, funding opposition groups | e.g. support for paramilitary groups, assassination |

Figure 5.1   The intensification of surveillance: external

values and commitments between the two sides. We might summarize these resources as *symbolic*. Actual patterns of power may, of course, combine these different forms in varying ways.[60]

In the figures symbolic, material and physical sanctions are deployed along a spectrum, but, note, this is for analytical purposes. Moving from left to right along the spectrum, we can see an escalation in the deployment of power such as would be familiar to international relations students;[61] but, perhaps more usefully, it is the varying combinations of the three resources deployed in any situation that indicate the seriousness with which the issue is viewed by the power-holder.[62] In the second row of figure 5.2 there are some examples of 'above-the-line' policies that might be deployed. These are overt in the sense that resources are deployed openly: ambassadors and ministers urging particular forms of behaviour on other states or non-state actors make public speeches. They may also lobby in private, but the point is that the people they are trying to influence know exactly where the effort is coming from. More materially, loans or 'most favoured nation' trade status are offered as an inducement, while economic sanctions may be applied unilaterally or multilaterally through UN procedures. Examples include South Africa during the later years of apartheid, Iraq following the 1991 Gulf War, and the Taliban in December 2000. Physical resources will normally be military forces available for an invasion or a naval blockade – for example, President Kennedy's blockade of Cuba to prevent Soviet ships from delivering missiles to Cuba in 1962. Sometimes states may openly support the use of force by proxies or openly provide support for domestic opponents of a regime to mount a *coup*. Note that referring to these measures as 'above the line' indicates that responsibility for the actions can be clearly seen – it does not necessarily mean that they are legal, Usually they will be, since states prefer

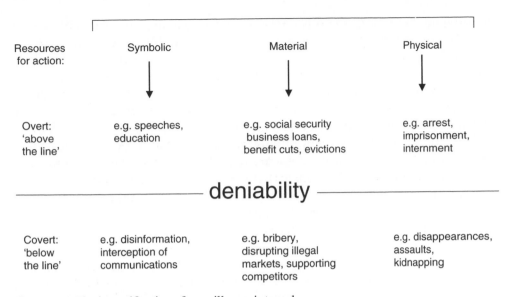

Figure 5.2   The intensification of surveillance: internal

not to take actions generally acknowledged as illegal,[63] but international law is often sufficiently ambiguous for legality to be claimed even if not all others agree, as the US-led invasion of Iraq in 2003 demonstrated.

Figure 5.2 shows the same processes at work *internally* when governments seek to translate information into policy. Activities that are seen as threatening to the social, political and economic fabric of societies may be defined as breaches of the criminal law, as infringements of regulations, or will remain legal. Symbolic attempts will be made through speeches and education to discourage people from engaging in these activities. Also material resources may be deployed: for example, the UK government in recent years has been making increasing efforts to discourage 'anti-social behaviour' – officially, this is a level of disorderly behaviour remaining just below the line of criminality – and has supported local authorities in establishing special administrative units to deploy professional 'evidence-gatherers' whose evidence is used to support eviction proceedings against those committing the behaviour. Examples of physical resources are those with which we are more familiar – police retain the power to arrest and detain those whose behaviour is 'reasonably suspected' of being criminal, and in a small minority of cases these cases will proceed through the criminal justice system and result in a conviction that may result in imprisonment.

Since policy and operations above the line are openly avowed, they will be carried out by a variety of state agencies, including the military and police. The 'line' is defined in the figures by the concept of deniability – in the same way that most actions above the line are arguably legal, so most (but not all) below the line are demonstrably illegal. This is the primary reason why states wish to be able plausibly to deny that they are responsible, but there are others.

Carrying out operations secretly appears to provide a number of advantages for officials: they avoid having to explain anything in public, they retain greater operational flexibility, and, if successful, they avoid the risk of retaliation from the target. On the other hand, they may involve great costs: the more complex the operation, or the greater the number of people involved, the harder it becomes to maintain secrecy. If operations are exposed, the sponsoring state may face great embarrassment and a lack of trust in its future actions. A variation on this theme is the use of intelligence agencies as a means of providing 'back channels' to adversaries; these are useful precisely because, for example, governments cannot admit publicly that they are 'talking with terrorists'. So, in Northern Ireland, while police, security and military agencies sought to defeat the PIRA, some MI6 officials tried to keep talking with a view to developing a peaceful political process.[64] It is as likely that this reflected different attitudes and organizational mandates as any sophisticated grand strategy.

The question of trust raises the ethical issue of whether states that claim to be democratic should be involved at all in deniable actions against others. It would not make sense for states to deny themselves the possibility of clandestine diplomacy to achieve peaceful solutions to intractable problems. Hence some argue that where covert action can provide states with cheaper, more convenient means of protecting themselves, they would be foolish not to take advantage of it.[65] But others argue that such actions violate acceptable norms of international behaviour for which officials will not be held accountable. There will be others who do not take either of these absolute positions, but argue that the so-called quiet option is rarely as effective as some claim.[66]

In terms of their formal mandate, not all security agencies will be empowered to take action at all. CSIS, for example, is instructed to collect, analyse and retain information regarding activities threatening Canadian security, 'and report to and advise the Government'.[67] In the UK, by comparison, MI5's function is defined more broadly as 'the protection of the national security',[68] thus incorporating a mandate to take action as well as gather information. The Intelligence Services Act 1994 that provided MI6 and GCHQ with a statutory mandate for the first time also included a section seeking to indemnify officers who took actions abroad for which they would be criminally liable if committed in the UK[69] – a clear acknowledgement that covert operations are conducted. Police also have a broader mandate: since the introduction of the 'new police' in London in 1829, a central function has been the 'prevention' of crime that, similarly, involves both the collection of information and some form of action.[70]

Again, the figures give examples of some of the most frequently deployed techniques: symbolic resources are most often used as part of disinformation or propaganda campaigns. The information disseminated by radio or pamphlet or website may or may not be accurate, but what these techniques have in common if they are 'below the line' is that the true origin of the information is disguised. The history of deception in intelligence can be traced back to at least Leonidas and Themistocles in the Persian Wars.[71] Michael Herman tells us that intelligence 'works closely with deception. Military deception is an operational activity; strictly speaking it is not intelligence. But intelligence should be the expert on the foreign intelligence organizations to be deceived, and if it controls a double agent it provides the deception channel.'[72] Deception can be used to manipulate perceptions of a state's capabilities or perceptions of its intentions. Susceptibility to deception clearly limits the accuracy of intelligence.

States may seek to provide material support to opposition or dissident groups in another country,[73] may bribe officials, and may disrupt their raising of funds.[74] A very modern method is to deploy information warfare in which the ICT networks of the target are attacked.[75] Military force may be applied covertly in different ways – this is not really an option available to many nations, but major countries tend to have some 'special operations' units for covert work – the USA now has a Special Operations Command (SOCOM), and the UK deploys the Special Air and Special Boat Services (SAS and SBS).

Another technique will be to offer support to indigenous paramilitary groups – such as the Northern Alliance in Afghanistan[76] – to carry out the action or, increasingly in these days of 'out-sourcing', to subcontract the operation to a private military company (PMC). For example, Sandline International was contracted to help re-install the elected President of Sierra Leone, Ahmed Kabbah, who was ousted in a *coup* in 1997. Sandline's involvement was underwritten by the financier Rakesh Saxena, memorably described by Foreign Secretary Robin Cook as 'an Indian businessman, travelling on the passport of a dead Serb, awaiting extradition from Canada for alleged embezzlement from a bank in Thailand',[77] in return for diamond concessions in Sierra Leone. In March 1998 the company assisted a Nigerian-led force to retake the capital. However, Sandline's shipment of arms was held to be a violation of a UN embargo, and HM Customs raided the firm's London offices in pursuit of their investigation. In an echo of the arms-to-Iraq affair a few years earlier, Sandline responded that their operation had been undertaken with the full knowledge of the Foreign Office.[78] This was originally denied, but later shown to be true, and exposed contradictions in the 'ethical foreign policy' that Cook claimed to be following.[79]

Northern Ireland provides many examples of the dangers of uncontrolled covert action in counter-terrorism. After many years of official denials, inquiries by a Canadian judge and a senior British police officer indicate that state agencies 'colluded' with loyalist paramilitaries in the killing of lawyers and others alleged to be Republicans. 'Colluded' is a slightly euphemistic term to describe the subcontracting of murder to paramilitary groups in such a way as to conceal state involvement. Judge Cory's report into the murder of Patrick Finucane, a Catholic lawyer, concluded 'that there is strong evidence that collusive acts were committed by the Army (Force Research Unit), the Royal Ulster Constabulary Special Branch and the Security Service'.[80] Sir John Stevens, then Commissioner of the London Metropolitan Police, concluded his Third Report into the Finucane

---

Box 5.3 The 'chilling' of covert action

'After the Watergate era, Congress established oversight committees to ensure that the CIA did not undertake covert action contrary to basic American law. Case officers in the CIA's Clandestine Service interpreted legislation, such as the Hughes–Ryan Amendment requiring that the president approve and report to Congress any covert action, as sending a message to them that covert action often leads to trouble and can severely damage one's career. Controversies surrounding Central American covert action programs in the mid-1980s led to the indictment of several senior officers of the Clandestine Service. During the 1990s, tension sometimes arose, as it did in the effort against al Qaeda, between policymakers who wanted the CIA to undertake more aggressive covert action and wary CIA leaders who counselled prudence and making sure that the legal basis and presidential authorization for their actions were undeniably clear.'

Source: 9/11 Commission Report, p. 90

---

and other murders thus: 'there was collusion in both murders and the circumstances surrounding them. Collusion is evidenced in many ways. This ranges from the failure to keep records, the absence of accountability, the withholding of intelligence and evidence, through to the extreme of agents being involved in murder.'[81]

As this example indicates, covert action is not limited to foreign countries. Famously, under J. Edgar Hoover from the 1950s onwards, the FBI developed a range of covert programmes that were deployed against the Ku Klux Klan, the Communist Party, Black power, civil rights and antiwar movements. COINTEL-PRO incorporated a range of techniques, including false documents aimed at fomenting splits within political groups, inciting violence, and spreading false rumours about activists' personal lives.[82] The controversies when these techniques were revealed, Hoover's death in 1972, the Watergate investigations, and legal actions against the Bureau all contributed to a significant shift in its targets and internal procedures so that, by the later 1970s, it was concerned more with white-collar and organized crime than with political and security targets.[83] However, the widespread criticism of the FBI for its contribution to the intelligence failure of 9/11 has led to a rapid reappraisal of the Bureau's role, with attempts to reorient it towards counter-terrorism, including the resurrection of COINTELPRO tactics of the 1960s.[84]

An abiding dilemma for security agencies is, having identified and located targets, whether to maintain surveillance in the interests of developing intelligence (and/or evidence) while risking the perpetration of an attack or whether to intervene earlier to disrupt/arrest/interrogate and risk cutting off the information flow. 9/11 has shifted this balance clearly towards the latter, because of the heightened fears of WMD attacks (however fanciful some of these may be). Police may also deploy 'covert action' towards crime, though that is not what it will be called. In the UK during the 1990s, police increasingly made use of 'disruption' as a way of countering the activities of professional or organized criminals. This might involve passing information or disinformation regarding the presence of informers within a group through more physical measures such as overt surveillance at the site of an anticipated crime. Drugs might be confiscated even if no arrests or charges followed because of evidential difficulties, or people might be arrested not with a view to prosecution but in order to obtain information or disrupt a planned crime. The advantage to police of these tactics is that they can avoid the costs and uncertain outcomes of the full criminal justice process. The idea of targeting criminals and then disrupting their activities is the essence of the 'intelligence-led' model of policing.[85]

Conclusion

In this chapter we have discussed the processes whereby information gathered by intelligence agencies is translated into what we call 'intelligence', how it is passed on to others, and how it informs police or government action. As a result of the controversies around the (ab)use of information and intelligence with respect to the decision to invade Iraq, we now have access to a good deal more information about these processes than previously. Although there is an increasing array of highly sophisticated software that increases the possibilities of carrying out indepth analysis of the relationships between data, analysis remains at heart an intellectual exercise in which analysts struggle to ascribe meaning to information. But this is a process carried out within organizational contexts, and therefore, to the cognitive problems that may afflict individuals, have to be added organizational problems that can range from an excess of conformity ('groupthink') to political battles over turf and interpretations. We examine the specific impact of these regarding Iraqi WMD in chapter 7.

In the same way that much of what is gathered may not actually be analysed beyond an initial assessment of credibility, much of what an agency produces by way of intelligence may not be disseminated. This is not necessarily because of short-sightedness or incompetence. A reluctance to share information may indicate a concern to protect sources or simply result from a lack of appreciation that some other body would be interested (one problem with a simple market model of intelligence in which producers simply give consumers what they ask for is the assumption that consumers understand what they need). How dissemination takes place (verbal? visual? written? how long? including examples of raw data?) will be only one factor in determining how it is received, but the policy interests of the consumer will also affect what they hear. This factor is reinforced by the nuanced way in which intelligence is written – analysts deal with uncertainty, and this gives consumers more 'space' within which to hear what they want to hear.

Finally, we discussed the relationship between intelligence and action more generally. As well as intelligence providing the knowledge base for governments' publicly acknowledged foreign diplomatic policies and domestic security policies, it provides also the basis for secret policies conducted to counter or disrupt social, economic, military or political threats. Such policies can be very attractive to officials, because they *seem* to offer relatively 'quick fixes' to complex problems; but they can be highly problematic if examined in a broader light and over a longer term. President Clinton recalled remarking at some point to his chairman of the Joint Chiefs of Staff, 'You know, it would scare the shit out of al-Qaeda if suddenly a bunch of black ninjas rappelled out of helicopters into the middle of their camp.'[86]

Prior to 9/11, no such operation was launched, but secrecy means that officials can avoid accountability, and where their actions do cause death and destruction, then this must raise issues about the legitimacy of regimes that, in all probability claim to be democratic and law-abiding. Covert action is a kind of institutionalized hypocrisy in which ethics and the rule of law are subjugated to the achievement of short-term political gains, when the costs are borne by some national or ethnic or political 'other'. In the longer term, of course, such policies may come back to haunt the perpetrators – most notably in recent times, the presence within al-Qaeda of *mujahideen* initially trained and equipped by the USA to fight the Soviet Union in Afghanistan.[87] The success or failure of all policies, whether overt or covert, depends at least in part on the reaction to them from those they are intended to affect – specifically, in the security field, the amount of resistance. Even if policy is developed in a relatively open process, predicting its outcomes – intended and unintended – is notoriously difficult; in the closed world of intelligence, where covert actions may be planned by a small group, the danger of wishful thinking is paramount.

CHAPTER 6

Why Does Intelligence Fail?

Reports that say that something hasn't happened are always interesting to me, because as we know, there are known knowns; there are things we know we know. We also know there are known unknowns; that is to say we know there are some things we do not know. But there are also unknown unknowns – the ones we don't know we don't know.

Donald Rumsfeld, February 2002

Introduction

THIS chapter discusses the limits of intelligence. In doing so, it draws almost exclusively on examples of US intelligence failure, for the good reason that such failures are debated more openly in the USA than in any other political system; hence evidence on which to base analysis is more readily available. This allows us better to understand the nature of intelligence failure, by locating its primary source at a given point in the intelligence cycle. However, this should not lead us to the enticing conclusion that intelligence failure can always be so easily pigeon-holed. As chapter 7 makes clear, intelligence failure is not necessarily mono-causal or confined to just one point of the cycle. Nevertheless, the concept of the intelligence cycle does act as a useful mechanism for locating the causes of intelligence failure and considering reforms aimed at reducing the risk of its recurrence.[1]

The creation of the CIA was meant to ensure that there would be no future catastrophic security failure like the December 1941 Japanese surprise attack on Pearl Harbor. The elimination of surprise was central to its purpose.[2] However, popular notions that intelligence can provide a fail-safe mechanism have created false expectations as to just what intelligence can deliver. At the outset it is worth highlighting the scope of activity to which these false expectations attach. For example, a 1995 CIA publication, *A Consumer's Guide to Intelligence*, defined intelligence in its national security context as covering 'all military, economic, political, scientific, technological, and other aspects of foreign developments that pose actual or potential threats to US national interests'.[3] To claim capabilities over such a broad and unpredictable range of variables is to invite both false

103

expectations and disappointment and anger when intelligence visibly falls short of these. Indicative of this, in 2005 the *Economist* characterized the CIA as 'an unreformed, substantially unaccountable bureaucracy, which has almost never sacked anyone, which appears deluded by its own mythology and which, despite some notable successes, is burdened by a miserable run of failures'.[4] Hence, Enoch Powell's adage that 'All political lives, unless they are cut off in midstream at a happy juncture, end in failure'[5] could well be employed to US DCIs – Dulles, Helms, Colby, Casey, Woolsey, Deutch and Tenet have all vacated the office in response to varying degrees of failure.

The Limits of Intelligence

However, some of the 'limits' of intelligence are more apparent than real, and arise as a consequence of the fact that intelligence is poorly understood. At times, its advocates have made unjustifiable claims for what it can achieve; at other times, decision-makers, especially those with limited experience of intelligence, have had unrealistic expectations of what it can deliver. Failures of power are at least as frequent as failures of 'knowledge'. 'Intelligence' is not the holy grail; it cannot, and should not claim to, offer a crystal ball for seeing the future clearly. As we saw in chapter 5, the process by which intelligence is developed is fraught with potential distortions and problems that can derail the production of accurate intelligence. Some of these relate to the inherent shortcomings and cognitive limits of personnel; others are to a greater or lesser extent inherent in the process. These include the intrinsic difficulties of identifying targets and the tendency to concentrate, for practical or ideological reasons, on the 'usual suspects'; internal bureaucratic obstacles (intelligence agencies are prone to 'turf wars'); and failures to share information that derive, in part, from the very concern with 'secrecy' that is seen as the *sine qua non* for effective intelligence. Finally, as we have seen, those states, organizations, groups or people who are the targets of intelligence operations are unlikely to remain passive. They have their own objectives and deploy their own techniques to counter attempts to discover their secrets. These may just be defensive (secrecy), but may also attempt to deliberately mislead and thus disrupt an opponent's operations.

In the wake of 9/11, Iraq and 7/7, it is clearly essential to identify and understand the nature of intelligence failure and where it occurs, so as to be able to improve systems and processes, and thereby minimize the risk of future failures, even if it is true that such modifications can bring about only marginal improvements in the efficacy of intelligence agencies. This is essentially the argument put forward some years ago by Richard Betts (see figure 6.1). As noted in chapter 1, Betts contended that:

> In the best-known cases of intelligence failure, the most crucial mistakes have seldom been made by collectors of raw information, occasionally by professionals

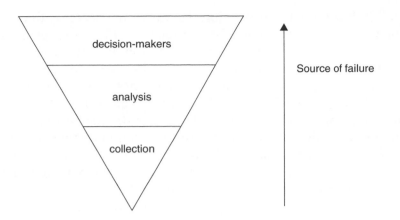

Figure 6.1 Betts's sources of intelligence failure

who produce finished analyses, but most often by the decision-makers who consume the products of intelligence services. Policy premises constrict perception, and administrative workloads constrain reflection. Intelligence failure is political and psychological more often than organizational.[6]

Secondly, Betts argues that

Observers who see notorious intelligence failures as egregious often infer that disasters can be avoided by perfecting norms and procedures for analysis and argumentation. This belief is illusory. Intelligence can be improved marginally, but not radically, by altering the analytic system. The illusion is also dangerous if it abets overconfidence that systemic reforms will increase the predictability of threats.[7]

Hence, the limits of intelligence dictate that intelligence failure is inevitable. Partly, this is a consequence of the impossibility of perfect predictive success; partly it is a consequence of decision-makers' (politicians with regard to states) natural tendency to err on the side of caution by subscribing to worst-case scenarios, or to simply ignore intelligence that does not fit their own preferences. The extent to which they do this is related to a strategic environment and past history, but given that their core function is the security of the state and its citizens, they all share essentially the same commitment to ensuring that vulnerabilities are not exposed and that they themselves are not exposed as a consequence of unpreparedness or failure to act on what is subsequently demonstrated to have been actionable intelligence. This tendency is heightened in the aftermath of an attack or failure to prevent some other form of strategic surprise.[8]

Failure Located in Collection and Analysis

Failure at the levels of collection and analysis can occur for a wide range of reasons. The reliability of sources of information clearly helps to determine the accuracy of analysis. If the information is inaccurate, beyond being merely worthless, it will invite policy failure. Linguistic barriers may limit the number of analysts not susceptible to basic mistakes of translation or interpretation. The more difficult accurate, first-hand understanding of the target state is, the easier it becomes for politicians to apply their own ideologically informed explanations to specific behaviour and to see these explanations carry the day. There will simply be few qualified dissenting voices. Elsewhere, as we saw in chapter 5, members of the analytical community may consciously or subconsciously engage in a process of 'groupthink' whereby they accept dominant analyses or arguments and refrain from rocking the boat by registering their analytical dissent, for a variety of reasons. It is a phenomenon that acts as a barrier to the application of intuition and to taking imaginative approaches to the study of problems. Moreover, given the requirement for instant analysis, the short time-scales that are often involved serve to reinforce this disincentive to take more imaginative approaches and inhibit the process of abduction – testing emerging information against competing hypotheses rather than just against the dominant assumption.[9] Then there are the simple blunders. Notable post-Cold War blunders include the intelligence that formed the basis of the 1998 attack on a pharmaceutical plant in Sudan and on the Chinese embassy in Belgrade during the 1999 Kosovo war.

Lack of imagination has been a notable contributory factor to intelligence failures; for example, the 9/11 Commission identified this as one of the four kinds of failure the attacks revealed.[10] Other examples would include the failure to predict the 1973 Arab–Israeli war. Often such failure takes the form of an organizational inability to see beyond the dominant assumption, or an unwillingness to challenge it. Understandably, this inability or unwillingness is likely to increase in direct proportion to the volume of intelligence seemingly supporting the dominant assumption. Oft-mooted ways of overcoming this reluctance involve institutionalizing a degree of competitive analysis or formalizing the role of devil's advocate within the analytic process.

However, there are weaknesses with both proposals. With regard to competitive analysis, this carries with it the legacy of the Team B experiment of the 1970s, now joined by the Office of Special Plans' activities (discussed below) in presenting the case for war against Iraq in 2003. In both cases the competitive analysis was rooted in assumptions about the character and likely behaviour of the target state, so much so with regard to Team B that Lawrence Freedman has characterized its 1976 report as 'not so much an alternative estimate as a critique of the performance of the intelligence community over the previous decade', which was seen as being flawed because rooted in a fundamental failure to appreciate the reality of Soviet attitudes and goals.[11] Moreover, competitive analysis would result in a product that runs counter to customer requirements with regard to intelligence:

> Outsiders called in to refute or [challenge] intelligence estimates would only
> muddle the process from the decision-makers' perspective. Policymakers need
> abbreviated, focused analytical products from the intelligence community. Even

with the lengthier estimates, the intelligence community should be affirming to policymakers the most likely course of events after processing and evaluating the available evidence. Only through these types of estimates can strategic-level intelligence agencies properly 'serve' the policymakers.[12]

Once formalized, the utility of a devil's advocacy approach is immediately compromised – it does not come from a broad range of subject experts but from one source or group of sources and takes on a ritualistic character which lessens the likelihood of it consistently being taken seriously. However, without such a formalization of the position, finding people willing to act as devil's advocates encounters the organizational problem that dissent can be seen as a barrier to promotion. As Bob Woodward notes with regard to the dominant assumption within the CIA regarding Iraqi WMD in late 2002: 'The alternative view was that Saddam didn't have WMD. No one wanted to say that because so much intelligence would have to be discounted.'[13]

Conversely, imagination can also be a source of intelligence failure. A good example of this relates to an end of 2003 terror alert issued by the US Department of Homeland Security, which raised the (US) national threat level to high ('orange'). One impact of this was long delays and even cancellations of flights into the USA from the UK, France and Mexico. At the time, this decision was said to have three bases:

- A rise in the *level* of intelligence 'chatter' picked up electronically, which is itself used as a gauge of terrorist activity.
- Both this and information from informants pointed to concern about specific flights – those from London to Washington, Paris to Los Angeles, and Mexico City to Los Angeles.
- Added to this, the Christmas holiday period was already considered a high-risk time because it was when 'shoe bomber' Richard Reid had attempted to ignite his shoes – during a Paris–Miami flight on 22nd December 2001.[14]

Flight delays and cancellations were partly a product of the recent demand by the USA that all aircraft flying into US airspace pass on a flight list prior to take-off.[15] Clearly, the analysis of these lists played a crucial role in the identification of a terrorist threat. In the absence of a centralized database, many of the delays seemed to result from a checking process which was technologically limited and unsophisticated, given the budgets of the agencies involved in conducting them. Cancellations of French flights, for example, turned out to be based on the similarity of passenger surnames with those on a list of wanted al-Qaeda activists derived from interrogations of prisoners held at Guantánamo Bay, leading to a Welsh insurance agent and an elderly female Chinese restaurant owner being questioned over terrorist links.[16] It subsequently transpired that the alert was also attributable to CIA analysts' belief that al-Qaeda was sending secret messages via Arabic satellite television channel al-Jazeera, which gave details of specific flights and targets into which they would be flown.[17] This belief arose from their use of a process called 'steganography', which was used to divine hidden messages from the television images. Head of Homeland Security, Tom Ridge, later conceded that this approach to intelligence was 'bizarre, unique, unorthodox, unprecedented', adding that, 'speaking for myself I've got to admit to wondering whether or not it was credible'.[18]

Failure can also be rooted in structures and management approaches. Most obviously, in fragmented intelligence communities, limits to communication possibly fostered by an internally competitive environment can be a source of failure. Management style and willingness to encourage an environment in which competing hypotheses can be explored is another potential source. So too is the strength of the 'dominant assumption', partly because it can be handed down as a given in training programmes. For example, Frank Snepp, principal analyst for the CIA on North Vietnam for a time from the late 1960s, has recalled how: 'When I was training in the Agency to go to Vietnam, I was hit over the head with the domino theory. I was told that it was what would define the future of South Vietnam. The ideology that propelled us into the war obscured history, and it was obviously a terrible oversight because in embracing the domino theory we perpetuated our presence there, we justified staying in.'[19] Dominant assumptions similarly constrained responses to developments in the US relationship with the Soviet Union. In 1983, a series of factors ranging from the heightened confrontational rhetoric of President Reagan's references to the Soviet Union, reaction to the downing of Korean Airlines' flight 007 over Soviet airspace, and the unveiling of the 'Star Wars' missile defence concept convinced the Soviet leadership that the USA was preparing to launch an attack. When Soviet defector Oleg Gordievsky visited Washington in 1986, he found that analysts had completely misread this state of Soviet paranoia, recalling that 'one important analyst told me it was a huge deception plan by the Soviet leadership to deceive us. So they were so deeply rooted in their own dogmas of the previous time, when they received fresh and different information which clashed with their dogmas, they didn't like it. They were not flexible enough.'[20]

Additionally, intelligence needs to be alert to the possibility of, and hence able to overcome, the concealment and deception strategies discussed in chapter 5. All of the above limitations have been evident to a greater or lesser degree in relation to US and Western attempts to gain reliable information concerning non-conventional weapons programmes in Iraq, Iran and North Korea.[21] Where the target is not a state, but a group of sub-state actors such as the leadership of al-Qaeda, these difficulties are amplified by the kinds of difficulties well illustrated in the drawn-out efforts to apprehend bin Laden and his closest associates.

Failure, then, is inevitable in intelligence. Predictions drawn from analysis as to future behaviour will never be 100 per cent accurate. In this, intelligence work has something in common with meteorology, the science of weather forecasting. The latter, resting on a firmer scientific basis, can predict general trends with a high degree of confidence, but it cannot always predict accurately, nor can it always be relied on reliably to predict the *impact* of poor or freak weather, especially where this differs markedly from past experience. For example, the US government appeared completely unprepared for the inundation of New Orleans after Hurricane Katrina in September 2005, despite a warning from the Federal Emergency Management Agency (FEMA) in early 2001 that it was one of the three most likely disasters to happen – the other two being a terrorist attack on New York and a Californian earthquake.[22]

Intelligence services are not only expected to be able to assess trends and anticipate deviations from trends; they are also expected to be able to gauge the *impact* of these. In this, there is a risk that too much is being expected of intelligence. For example, there were clear failings of US intelligence in relation to its analysis of the immediate post-war situation that would face US forces in Iraq, so much so that

> Intelligence officials were convinced that American soldiers would be greeted warmly when they pushed into southern Iraq [hence] a CIA operative suggested sneaking hundreds of small American flags into the country for grateful Iraqis to wave at their liberators. The agency would capture the spectacle on film and beam it throughout the Arab world. It would be the ultimate information operation.[23]

This erroneous macro-analysis bears responsibility for numerous micro-failures, including the failure to anticipate the resistance role of paramilitary forces in southern Iraq during the US advance towards Baghdad, the failure to identify and secure arms caches across the country, subsequently raided by or on behalf of resistance forces, underestimation of both the devastation brought about by a combination of sanctions and war to Iraq's infrastructure, and hence of the extent of reconstruction required, and overestimation of the professionalism of the Iraqi police force. Echoing one of the explanations for intelligence failures over Vietnam some thirty years earlier (and discussed below), former CIA deputy director Richard J. Kerr explained that 'The intelligence accurately forecast the reactions of the ethnic and tribal factions in Iraq,' but that, nevertheless, 'collection was poor. Too much emphasis was placed on current intelligence and there was too little research on important social, political and cultural issues.'[24] The Butler Report made a similar point in relation to gaps in pre-war UK intelligence.[25]

The limits of intelligence can be understood by examining intelligence successes as much as failures. For example, with regard to the 1967 Arab–Israeli war, the CIA was able to predict the likely outbreak, the duration of the war, and its outcome. In this case, intelligence success was attributable to several factors, including the fact that policymakers asked one clear question, 'Who will win if the US stays out?', and the fact that the estimation was based on comparative military data. Hence, 'analysts did not have to advance vague medium- or long-term predictions that could go wrong because of unforeseen or high impact/low probability events', and were dealing with hard fact as opposed to 'tea leaves'.[26]

The fact that there are clear limits to intelligence is easily demonstrated by reference to a few of the defining events of the last century that US intelligence failed to anticipate. Any such list would have to include predictive failures regarding the Soviet testing of its first atomic bomb, the North Korean invasion of South Korea, the construction of the Berlin Wall, an apparent string of failures over Vietnam, the Soviet invasion of Czechoslovakia in 1968, and of Afghanistan in 1979, the Iranian revolution of the same year, the Polish crisis of 1980–1[27] and, more centrally given that its primary focus for over forty years was the USSR, the end of the Cold War. We discuss Vietnam and Iran in more detail below. With regard to the Soviet atomic bomb, just five days before it was exploded, the CIA produced a report echoing earlier analyses that mid-1953 was the most probable date for Soviet acquisition.[28] Although U-2 spy planes identified Soviet missile sites under construction in Cuba, US intelligence had failed to anticipate their siting there. With regard to the North Korean invasion of South Korea, the CIA reported as early as March 1950 that an invasion *could* occur in June, and subsequently sent over 1,000 reports covering the North Korean military buildup, only for these to be overridden by the military because they conflicted with the prevailing strategic consensus of the day, that North Korea would not risk such an adventure.[29] As the British Ambassador to Japan told the Foreign Office at the time: 'While the actual attack itself came as a complete surprise to everybody both here and in Korea, my Military Adviser tells me that Military Intelligence had learnt in April last that preparations were being made for such an attack. The Americans therefore should have been ready for it at least to the point of making up their minds exactly what should be done, in the technical way, when the storm broke.'[30]

The failure to anticipate the Soviet invasion of Afghanistan represents another analytical failure, based on a persistent belief that the USSR would not introduce large numbers of conventional forces into the neighbouring country. As a March 1979 CIA assessment concluded:

> The Soviets would be most reluctant to introduce large numbers of ground forces into Afghanistan to keep in power an Afghan government that had lost the support of virtually all segments of the population. Not only would the Soviets find themselves in an awkward morass in Afghanistan, but their actions could seriously damage their relations with India, and – to a lesser degree – with Pakistan. As a more likely option, the Soviets probably could seek to reestablish ties with those members of the Afghan opposition with whom Moscow had dealt profitably in the past.[31]

Hence the invasion caught the intelligence community off guard. The failure was not a consequence of an absence of information that could be held to point in the direction of an imminent Soviet invasion. Rather, it was a consequence of a mindset that did not consider an invasion to be a rational choice and so discounted it, and which sought to fit subsequent, potentially contradictory, evidence into this mindset rather than assess how far it undermined the validity of the prevailing assumption. Hence, this case illustrates a problem highlighted by Jack Davis: 'Whatever the analyst's level of expertise, the "hard-wiring" of the mind tends to make confirming information seem more vivid and authoritative than information that would call an established bottom-line judgment into question.' Compounding this problem is the fact that 'general recognition of cognitive vulnerability does not remove risk of unmotivated bias in evaluating information'.[32]

In 1983 the case of Afghanistan was included in a report commissioned to examine the quality of intelligence relating to 'significant historical failures over the last twenty years or so'.[33] This situated the core analytical error as being a misunderstanding of Soviet intentions rooted in an accurate assessment of the costs, but one to which US analysts then attached an inappropriate cost–benefit measure. 'In hindsight', the report concluded,

> the intelligence community accurately estimated the advantages and disadvantages of intervention. The community held to a premise that the disadvantages of intervention outweighed the advantages and concluded therefore that the Soviets would act rationally in accordance with our perception of Soviet self-interest. As real as the penalties to the Soviets have proved to be, we failed to comprehend the imperatives of Soviet policy as they perceived them. We had a clear understanding of their capabilities, but we misjudged their intentions.[34]

The extent of the apparent failure to predict the end of the Cold War is contested. Douglas J. MacEachin has contended that from the mid-1970s the Soviet Union was correctly described by CIA analysts as being 'plagued by a deteriorating economy and intensifying societal problems'.[35] Nevertheless, others have argued that the CIA's overestimation of Soviet economic growth shows that they were wide of the mark. On Soviet military strength, it has been claimed that the CIA was misled by double agents who exaggerated the preparedness and strength of the Soviet military, feeding into CIA reports that helped to persuade Congress to grant funding for projects such as the F-22 fighter aircraft.[36] MacEachin points to a CIA assessment produced in autumn 1989 which pointed to turbulent times ahead for the USSR, which it was 'doubtful at best' that Gorbachev would be able to control. However, this concern over the domestic impact of Gorbachev's reforms is not the same as predicting his acquiescence in the downfall of communism in East Germany or his role in dismantling the Warsaw Pact as a unified military alliance. MacEachin is correct to note that the CIA identified trends that could lead in a given direction with the assistance of the appropriate agency, which arrived in the shape of Gorbachev,[37] but it could not predict when this would happen, or its scale or impact – as noted above, much like the meteorologists who struggle to translate weather indicators into precise predictions.

The post-Cold War world has also featured significant failures at the levels of collection and analysis. In May 1998, Clinton Administration officials found out about India's nuclear tests from media coverage of the Indian government's official announcement. Senate Intelligence Committee chairman Richard C.

Shelby called it a 'colossal failure'. The subsequent Jeremiah Report pointed to mirror-imaging (the assumption that a target would behave in the same way as the customer of the intelligence would in similar circumstances) as a key cause of the failure, along with limited co-operation within the fragmented US intelligence community. In addition, an almost complete absence of human intelligence inside India had left the US dependent on satellite imagery.[38] The utility of this had been hampered by a meeting in 1995 at which the US Ambassador to India had shown Indian officials spy satellite photographs showing test preparations, allowing the Indians to improve concealment techniques. In fact, US satellites had picked up evidence of test preparation during the night before the detonation, but CIA satellite intelligence analysts slept through it, not having been put on alert.[39] As George Tenet told the Senate Select Committee on Intelligence: 'There is no getting around the fact that we did not predict these particular Indian nuclear tests. . . . We did not get it right, period.'[40]

In all of the above cases, what intelligence failed to do was to anticipate strategic shifts in behaviour, leaving its customer vulnerable to strategic surprise. However, the anticipation of strategic shifts is problematic. It is far easier for analysts to predict on the basis of the continuation of identified trends. Deviation from these trends by an intelligence target can be anticipated with certainty only via information from sources close to decision-makers – the 'what do they think?' dilemma.

This can lead to what could be termed 'the Knightley position', after journalist and intelligence writer Phillip Knightley articulated over a long period that seemed to offer ever more examples to show that 'most intelligence is useless, and spies who promise to provide reliable information are guilty of the biggest confidence trick of our age'.[41] He recalls a 1994 conference in Germany, 'attended by a panel of spymasters from east and west. I challenged them to name a single important historical event in peacetime in which intelligence had played a decisive role. No one could do so.'[42] Then again, there are even those, such as military historian John Keegan, who are sceptical about the decisiveness of the contribution that intelligence has made in wartime.[43] It is a scepticism that extends to diplomatic historians as well.[44] Knightley argues that the success of intelligence services in sustaining their operations outside wartime has rested on them successfully selling three propositions to politicians (and, implicitly, most of the mainstream media):

- 'In the secret world it may be impossible to distinguish success from failure. A timely warning of attack allows the intended victim to prepare. This causes the aggressor to change his mind; the warning then appears to have been wrong.'
- 'Failure can be due to incorrect analysis of the agency's accurate information – the warning was there but the government failed to heed it.'
- 'The agency could have offered timely warning had it not been starved of funds.'[45]

The Policymaker–Intelligence Interface as a Site of Intelligence Failure

It is at the level of the policymaker–intelligence community nexus that, if Betts's model is to hold good, we would expect to find the most serious sources of potential failure. For Loch Johnson, 'disregard of objective intelligence' by policymakers was one of the 'seven sins of strategic intelligence'.[46] As with Stalin's refusal to believe intelligence that the Nazis were preparing to invade the Soviet Union in 1941, 'no shortcoming of strategic intelligence is more often cited than the self-delusion of policymakers who brush aside – or bend – facts that fail to conform to their Weltanschauung'.[47] This kind of 'intelligence failure' is essentially a political failure, in that the failure is not primarily that of the intelligence community, beyond failing to convince the policymaker of the validity of its analyses, and is closely related to the politicization of intelligence – that is, the manipulation of evidence to fit preferred and pre-existing explanations, or the selection of evidence (involving omission as well as inclusion) to fit a known desired outcome.

Vietnam

Where intelligence does not fit policy preferences, it can be ignored by policymakers. This was the case with large numbers of pessimistic CIA analyses during the 1960s (and before) on the situation in Vietnam. One illustrative example concerns an evaluation of a new Vietnam initiative drafted by Director for Intelligence R. Jack Smith, who has recalled how

> If one based one's decision on the conclusions of our study, the result was obvious: the gain was not worth the cost. Nevertheless, the President announced the next day that he intended to go ahead. Distinctly annoyed that an admirable piece of analysis, done under forced draft at White House request, was being ignored, I stomped into Helms's office. 'How in the hell can the President make that decision in the face of our findings?' I asked.
>
> Dick fixed me with a sulphurous look. 'How do I know how he made up his mind? How does any president make decisions? Maybe Lynda Bird was in favor of it. Maybe one of his old friends urged him. Maybe it was something he read. Don't ask me to explain the workings of a president's mind.'[48]

For his part, Chester Cooper, a former NSC staff officer, noted how Lyndon Johnson's memoirs,

> which are replete with references to and long quotations from documents which influenced his thinking and decisions on Vietnam, contain not a single reference to a National Intelligence Estimate or, indeed, to any other intelligence analysis. Except for Secretary McNamara, who became a frequent requester and an avid reader of Estimates dealing with Soviet military capabilities and with the Vietnam situation, and McGeorge Bundy, ONE [Office of National Estimates] had a thin audience during the Johnson administration.[49]

It would be wrong to present CIA thinking on the Vietnam War as constituting a unified vision. There was a considerable gap between the views of officers
involved in the operational side of the war and those involved in producing
analysis, and even within these two groups there were divisions. While, opera-
tionally, the CIA was centrally and enthusiastically involved in the Phoenix
program,[50] one of the least glorious episodes of the entire conflict, analysts
tended to offer policymakers consistently pessimistic assessments. However,
analysts were susceptible to pressure. Harold Ford concedes that 'at times some
CIA analysts overreacted to certain assertive personalities from other offices
who happened to be arguing wholly unsupportable optimism', and that in a
'handful' of cases, 'analytic officers caved in to pressures from above and
produced mistakenly rosy judgments'.[51] One source of pressure was DCIs themselves, certain of whom 'brought pressure on Agency officers to make their
Vietnam analyses more palatable to policymakers'.[52] One of these was John
McCone. Ford gives an example from early 1963, weeks before the riots in Hue
that led to a deterioration in the situation in South Vietnam which culminated
in the self-immolation of Buddhist monks and the assassination of South
Vietnamese president Diem. At this time McCone, the Joint Chiefs of Staff, the
US Embassy in Saigon, and other policymakers objected to a draft NIE which
concluded that Vietnam suffered from a catalogue of debilitating woes, including an absence of 'aggressive and firm leadership at all levels of command, poor
morale among the troops, lack of trust between peasant and soldier, poor tactical use of available forces, a very inadequate intelligence system, and obvious
Communist penetration of the South Vietnamese military organization'.
As Ford recounts:

> Those criticisms by Community analysts raised a firestorm of protest among the
> policymaking officers. They brought such pressure on DCI McCone and ONE that
> the latter caved in and agreed to a rewritten, decidedly more rosy NIE, in which
> the earlier criticisms of the ARVN [South Vietnamese Army] were muted and the
> tone of the Estimate changed: the first sentence of the revised NIE now read, 'We
> believe that Communist progress has been blunted [in South Vietnam] and that
> the situation is improving.' This was not one of the CIA's proudest moments.[53]

This was not an isolated incident. For example, while intelligence community analyses were sceptical of the validity of the 'domino effect', McCone sided
with the military in their belief in it, and, as the individual charged with
'telling it like it is' to policymakers, failed to challenge this belief by pointing
out his Agency's own scepticism.[54] McCone was not alone in failing to represent
and defend analysis, however unpalatable to policymakers. The CIA's Special
Assistant for Vietnam Affairs, George Carver, regularly gave policymakers more
upbeat assessments of the situation in Vietnam than the analyses supported.
All of which points to the biggest hurdle facing analysts seeking to get their
message across to policymakers, 'the fact that the decisions on what to do in
Vietnam were not taking place in a vacuum but in a highly charged political
arena'.[55] In such an atmosphere, policymakers were unlikely to be receptive to

intelligence unless it supported the positions they were already defending. It also presented McCone with a conundrum as DCI. Challenging core policy-maker assumptions would affect his credibility, and perhaps even his access. Yet, while not challenging these assumptions, his access was ineffective. After he did diverge from Johnson on the best way forward, his access was duly affected. McCone was frozen out, and resigned in April 1965. The lessons of McCone's experience cannot have been lost on subsequent DCIs, including George Tenet. The credibility/access conundrum remains for DCIs, and it may well be that Tenet's 'slam dunk' reassurance on Iraqi WMD is just the most recent expression of it.[56]

Iran

Similar problems around 'telling it like it is' contributed to the failure to predict the coming of revolution in Iran, so much so that in just a year before the Shah fell, President Carter, during a visit to Tehran, publicly praised him as 'an island of stability in one of the more troubled areas of the world'.[57] In a classic example of confusing intelligence with policy, Carter's DCI, Admiral Stansfield Turner, subsequently offered the view that

> For us in the intelligence world to have gone to the President and said, 'We think Iran is about to crumble,' would have been a major change in US policy. It's hard for anybody to go that much against the opinion that has built up in this country as to what the relationship with Iran should be . . . to come to the conclusion that this was the truth would have been very difficult because it would have been running so contrary to the tide of opinion about what our relationship with Iran was.[58]

However, the failure over Iran went beyond a failure at the level of the intelligence community–policymaker interface. It stands out because of the scale of the US stake in the stability of the Shah's rule. Others have criticized the short-term character of analyses on Iran, focused on individual disturbances or riots at the expense of attention to the wider trend and, linked to this, the role the USA could play in attempting to persuade the Shah to moderate or change his approach to governance.[59] Analyses were based on a dominant assumption that the Shah would survive the crisis. It may well be that this insistence on the solidity of the Shah's rule was based on the fact that, as Gary Sick, a former National Security Council staffer with responsibility for Iran, has observed, 'the CIA were not a neutral observer and they had something at stake. And the stake was their relationship with the Shah and his regime that was extremely important to them. They were simply not prepared to sit back and look at it objectively.'[60] Crucially, the CIA's focus was not Iranian domestic politics, but the Cold War advantage that close alliance with the Shah offered and backing his rule in order to aid its continuation:

> The Shah was prepared to co-operate very actively with regard to intelligence on the Soviet Union – we had several big sites located in Iran, secret sites that tracked

missile development in the Soviet Union – and to keep track of regional affairs, the co-operation between the Shah and the station chief in Iran was very, very close. So the station chief basically had an appointment to see the Shah on a regular basis, like once a week. And they had a long, detailed discussion and an exchange of information in which the CIA found this to be just an extraordinarily useful relationship. And, as a result, they were probably the last who were willing to admit that something terrible was going on here when the Shah started to fall. They were far, far behind the game.[61]

At the same time, as Michael Donovan has emphasized, even though the US–Iranian relationship was very close, Iran remained a 'hard target' for US intelligence, and the eventual outcome so hard to predict that, as Donovan writes, 'in 1976–77, to have concluded that the Shah of Iran would fall to millions of Iranians rallied by an aging cleric in exile, one would have needed the Oracle of Delphi'.[62] Yet there were fundamental failures. As a 1979 House of Representatives inquiry into the débâcle concluded: 'In the case of Iran, long-standing US attitudes toward the Shah inhibited intelligence collection, dampened policymakers' appetite for analysis of the Shah's position, and deafened policymakers to the warning implicit in available intelligence.'[63]

Politicization of Intelligence

Robarge has termed the CIA's success in relation to the 1967 Arab–Israeli war 'one of those rare instances when unpoliticized intelligence had a specific, clear-cut, and immediate impact on US foreign policy',[64] further suggesting that this interface is a key site of contestation and resistance. Clearly, the degree of DCI access to the White House and a President's respect for the DCI (which determines credibility) are important variables here. It is important not to equate access with credibility – the latter does not automatically flow from the former.[65]

Martin Petersen has suggested four sources of policymaker resistance to unwelcome intelligence, particularly when it comes from political or country analysts rather than economic or scientific analysts:

- Policymakers consider themselves highly competent political analysts: 'What money is to New York and celebrity is to Los Angeles, politics and the knowledge of politics is to Washington. Policymakers know they are politically savvy – that is why they are in the positions they are in – and they have tremendous and justified confidence in their own political judgment.'[66]
- Policymakers are essentially 'people people' who, 'think in terms of people, not history or trends. They see politics as people making deals, people maneuvering for advantage, people acting. Historical precedents and larger political, military, economic, or social forces register less than individuals. From a policymaker's perspective, France, China, Russia, etc. do not act; their

counterparts in these countries act. History is made by powerful people like themselves.'[67]

- Policymakers have met the people whom intelligence analysts write about.
- Policymakers believe that they read all people equally well.

Moreover, policymakers naturally form their own policy preferences in advance of receiving intelligence analysis on an issue, a product of a combination of their own backgrounds, experiences, interests and world-view. They then seek supporting evidence for these preferences from the intelligence, and can be resistant to any intelligence that points in a different policy direction.

There is, however, a legitimate question – with no clear answer – concerning the appropriate distance and independence that intelligence should have from policy making. Michael Herman has written that 'Intelligence is part of the government system, and has to have empathy and credibility with the policy-makers it serves. It cannot adopt an Olympian objectivity, or detach itself completely from government's policies and preconceptions. It has to sell its product, and has to be sensitive to its audience to do so.'[68] This does not automatically mean agreeing with policy-makers.[69] As Richard Helms reflected, looking back to his time as DCI during the Vietnam War:

> My view was that the DCI should be the man who called things the way he saw them, the purpose of this being to give the president one man in his administration who was not trying to formulate a policy, carry out a policy, or defend a policy. In other words, this was the man who attempted to keep the game honest . . . when the bombing wasn't working, we told him so. . . . And presidents get mad about this. But presidents are usually better than their secretaries of State and Defense, who feel that they've got to carry out the president's wishes and that if they're not really in there extra strong, they're not really doing right by their patron.[70]

Complicating matters somewhat, there is also the view that analysts' training has placed too great an emphasis on 'straight line, single outcome' analysis, a view that finds perfect harmony with policymakers' natural belief in their own ability to divine outcomes. As articulated by US Defense Secretary Donald Rumsfeld, this can be taken to mean that 'If you think about it, what comes out of intelligence is not fixed, firm conclusions. What comes out are a speculation, an analysis, probabilities, possibilities, estimates. Best guesses.'[71] In this context it can be argued, as Jack Davis does, that 'Policy officials have the licence to . . . ask that assumptions and evidence be examined more thoroughly, and to request customized follow-on assessments. That is part of their job description, whether they are seeking fresh insights or analytic support for their established views.'[72] However, the idea that analysts offer just one view is dangerous, the thin end of a wedge that raises the unwelcome spectre of an internal market in analysis, and which can lead to policymaker demands for access to raw intelligence and exclusion of analysts from the generation of assessments. This is precisely what John Bolton did as Under-Secretary of State for Arms Control, explaining that 'I found that there was lots of stuff that I wasn't getting and that the INR analysts weren't including. I didn't want it filtered, I wanted to see everything – to be fully informed. If that puts someone's nose out of joint, sorry about that.'[73] When Bolton's subsequent nomination to be US Ambassador to the UN was held up in Congress, one of the areas of controversy was Bolton's attempt to sack the national intelligence officer for Latin America, a career intelligence official, who would not agree with Bolton's assertion that Cuba had biological weapons.[74]

It is clear from the cases cited in this chapter that strong pressure from policy-makers can have a corrupting effect on the production of analysis, although it is worth noting at this point that intelligence is not the only area where governments have pressured experts to produce findings in line with their policy preferences – the tendency is more widespread.[75] In the terms of chapter 2, knowledge does not inform the exercise of power, but power determines what is to be defined as knowledge. For example, in relation to the 1973 Arab–Israeli war, Avi Shlaim identified the omnipresent risk that

> Individuals who work for an organization that displays a strong commitment to a policy or outlook will be tempted to send back news which shows that they are on the right side, and to ignore or underplay uncomfortable facts so as not to risk unpopularity with their colleagues and superiors. In these circumstances, it is not always possible to distinguish between what is seen and what is regarded as expedient to see. . . . If the intelligence is dominated by a group of powerful decision-makers, it will become the prisoner of these decision-makers' images, dogmas, and preconceptions. Instead of challenging these dogmas and correcting these images when they clash with its objective findings, the intelligence service will be no more than a rubber stamp of these preconceptions.[76]

We noted in chapter 5 that analysts must be 'entrepreneurs', knowing how to attract the attention of policymakers to get their analysis seen, creating the dilemma highlighted by Michael Herman:

> The recurrent problem for American intelligence professionals has been getting sufficiently close to policy to be heard at all, amid all the size, diffusiveness and clamour of Washington. Alternative interpretations are always available to help policymakers pick and choose what suits them. Cherry-picking leaders can have a ball, at least in the short term.[77]

And, if policymakers do not get what they want, bodies can be created to produce it, as with the Paul Wolfowitz-inspired Pentagon Office of Special Plans (OSP). By mid-2002 intelligence was being 'stove-piped' from the Pentagon, via the Vice-President's office, to the White House, without any professional intelligence filtering. Seymour Hersh felt that Wolfowitz, along with Donald Rumsfeld, 'came into office openly suspicious of the intelligence community and the bureaucracy. They thought they were too soft on Iraq, not tough enough with Saddam, not able to make the decisive choices. So what you have is a bunch of people who weren't lying; they simply had fixed the system so it couldn't give them information they did not want to hear.'[78] As one disaffected former intelligence official told Seymour Hersh: 'One of the reasons I left was my sense that they were using the intelligence from the CIA and other agencies only when it fit their agenda. They didn't like the intelligence they were getting, and so they brought in people to write the stuff. . . . If it doesn't fit their theory, they don't want to accept it.'[79] In this context, devil's advocacy was unwelcome, whereas worst-case assessments on Iraqi WMD issues were regularly requested by the Vice-President's office. Ironically, in his pro-war manifesto, *The Threatening Storm*, Kenneth Pollack highlighted Saddam's unwillingness to accept intelligence he did not want to hear, and the consequent tendency of those in government and military circles to furnish him with just what he wanted to hear, arguing that this was one of the sources of the threat posed by him.[80] Politicization, then, remains a constant danger, seemingly transcending regime type. It was one of the principal contributory factors to the intelligence failures over Iraq's WMD, although, as chapter 7 makes clear, the very nature of the process means that this is keenly contested. There are analyses that seek to explain the post-9/11 limits of intelligence without reference to politicization, but they are the weaker for it.[81]

The *9/11 Commission Report*: Explaining Intelligence Failure?

There was never any doubt that the events of 9/11 represented the kind of surprise attack that the CIA had been formed to secure against, and hence a catastrophic intelligence failure. The task of the 9/11 Commission was essentially to identify the nature of the failure, and in so doing, locate its source and make recommendations to prevent further catastrophe. A close reading of the report shows clearly where failures occurred, although the evidence that policymakers failed to act on intelligence warnings was not translated into criticism of the principals in the Bush Administration. Perhaps fearing criticism for failure to heed intelligence warnings, the Bush Administration was initially reluctant to establish the Commission, and once it had done so, was hardly enthusiastic in its co-operation. It attempted to prevent NSA Condoleeza Rice from testifying, and insisted that the President himself would testify only if he could be accompanied by Vice-President Dick Cheney and would not be required to testify on oath. As with the later Butler Inquiry in the UK, a compromise agreement kept any 'individual blame' out of the report.[82]

In terms of timely intelligence warnings and the political failure to act on them, chapter 8 of the report, 'The System Was "Blinking Red"', is key; with its headings 'The Drumbeat Begins', 'High Probability of Near-Term "Spectacular" Attacks', 'The Calm Before the Storm', and 'Government Response to the Threats', it effectively conveys the same story as former Clinton and Bush Administration terrorism co-ordinator Richard Clarke had already told, of serial warnings but no policy response.[83] In part, this reflected the dominant assumptions among the foreign policy experts whom the new President relied upon. These dominant assumptions were still shaped by the experience of the Cold War, and their view of threats as being essentially state-centric in nature meant that they were insufficiently flexible to make the cognitive adjustments required in order to recognize the warnings. The key document to alert the Administration should have been a 6 August 2001 PDB, containing an item headed 'Bin Laden Determined to Strike in US' (see box 6.1). It was the thirty-sixth time in 2001 that bin Laden or al-Qaeda had figured in a PDB.[84] The analysts who produced the item were responding to an inquiry by the President about whether any threats to the USA existed, and to them 'represented an opportunity to communicate their view that the threat of a Bin Laden attack in the United States remained both current and serious'.[85] The President told the inquiry that the report 'was historical in nature', and that 'if his advisers had told him there was a cell in the United States, they would have moved to take care of it'.[86] However, the PDB contained a number of potential warnings, including the fact that FBI information 'indicates patterns of suspicious activity in this country consistent with preparations for hijackings or other types of attacks, including recent surveillance of federal buildings in New York'.

At the same time, analysts' fears about the possibility of an attack on the USA were not reaching the right people. The Commission reported that 'Most of the intelligence community recognized in the summer of 2001 that the number and severity of threat reports were unprecedented.' However, despite the *number* of fragments, there were too few specifics to point to a named target. Moreover, the 9/11 planning fell into 'the void between foreign and domestic threats', which made it harder to make sense of the fragments: 'The foreign intelligence agencies were watching overseas, alert to foreign threats to US interests there. The domestic agencies were waiting for evidence of a domestic threat from sleeper cells within the United States. No one was looking for a foreign threat to domestic targets. The threat that was coming was not from sleeper cells. It was foreign – but from foreigners who had infiltrated into the United States.'[87]

The President's style of governance, and indeed level of engagement with the material, can itself be interpreted as being a contributory factor in the 9/11 failure. No NSC meetings were called to discuss the threat outlined in the 6 August briefing, and the Commission could find 'no indication of any further discussion before September 11 among the President and his top advisers of the possibility of a threat of an al Qaeda attack in the United States'.[88] One reason for this is that the President retired to his Texas ranch for the summer. DCI Tenet visited him there on 17 August, but 'did not recall any discussions with the President of the domestic threat during this period'.[89] The report saw 'little evidence that the progress of the plot was disturbed by government action. The US government was unable to capitalize on mistakes made by al Qaeda. Time ran out.'[90]

Box 6.1   6th August 2001 PDB: Bin Laden Determined to Strike in US

Clandestine, foreign government, and media reports indicate bin Laden since 1997 has wanted to conduct terrorist attacks in the US. Bin Laden implied in U.S. television interviews in 1997 and 1998 that his followers would follow the example of World Trade Center bomber Ramzi Yousef and 'bring the fighting to America.'

After U.S. missile strikes on his base in Afghanistan in 1998, bin Laden told followers he wanted to retaliate in Washington, according to a —— service.

An Egyptian Islamic Jihad (EIJ) operative told —— service at the same time that bin Laden was planning to exploit the operative's access to the U.S. to mount a terrorist strike.

The millennium plotting in Canada in 1999 may have been part of bin Laden's first serious attempt to implement a terrorist strike in the U.S.

Convicted plotter Ahmed Ressam has told the FBI that he conceived the idea to attack Los Angeles International Airport himself, but that in ——, Laden lieutenant Abu Zubaydah encouraged him and helped facilitate the operation. Ressam also said that in 1998 Abu Zubaydah was planning his own U.S. attack.

Ressam says bin Laden was aware of the Los Angeles operation. Although Bin Laden has not succeeded, his attacks against the U.S. Embassies in Kenya and Tanzania in 1998 demonstrate that he prepares operations years in advance and is not deterred by setbacks. Bin Laden associates surveyed our embassies in Nairobi and Dar es Salaam as early as 1993, and some members of the Nairobi cell planning the bombings were arrested and deported in 1997.

Al Qaeda members – including some who are U.S. citizens – have resided in or traveled to the U.S. for years, and the group apparently maintains a support structure that could aid attacks.

Two al-Qaeda members found guilty in the conspiracy to bomb our embassies in East Africa were U.S. citizens, and a senior EIJ member lived in California in the mid-1990s.

A clandestine source said in 1998 that a bin Laden cell in New York was recruiting Muslim-American youth for attacks.

We have not been able to corroborate some of the more sensational threat reporting, such as that from a —— service in 1998 saying that Bin Laden wanted to hijack a U.S. aircraft to gain the release of 'Blind Sheikh' Omar Abdel Rahman and other U.S.-held extremists.

Nevertheless, FBI information since that time indicates patterns of suspicious activity in this country consistent with preparations for hijackings or other types of attacks, including recent surveillance of federal buildings in New York.

The FBI is conducting approximately 70 full-field investigations throughout the U.S. that it considers bin Laden-related. CIA and the FBI are investigating a call to our embassy in the UAE in May saying that a group of bin Laden supporters was in the U.S. planning attacks with explosives.

Source: 9/11 Commission Report, pp. 261–2. Redactions are indicated by ——.

The 7 July 2005 London Bombings: An Intelligence Failure?

Did the 7 July 2005 London suicide bombings represent an intelligence failure? Not in the broadest sense, as ever since 9/11 security and police officials had warned of the risk. However, there were certainly instances of missed opportunities. Moreover, in the immediate aftermath of the bombings, the intelligence services and police seemed to have little idea of the scale of the potential problem. Indicative of this is that police and security officials' estimates of the number of individuals who had trained in al-Qaeda camps abroad and subsequently returned to the UK varied between 200 and 3,000.[91]

In other words, there was little concrete idea of the scale of the potential problem, or of whether the bombers were foreign nationals or radicalized British Muslims. Indeed, for the first week after the bombings, in off-the-record briefings, police and intelligence officials indicated that they believed that the bombers had escaped – they did not think that they were looking at a case of suicide bombing.[92]

One possible explanation for this uncertainty related to a historical focus on Irish terrorism, now viewed to have been at the expense of other forms.[93] However, in the immediate aftermath of 9/11, £54 million was pumped into MI5, MI6 and GCHQ, and 'directed towards more collection (including surveillance, interception and agent-running), investigation, and dissemination of intelligence'.[94] Annual budgets have increased year on year since then.[95] The proportion of MI6 and GCHQ resources devoted to counter-terrorism is classified information, but we know that MI5 regularly devotes between two-thirds and three-quarters of its resources to the task, and that since 9/11 the majority share has been focused on international, not Irish, terrorism (see table 3.1). Moreover, by the mid-1990s the UK's intelligence agencies and police knew that London was increasingly being used as a base for terrorism in the Balkans and the Middle East. In particular, a number of young British Muslims fought in Bosnia in the mid to late 1990s. One report estimated that up to 200 British Muslims trained in camps in Pakistan before going on to fight in Bosnia.[96] However, these individuals were not considered a threat to UK national security, and so there was no attempt to intervene and prevent their activities.

Similarly, from 2003 a steady flow of young British Muslims travelled to Iraq to join the insurgency/resistance there. Whereas in the case of Bosnia in the 1990s, such individuals were not thought likely to pose a significant threat to the UK if they returned, in this case the potential threat was recognized, but the clear expectation was that a proportion would die in Iraq, some as a result of suicide bombings, others killed by US, UK or Iraqi forces. As one intelligence source put it, 'We have monitored some of them leaving, sometimes via France, but we haven't yet seen them returning. Some of them have multiple identities, which makes them difficult to track.'[97]

The month before the 7/7 suicide bombings, the JTAC reduced the level of threat from al-Qaeda from 'severe-general' to 'substantial', reflecting their belief that 'at present there is not a group with both the current intent and the capability to attack the UK'.[98] Clearly, this did represent an intelligence failure, in that analysis was moving in the wrong direction, raising fundamental questions about how intelligence is collected and analysed.[99]

So too did a further revelation. The man thought to have been the ringleader of the 7/7 bombers, Mohammad Sidique Khan, had come to the attention of MI5 in

2004 when he was involved on the fringes of an alleged bomb plot. Khan's details had been found on one of those arrested, but the intelligence services chose not to place him under surveillance.[100] Hence, the idea that all of the bombers were 'clean skins', unknown to the intelligence services, was inaccurate.

A further apparently missed link concerns the trip to Pakistan made by two of the bombers, Khan and Shahzad Tanweer, in November 2004. They stayed in Pakistan for almost three months, returning in February 2005. It is not clear whether MI5 was aware of this trip prior to the bombings, and debatable as to whether they should have been. One newspaper report claimed that Pakistani Inter-Services Intelligence (ISI) officials believed that Khan spent time there liaising with an al-Qaeda operative and explosives expert.[101] A later report claimed that Shahzad Tanweer spent time at a training camp near the Kashmir border run by Harkat ul-Mujahedin ('Movement for Holy Warriors'), a group implicated in the kidnap and murder of American journalist Daniel Pearl in 2002.[102] A mobile phone SIM card found on Tanweer's remains after the bombings contained a list of telephone numbers in Pakistan, follow-up of which led to arrests but no significant advances in the investigation. Nevertheless, it seems clear that Khan and Tanweer had contacts amongst extremist clerics and possibly even rump members of the Afghan-era al-Qaeda in Pakistan.[103]

Do the suicide bombings of 7/7, then, represent an intelligence failure? Clearly, to an extent, they do; although it is important to emphasize again that popular notions that intelligence can provide a fail-safe mechanism have created false expectations as to just what intelligence can deliver.[104] In the case of the London bombings, efforts to guard against such an attack could have been complicated by the inability of politicians to publicly admit the link between radicalization of British Muslim youth and the war in Iraq, leading to fuzzy characterizations of terrorist motivation and the nature of al-Qaeda. This also raises the question of whether the attacks represent more of a policy failure than an intelligence failure, a question which arises in a number of other cases, including the Argentine invasion of the Falklands[105] and WMD in Iraq, and whether in this case government policy created a potential threat of a scope well beyond that which the intelligence services could reliably guard against in their current form and scale and in the context of existing liberal-democratic norms.

Conclusion

One significant factor in explaining why intelligence failures take the form they do, and where responsibility for them resides, is in the area of 'intelligence learning'. In the early days of the CIA, significant intelligence failures occurred at the analytical level – as with the failure to predict the Soviet testing of the atomic bomb. However, in reflecting on analytical failure, and on failures rooted in faulty collection or in bureaucratic factors, the intelligence community was able to apply what might be termed 'intelligence learning' and thereby reduce the risk of the application of the same processes leading to comparable failures in future. However, 'intelligence learning' has not been carried into the level of the policymaker–intelligence community interface and is not, in any case, the solution where failures are more to do with policy than intelligence. As the cases in this chapter have shown, present-day policymakers remain susceptible to the same tendencies that led to, or contributed to, intelligence failures in the past. Nowhere is this clearer than in the case of Iraqi WMD, the subject of chapter 7.

Intelligence on Iraqi WMD: What Kind of Intelligence Failure?

It is time to begin the fundamental analysis of how we got here, what led us here and what we need to do in order to ensure that we are equipped with the best possible intelligence as we face these issues in the future. Let me begin by saying, we were almost all wrong, and I certainly include myself here.

David Kay to the Senate Armed Services Commitee, January 2004

Introduction

THROUGHOUT the book, we have highlighted both what intelligence can deliver and also its limitations. Since the events of 9/11, questions about the limits of intelligence and concerns about the possible politicization of intelligence have come to the fore. The controversy over the US and UK governments' case for war on Iraq contributed to making these the key questions in the study of intelligence at this time, for now at least re-focusing debates about accountability.

The official case for war on Iraq rested heavily on intelligence acquired by US and UK agencies apparently showing that Iraq represented a real and growing threat. However, in the aftermath of the 2003 Iraq War, the WMD that had been invoked as justification for it could not be found. At the end of an exhaustive search, in January 2004 arms expert David Kay, the man charged with leading the post-war hunt for Iraq's WMD, told the Senate Armed Services Committee that 'we were all wrong', that Iraq had no WMD, having destroyed them – possibly even as early as 1991. The intelligence that had been consistently cited from mid-2002 as indicating the urgency of the task ahead was thus called into question. Investigations were launched in the three countries that had cited intelligence evidence of Iraqi WMD as justifying the war and then committed troops to its conduct – the USA, the UK and Australia. This chapter analyses these national inquiries, applying their insights into the intelligence process discussed in earlier chapters, in particular the Betts framework outlined in chapter 6, thereby drawing out common themes and helping shed light on the location(s) of a failure that the Silberman–Robb Commission termed 'one of the most public – and most damaging – intelligence failures in recent American history'.[1] It begins with a detailed analysis of the Senate Select Committee inquiry, considers how far the Silberman–Robb Commission concurred with these findings, and then considers the Butler Inquiry in the UK and the investigations by parliamentary committee and the Flood inquiry in Australia.

US Senate Select Committee on Intelligence

The US Senate Select Committee on Intelligence (SSCI) inquiry into *The US Intelligence Community's Pre-war Intelligence Assessments on Iraq*, beginning in June 2003, set out to consider key issues such as 'the quantity and quality of US intelligence on Iraqi weapons of mass destruction programs' and ties to terrorist groups; 'the objectivity, reasonableness, independence, and accuracy of the judgments reached'; whether these were properly disseminated to the executive and legislative branches; and whether any political pressure affected these assessments.[2]

In February 2004, it was announced that the Committee's investigation would be conducted and published in two phases, the second of which would appear only after the 2004 presidential election. This was intended to cover the more politically contentious issues, such as 'whether public statements, reports and testimony regarding Iraq by US Government officials made between the Gulf War period and the commencement of Operation Iraqi Freedom were substantiated by intelligence information'; pre-war intelligence assessments on post-war Iraq; 'any intelligence activities relating to Iraq conducted by the Policy Counterterrorism Evaluation Group (PCTEG) and the Office of Special Plans within the Office of the Under Secretary of Defense for Policy'; and the use of information provided by the exile-based Iraqi National Congress.[3]

In producing its *Report*, the Committee was given access to more than 15,000 pages of intelligence community analysis on Iraq, supplemented by a further 30,000 pages submitted as a result of requests arising from initial analysis and, for example, involving intelligence community analyses that contradicted the dominant analyses on Iraqi WMD or links to al-Qaeda. It was, however, denied access to the CIA-produced PDBs, leaving it 'unable to determine fully whether Intelligence Community judgments were properly disseminated to policymakers in the executive branch, one of the tasks outlined for review'.[4]

The *Report* focuses on the production and content of one document – the October 2002 NIE *Iraq's Continuing Programs for Weapons of Mass Destruction*, a more basic declassified version of which, *Iraq's Weapons of Mass Destruction Programs* (discussed below), was made available at the same time. According to the CIA, the NIE process is designed to provide the 'best, unvarnished, and unbiased information – regardless of whether analytic judgments conform to US policy'.[5] This focus allowed the Committee to consider how close the CIA came in the case of Iraq to achieving its Directorate of Intelligence's goals of producing analysis that is rigorous, well-reasoned and appropriately caveated.[6] As the

Report makes clear, it failed in all of these. The key questions are why, and where does responsibility lie? Was the balance of responsibility consistent with the model suggested by Betts in 1978, or did it differ? Does the evidence unearthed necessitate a rethinking of Betts's model?

There are two key issues around the production of this particular NIE that are worthy of note at the outset. The first concerns its genesis. Despite the ominous and frequent warnings about the Iraqi peril emanating from the executive branch, the October 2002 NIE was a response to Congressional pressure rather than an executive branch request. In September 2002 (in the wake of a Bush–Blair summit at Camp David, and the month of the UK Downing Street dossier on Iraq's WMD), three members of the SSCI wrote to the DCI, George Tenet, requesting the production of a NIE.

Another is the time-scale for production of NIEs. The drafting guidelines of 1994 contain three broad time-scales for drafting: a two- to three-week 'fast track'; a four- to eight-week 'normal track'; and a two months or more 'long track'.[7] In a mid-1970s essay on the matter, Sherman Kent observed that up to that point NIEs had historically taken six to eight months to produce, although in the case of the 1956 Suez crisis a draft NIE, bypassing key stages, was produced in a record 30 minutes.[8] The time-scale for the Iraqi WMD NIE was 'fast track'. The process began on 12 September (concurrent with the production in the UK of the Downing Street dossier), a draft was prepared by 23 September, discussed at an all-day co-ordination meeting on 25 September, and a second draft sent out the following day.

While the 1994 drafting guidelines indicate that at this point the draft should have been submitted to intelligence community peers and a panel of intelligence community experts for review, and that a summary of the outside experts' views should be included in the NIE, the Iraq NIE bypassed these stages. The National Intelligence Council vice chairman explained to the SSCI that 'I think all you could have called in is an amen chorus on this thing, because there was nobody out there with different views.'[9] The NIE was approved and printed on 1 October 2002. Despite this attenuated route to publication, the SSCI concluded that the 'fundamental analytical flaws' it contained were not a consequence of this limited time frame.[10]

Betts's model would suggest that the major responsibility for failure lies with policymakers, with the additional possibility of some analytical errors, and even of some failings in collection. The overall SSCI conclusion regarding intelligence on Iraqi WMD is damning. 'Most of the major key judgments', it concluded, were 'either overstated, or were not supported by, the underlying intelligence reporting. A series of failures, particularly in analytic trade craft, led to the mischaracterization of the intelligence.'[11] The failure is firmly located as one of analysis, with some failures in collection, all compounded by poor management and an environment that seemed to militate against information sharing.[12] In short, the *Report* assigns responsibility for the failure, first, to analysts; second, to managers and bureaucratic structures; and third, to failures in collection. This would appear to call into question the applicability of Betts's model. We will now consider the SSCI's location of failure in more detail, beginning with collection.

Failures in collection

The *Report* identifies some responsibility for failure as lying in the field of intelligence collection. It criticizes the heavy reliance during the 1991–8 period on UNSCOM inspectors. It is also critical of the fact that the intelligence community did not use the period of the inspections to establish HUMINT sources that could replace the inspectors in the event of their departure. Incredibly, in light of the certainty of the conclusions contained in the October 2002 NIE, after 1998 the intelligence community (IC) did not have any HUMINT source of its own reporting on Iraqi WMD.[13] With hindsight, this is not surprising – such sources did not exist. A CIA official told the SSCI that, 'despite an intense, vigorous recruitment campaign against Iraq WMD targets . . . we were never able to gain direct access to Iraq's WMD programs',[14] but this difficulty apparently failed to generate any competing hypotheses within the intelligence community as to why this was the case.

There is a reason for this, relating to the acknowledged difficulties in acquiring HUMINT in areas from which the collecting body is excluded. It is clear that HUMINT is most effective where the collecting body has an official presence in the target state. Without this, in the Iraqi case, collection 'depended too heavily on defectors and foreign government services'. Not having an official in-country presence meant that the intelligence community did not have direct access to HUMINT sources, making it difficult to assess their credibility, and leaving analysts reliant on judgements of other countries' intelligence services. Unimpressed by the CIA's explanation of the difficulties involved in parachuting agents into hostile environments and its argument that it 'takes a rare officer who can go in . . . and survive scrutiny . . . for a long time', the *Report* called this 'less a question of resources than a need for dramatic changes in a risk averse corporate culture'.[15]

Failures in analysis

The SSCI found that the assessment that Iraq 'is reconstituting its nuclear program' was supported by intelligence showing that dual-use equipment was being purchased, but failed to show that it was destined for an Iraqi nuclear programme.[16] As with the British government's dossier of the previous month, judgements that Iraq 'has chemical and biological weapons' overstated conclusions that could be safely reached on the basis of the available intelligence.[17] On chemical and biological weapons (CBW), suspicions based on Iraq's past technological capabilities in this area, deception practised against UNSCOM, and past failure to satisfactorily account for all CBW holdings and precursors could have supported a conclusion that Iraq *may have had* such weapons, but the leap to asserting that it *actually had* them was not justified by the raw intelligence. Hence, the claim in the NIE that 'Baghdad has biological weapons' went beyond what could be concluded on the basis of existing information.[18] Similarly, the claim that 'all key aspects – R&D [research and development], production, and weaponization – of Iraq's offensive BW program are active and that elements are larger and more advanced than they were before the [1991] Gulf War' was not supported by the intelligence.[19] Claims regarding a possible Iraqi mobile biological weapons programme (which could 'exceed the production rates Iraq had prior to the Gulf war'[20]), came mainly from a single HUMINT source subsequently exposed as unreliable, and in any case 'overstated what the intelligence reporting suggested'.[21] Claims that 'Baghdad has . . . chemical weapons' similarly overstated existing knowledge.[22] Several assessments of Iraq's chemical weapons programme contained within the NIE – for example, that 'Saddam probably has stocked at least 100 metric tons and possibly as much as 500 metric tons of chemical weapons agents – much of it added in the last year' – were not based directly on intelligence reporting, but were analytical judgements which built on earlier, with hindsight erroneous, analyses – that is, they were a consequence of 'layering'.[23] The claim that Iraq was 'vigorously trying to procure uranium ore and yellowcake' via Niger exaggerated the existing state of knowledge.[24] Moreover, once it emerged that claims as to Iraqi attempts to procure material via Niger were based on forged documents, both the CIA and the DIA, 'continued to publish assessments that Iraq may have been seeking uranium from Africa', and the CIA 'continued to approve the use of similar language in Administration publications and speeches, including the State of the Union'.[25]

Earlier chapters drew attention to the importance of use of the appropriate language in analysis. Here, the SSCI found that the language used throughout the NIE 'did not accurately portray the uncertainty of the information', and instead 'portrayed what intelligence analysts thought and assessed as what they knew and failed to explain the large gaps in the information on which the assessments were based'.[26] Policymakers were denied the context that open acknowledgement of the gaps in the intelligence picture would have provided. Moreover, where uncertainty was expressed (as was also the case in the UK and Australia), it was used to suggest that Iraq's WMD were even more extensive than indicated, but that clever Iraqi denial and deception techniques, refined throughout the period since 1991, had effectively concealed the scale.[27]

At an analytical level, the failure was one of a tendency towards 'groupthink', a risk inherent in organized intelligence analysis, and one also identified as a source of the intelligence failure that occurred in the UK and Australia. In this case it manifested itself in the unchallenged dominant assumption that Iraq possessed and was concealing WMD, and which 'led Intelligence Community analysts, collectors and managers to both interpret ambiguous evidence as conclusively indicative of a WMD program as well as ignore or minimize evidence that Iraq did not have active and expanding weapons of mass destruction programs'.[28]

A key reflection of this tendency to explain away evidence that apparently contradicted the dominant assumption, rather than view it as a challenge necessitating a reassessment, related to the return to Iraq of UN weapons inspectors under Dr Hans Blix in November 2002. To take one example, the October 2002 NIE referred to the Amiriyah Serum and Vaccine Institute as 'a fixed dual-use BW agent production' facility. When inspectors found no evidence to support this claim, the CIA response was to discount the findings 'as a result of the inspectors' relative inexperience in the face of Iraqi denial and deception'.[29] In this, they were following an established pattern. Former UN weapons inspector Scott Ritter's account of UNSCOM's operations demonstrates how, throughout the 1990s, US officials simply refused to believe UNSCOM reports when inspection teams failed to find the WMD that the Clinton Administration 'knew' existed.[30] In fact, most of the intelligence on this site had been provided by a HUMINT source, code-named CURVEBALL, subsequently deemed to be a fabricator (see below).[31] In another example, the assessment in the NIE that Iraq's development of unmanned aerial vehicles was 'probably intended to deliver biological warfare agents' not only overstated existing knowledge,[32] but was reached despite Air Force dissent and other agencies' belief that their purpose was reconnaissance.[33]

While HUMINT sources were sparse,[34] those that offered what, with hindsight, turned out to be the most accurate information, were the ones most readily dismissed as merely rehearsing official propaganda. The *Report* discusses how

> A former manager in the CIA's Iraq WMD Task Force also told Committee staff that, in retrospect, he believes that the CIA tended to discount HUMINT sources that denied the existence of Iraqi WMD programs as just repeating the Iraqi party line. In fact, numerous interviews with intelligence analysts and documents provided to the Committee indicate that analysts and collectors assumed that sources who denied the existence or continuation of WMD programs and stocks were either lying or not knowledgeable about Iraq's program, while those sources who reported ongoing WMD activities were seen as having provided valuable information.[35]

One important factor in the tendency of analysts to err on the side of worst-case scenarios was the nature of the issue under consideration – WMD – and hence the potentially catastrophic consequences of being wrong. In this, the intelligence community's then-recent failure to 'join the dots' and prevent the 9/11 attacks, and the criticism that this had generated, were an important factor in understanding the pessimistic nature of the analysis concerning Iraq. A further factor conditioning the response was that a decade earlier the community had failed to identify the active nuclear weapons programme that did exist in Iraq and that was discovered and destroyed after 1991.[36]

Failures in management and organization

So strong was this dynamic, according to the *Report*, that managers shared the same 'groupthink' presumptions,[37] and so did not utilize established mechanisms to challenge them. 'Red teams' or 'devil's advocacy' approaches were simply not used in this case. The *Report* concluded that managers 'did not encourage analysts to challenge their assumptions, fully consider alternative arguments, accurately characterize the intelligence reporting, or counsel analysts who lost their objectivity'.[38]

As in the UK case, excessive compartmentalization of HUMINT regarded as sensitive was identified as a factor inhibiting the production of the most effective analysis. The Committee concluded that the process whereby the intelligence community 'calculates the benefits and risks of sharing sensitive human intelligence is skewed too heavily toward withholding information'.[39] However, the Committee found that the problem of information sharing went further, and that there was a tendency for the CIA to deny information to more specialist agencies that could have allowed for input that challenged existing presumptions.[40] Known dissenting views from other parts of the intelligence community were not always included in assessments where they would have challenged the dominant assumption – as, for example, over the debate concerning the purpose of aluminium tubes.[41] In some cases, assessments that conformed to the dominant assumption bypassed specialist agencies that were in a position to challenge them.[42]

Elsewhere, concerns about the credibility of sources were not reflected in assessments or otherwise disseminated to policymakers. One such case concerned an Iraqi mobile biological weapons production programme cited by Secretary of State Colin Powell in his February 2003 speech to the UN. The intelligence on this was based on four sources. Of these, one was an Iraqi asylum seeker, another, an Iraqi major who had defected, was brought to the attention of the DIA by the Iraqi National Congress but discredited in May 2002.[43] The most important source on this question, known as CURVEBALL, was described as a project engineer involved in biological production facilities, whose debriefings produced 112 reports[44] that were shared with the SSCI, and who, as noted above, was subsequently deemed to be another fabricator. Such was his importance that an INR BW specialist told the SSCI that without his evidence, 'you probably could only say that Iraq would be motivated to have a mobile BW program and that it was attempting to procure components that would support that'.[45]

Shortly before Powell's UN speech, a Defense Department employee contacted the CIA to share concerns about the reliability of CURVEBALL. He had the distinction of having met CURVEBALL in May 2000, and was the only US intelligence official to have done so prior to the 2003 invasion of Iraq. He warned that at the time of his contact, he and his agency 'were having major handling issues with him and were attempting to determine, if in fact, CURVEBALL was who he said he was. These issues, in my opinion, warrant further inquiry, before we use the information as the backbone of one of our major findings of the existence of a continuing Iraqi BW program!'[46]

In response, the Deputy Chief of the CIA's Iraqi Task Force emailed him:

> Greetings. Come on over (or I'll come over there) and we can hash this out. As I said last night, let's keep in mind the fact that this war's going to happen regardless of what Curve Ball said or didn't say, and that the Powers That Be probably aren't terribly interested in whether Curve Ball knows what he's talking about. However, in the interest of Truth, we owe somebody a sentence or two of warning, if you honestly have reservations.[47]

Failures at the most senior level of management – that of the DCI – were also identified. Damningly, the *Report* concluded that while George Tenet was 'supposed to function as both the head of the CIA and the head of the intelligence community, in many instances he only acted as head of the CIA'.[48] By his own account, he was unaware of dissenting opinions within the intelligence community on the possible use of the aluminium tubes at the centre of speculation relating to Iraq's nuclear programme. The fact that he did not, as DCI, expect to be made aware of dissenting opinions until the end of the analytic process meant that 'contentious debate about significant national security issues can go on at the analytic level for months, or years, without the DCI or senior policymakers being informed of any opinions other than those of CIA analysts'.[49] As a result, the DCI was unable to fully perform his role as 'the President's principal intelligence adviser'.[50]

Such compartmentalization, denial of information to other agencies in the intelligence community, and lack of DCI awareness of dissenting opinions on key issues, created concerns about the integrity of the CIA-produced and presented PDBs, access to which the Committee was denied. The Committee concluded that these 'may or may not include an explanation of alternative views from other intelligence agencies. Other Intelligence Community agencies essentially must rely on the analysts who disagree with their positions to accurately convey their analysis to the nation's most senior policymakers.'[51]

SSCI conclusions on the nature of the US intelligence failure

As a result of this analysis, and contrary to the Betts hypothesis, the main body of the *Report* appears to absolve policymakers of responsibility for the intelligence failure, concluding that it found 'no evidence that the IC's mischaracterization or exaggeration' on Iraqi WMD was 'the result of political pressure'.[52] (By contrast, as discussed below, the Australian Parliamentary Joint Committee inquiry accepted the existence of a sense of career pressure to conform.) Further, it blames the intelligence community for not 'accurately or adequately' explaining to policymakers the uncertainties that lay behind the catalogue of erroneous judgements contained in the NIE.[53]

However, it is not at all clear that the characteristics of 'groupthink' identified by the SSCI as operating in this case – 'examining few alternatives, selective gathering of information, pressure to conform within the group or withhold criticism, and collective rationalization'[54] – were not themselves consequences of individual perceptions of political pressure. The visits to CIA headquarters (numbering between five and eight; surprisingly no exact number was determined) by Vice-President Dick Cheney, a key advocate of the case for war between September 2001 and February 2003 were not held to have influenced the thrust of analysis on Iraq.[55] Nor is it clear that the managerial failure to utilize mechanisms designed to test analyses was attributable solely to a shared set of assumptions and not, at least in part, to their closer proximity to policymakers who had been making the case for a developing and threatening Iraqi WMD programme for months prior to the drafting of the October 2002 NIE. In this respect, 'managerial failure' could be interpreted as a euphemism for 'politicization'. Moreover, the SSCI had to reconcile the fact that, anonymously, a number of officials had been prepared to voice concerns, but were unwilling to be identified publicly.[56] Ironically, it is not at all clear that, in this area of inquiry, the SSCI itself adopted the best analytical practices that it identified as being absent from the intelligence effort on Iraq.

Some intelligence professionals did go public on this question of political pressure. Former Deputy Director of Central Intelligence Richard Kerr was quoted as saying:

> There was a lot of pressure, no question . . . The White House, State, Defense, were raising questions, heavily on WMD and the issue of terrorism. Why did you select this information rather than that? Why have you downplayed this particular thing? . . . Sure, I heard that some of the analysts felt pressure. We heard about it from friends . . . . There were people who felt there was too much pressure. Not that they were being asked to change their judgments, but they were being asked again and again to restate their judgments.[57]

It is also significant that those who were requesting these restatements were 'senior customers', including 'the White House, the vice president, State, Defense, and the Joint Chiefs of Staff'. Neither was Kerr alone in detecting political pressure on analyses relating to Iraq. George Tenet agreed that 'some agency officials raised with him personally the matter of the repetitive tasking and the pressure it created during this time period'.[58] The CIA Ombudsman agreed, telling the Committee that 'he felt the "hammering" by the Bush Administration on Iraq intelligence was harder than he had previously witnessed in his 32-year career with the agency. Several analysts he spoke with mentioned pressure and gave the sense that they felt the constant questions and pressure to re-examine issues were unreasonable.'[59]

In dismissing charges of political pressure, the SSCI needed to consider why intelligence analysts in the USA and the UK, and then in Australia, all began to sound the Iraq alarm at the same time, whereas previous assessments on Iraq in all three of these countries had offered a more balanced analysis. If the October

NIE arose as a consequence of systemic problems, these would be highly unlikely to have simply coincided with a change of political gear on Iraq in 2002, but would have emerged gradually over the years following the end of the UNSCOM process in 1998.

Consideration of the context of the *Report*, a negotiated product of a political process, is essential to a full understanding of it. It was due to appear in a US presidential election year, and dealt with a topic likely to be at the centre of campaigning. How far did the whole Committee accept the *Report*'s conclusions as representing a complete explanation of the intelligence failure over Iraq, and hence challenge Betts's hypothesis on the loci of such failures? In their 'additional views' appended to the *Report*, Democratic members made it clear that they regarded the inquiry thus far (phase 2 was due after the 2004 elections) as providing only a partial explanation. As vice-chairman Rockefeller and Senators Levin and Durbin noted:

> The central issue of how intelligence on Iraq was used or misused by Administration officials in public statements and reports was relegated to the second phase of the Committee's investigation, along with other issues related to the intelligence activities of Pentagon policy officials, pre-war intelligence assessments about post-war Iraq, and the role played by the Iraqi National Congress, led by Ahmed Chalabi, which claims to have passed 'raw intelligence' and defector information directly to the Pentagon and the Office of the Vice President.
>
> As a result, the Committee's phase one report fails to fully explain the environment of intense pressure in which Intelligence Community officials were asked to render judgments on matters relating to Iraq when policy officials had already forcefully stated their own conclusions in public.[60]

As in the UK case, the context of the political chronology is essential to explaining certain facts. One is the manner in which, in both countries, as the political case for war intensified, involving a characterization of the Iraqi WMD programme as more ominous and threatening than was supported by the available intelligence,[61] so intelligence judgements shifted to become more pessimistic than previously and thus to back the political case being made. In the US case the alarmist nature of the rhetoric arguably intensified during the period in September during which the NIE was being produced.[62] Echoing Robin Cook's critique of the UK government case for war, Senator Ron Wyden argued that 'These events [i.e. the invasion of Iraq] did not occur simply because the Bush Administration relied upon poor intelligence. In reality, the Administration repeatedly and independently made the case for war not by relying on US intelligence, but by ignoring or directly contradicting the same.'[63] Similarly, Senator Durbin argued that 'Administration policymakers were not looking for the Intelligence Community's consensus conclusions regarding Iraq's WMD programs – the President, the Vice President, Secretary of Defense Rumsfeld and General Myers had already reached their own conclusions, including that the US needed to go to war to neutralize the perceived Iraqi threat.'[64]

Intelligence certainly seems to have followed the policy agenda, rather than vice versa. Richard Clarke has recorded how, as early as 12 September 2001, 'Rumsfeld complained that there were no decent targets for bombing in Afghanistan and that we should consider bombing Iraq, which, he said, had better targets. At first I thought Rumsfeld was joking. But he was serious and the President did not reject out of hand the idea of attacking Iraq.'[65] As one analyst told the Committee, 'I would also say that this NIE was written – the going-in assumption was we were going to war, so this NIE was written with that in mind.'[66] This is a view supported by leaked memos concerning the Blair Government, one of which contained the minutes of a July 2002 Downing Street meeting at which the head of MI6, reporting back on a visit to Washington, is recorded as saying that 'military action was now seen as inevitable', and that 'the intelligence and facts were being fixed around the policy'.[67]

Moreover, in the US case, as in the UK and Australia, many of these shifting judgements were not actually substantiated by the available intelligence. In the US and UK cases, the political presentation of the intelligence base misrepresented the certainty of the underlying intelligence. In the US case in particular, one consequence of the production of the NIE was arguably to introduce a circularity into analysis on Iraq: the political case informed the intelligence analysis, which in turn reinforced for policymakers the certainty of the case they had been making.

The Democratic half of the SSCI certainly recognized the policymaker–intelligence interface as representing one location of the failure, and to this extent did concur with the Betts hypothesis, with Senators Rockefeller, Levin and Durbin concluding their additional comments by echoing Betts's 1978 warning:

> Legislative fixes that improve collection, analysis, and sharing of intelligence are powerless, however, in preventing intelligence from being slanted or exaggerated in support of policy objectives. The long-standing wall separating the worlds of Policy and Intelligence was first weakened and then crumbled under the pressure from Administration officials in the year and a half preceding the Iraq War. Restoring the Intelligence Community's damaged credibility requires patience and leadership.[68]

The Committee's reluctance to see the political class as contributing to the intelligence failure may well prove to be self-defeating. As Thomas Powers has observed:

> This pattern of blaming the CIA for what presidents have ordered it to do is the single most important cause of the emergence within the agency of a 'risk-averse' culture – a learned caution about undertaking operations of the sort CIA officers have later been required to explain or deny under oath on the witness stand. Secretary of State Madeleine Albright once told Richard Clarke that it was not hard to explain the passive-aggressive behaviour of the CIA. 'It has battered child syndrome.'[69]

The Silberman–Robb Commission set up by the President to explore the reasons for the intelligence failure over Iraq's WMD reinforced the conclusions of the SSCI. It highlighted failures in collection, in particular spreading the blame to cover SIGINT and satellite imagery as well as HUMINT. It found that 'Our collection agencies are often unable to gather intelligence on the very things we care the most about. Too often, analysts simply accept these gaps; they do little to help the collectors identify new opportunities, and they do not always tell decision-makers just how limited their knowledge really is.'[70] As this might suggest, analysts once again were to the fore of criticisms. At some point, the Commission concluded, analysts' assumptions about Iraqi WMD

> stopped being working hypotheses and became more or less unrebuttable conclusions; worse, the intelligence system became too willing to find confirmations of them in evidence that should have been recognized at the time to be of dubious reliability. Collectors and analysts too readily accepted any evidence that supported their theory that Iraq had stockpiles and was developing weapons programs, and they explained away or simply disregarded evidence that pointed in the other direction.[71]

The fragmentary nature of the US intelligence community was also cited as a factor, together with weak leadership. The Committee was not authorized to investigate how policymakers used the intelligence they received, but still dismissed charges of politicization and, like the SSCI, criticized the intelligence community for failing to communicate effectively with policymakers.[72] Nevertheless, in dismissing charges of politicization, it did come far closer than the SSCI to recognizing the pressures emanating from the White House, to the extent that its conclusion on politicization can be regarded as somewhat contradictory:

> we closely examined the possibility that intelligence analysts were pressured by policymakers to change their judgments about Iraq's nuclear, biological, and chemical weapons programs. The analysts who worked Iraqi weapons issues universally agreed that in no instance did political pressure cause them to skew or alter any of their analytical judgments. That said, it is hard to deny the conclusion that intelligence analysts worked in an environment that did not encourage scepticism about the conventional wisdom.[73]

The Butler Inquiry

At the outset, it is worth noting that the Butler Inquiry was not one sought or welcomed by Downing Street. By the end of January 2004, Iraq had dominated the UK political agenda for nearly two years. Since the end of the war, as marked by the US military occupation of Baghdad, three separate investigations had considered its origins and the role of intelligence in making the case for war. The first of these, by the Foreign Affairs Committee, had been critical, yet limited by the nature of the evidence available to it.[74] However, one unforeseen outcome of its hearings was the series of events that culminated in the suicide of MoD biological weapons expert Dr David Kelly. By the time a second investigation, by the ISC (see chapter 8), reported in September 2003,[75] Blair had set up a judicial inquiry under a former Lord Chief Justice of Northern Ireland, Brian Hutton, 'urgently to conduct an investigation into the circumstances surrounding the death of Dr Kelly'. The public hearings conducted by the Hutton Inquiry and evidence available to it, notably internal Downing Street e-mail traffic concerning the production of the September 2002 dossier, suggested a critical outcome.[76] However, when the report finally appeared in late January 2004, it exonerated the government of any bad faith in relation to the creation of the Iraq dossier, and focused its criticisms on the collective failures of BBC management, which had allowed the allegations to be broadcast and which had then seen them defended in the face of attacks from Downing Street. Nevertheless, David Kay's testimony in Washington at the beginning of 2004 and Blair's failure to dissuade the USA from holding its own inquiry, left him little option but to follow suit and announce a fourth UK inquiry.[77]

The Butler Inquiry's terms of reference went beyond considering the intelligence on which the case for war in Iraq was based to considering intelligence coverage in relation to all countries of proliferation concern. Its procedures mirrored those of the Franks committee, which had investigated the origins of the 1982 Falklands War. Significantly, the Butler Report opened with a chapter devoted to a discussion of the nature and use of intelligence, which warned of the 'limitations, some inherent and some practical on the scope of intelligence, which have to be recognised by its ultimate recipients if it is to be used wisely'. Intelligence could be 'a dangerous tool if its limitations are not recognised by those who seek to use it'. Adopting the distinction between 'secrets' and 'mysteries',[78] the Report offered the Inquiry team's own reflections on the limits of intelligence:

> A hidden limitation of intelligence is its inability to transform a mystery into a secret. In principle, intelligence can be expected to uncover secrets. The enemy's order of battle may not be known, but it is knowable. The enemy's intentions may not be known, but they too are knowable. But mysteries are essentially unknowable: what a leader truly believes, or what his reaction would be in certain circumstances, cannot be known, but can only be judged. JIC judgements have to cover both secrets and mysteries. Judgement must still be informed by the best available information, which often means a contribution from intelligence. But it cannot import certainty.[79]

This was particularly significant in this case, because by September 2002, as the evidence uncovered by the earlier Hutton Inquiry clearly showed, Downing Street officials had decided on Iraqi intent and sought the intelligence and a form of presentation to then convey their account of this intent in appropriately stark terms. Intelligence was being sought to support political judgements already arrived at. Moreover, the Report gently suggested the possibility that

one failure in the lead-up to war was that the 'ultimate users of intelligence' –
by virtue of his *modus operandi*, essentially the Prime Minister and a small group
of Downing Street advisers – did not fully understand some of the limitations
inherent in intelligence – not a far-fetched idea in relation to a Prime Minister
who had not previously held an office which would have necessitated contact
with it:

> These limitations are best offset by ensuring that the ultimate users of intelli-
> gence, the decision-makers at all levels, properly understand its strengths and
> limitations and have the opportunity to acquire experience in handling it. It is
> not easy to do this while preserving the security of sensitive sources and methods.
> But unless intelligence is properly handled at this final stage, all preceding effort
> and expenditure is wasted.[80]

The picture that emerges from the Butler Report is one of sparse intelligence on
Iraqi weapons production, one consistent with the picture that emerges from
the US and Australian inquiries, and no surprise, given that they were pooling
and dealing in essentially the same material. In particular, primary HUMINT
sources were thin on the ground. (It is worth noting that the Report is silent on
SIGINT.) The 2002 push to secure intelligence of the quality required to prove
the desired case did produce HUMINT. However, the political imperative meant
that insufficient discrimination was applied to the different kinds of information that the limited number of sources supplied. In sum, the quality of intelligence gathered from human sources proved to be highly dubious, but at the
time it contributed to the capacity to produce intelligence in line with governmental requirements and so was gratefully accepted. The Report's scathing
conclusion on these sources of intelligence is that:

- One main SIS source was sometimes passing on authoritative reporting, but
  at other times merely passing on what was essentially gossip.
- Reports to a further main source of SIS intelligence from a sub-source, and
  that were 'important to JIC assessments on Iraqi possession of chemical and
  biological weapons must be open to doubt'.
- Reports from a third source were withdrawn because they were unreliable.
- Reports from a liaison service on biological agent production were so flawed
  that 'JIC assessments drawing on those reports that Iraq had recently-
  produced stocks of biological agent no longer exist'.
- Finally, two main sources produced intelligence regarded as reliable at the
  time of writing the Butler Report. However, their intelligence was down-
  played because it was less alarmist in nature.[81]

This is a dismal picture, and one that requires explanation. The Butler Report
seeks to do this via references to the length of reporting chains, the scarcity of
sources leading to more credence being given to untried agents than was the
norm, and hitherto reliable agents being quizzed on issues outside their areas of

usual reporting. Despite the collection problems, as in the US case, the explanation for the failure is identified as existing at analytical and managerial levels. There is no doubt that each of these contributed to the intelligence failure, but, as in the USA, they cannot of themselves constitute the entire explanation. Underpinning all of these is the political requirement and the time-scale surrounding it. This produced political pressure to find information that pointed in a given direction. This pressure corrupted the intelligence process. That the assessment process (at the level of the JIC) was either not alert to this possibility, especially as latterly more alarmist evidence was being unearthed on demand where previously it had been absent, or not sufficiently robust to resist it, represents a further intelligence failure – one of intelligence management.

Political pressure on the JIC

The Report is critical of both the Prime Minister and JIC chairman John Scarlett. It criticizes Tony Blair for his language in presenting the dossier to Parliament, which served to reinforce an impression that the actual intelligence struggled to support. Moreover, it concluded that 'the publication of such a document in the name and with the authority of the JIC had the result that more weight was placed on the intelligence than it could bear. The consequence was to put the JIC and its Chairman into an area of public controversy and arrangements must be made for the future which avoid putting the JIC and its Chairman in a similar position.'[82] Notionally, because Blair and the JIC shared the blame, the Report explicitly backed Scarlett's promotion to head MI6. However, Scarlett's weakness in the face of political pressure was noted elsewhere in the Report. At one point the Report notes that 'The assessment process must be informed by an understanding of policy-makers' requirements for information, but must avoid being so captured by policy objectives that it reports the world as policy-makers would wish it to be rather than as it is.'[83] Moreover, Scarlett's weakness is made explicit in the Report's observation that there is 'a strong case for the post of Chairman of the JIC being held by someone with experience of dealing with Ministers in a very senior role, and who is demonstrably beyond influence, and thus probably in his last post'.[84] It is also worth noting that Blair's pre-emptive decision to promote Scarlett may well have affected the nature of the criticisms contained in the Butler Report. Once his promotion had been announced, it was clear that any personal criticism would cost him that post.[85]

Moreover, although the Butler Inquiry team was clearly aware of the political pressures operating on and within the JIC, their conclusions do not always follow the logic of their analysis. There are two criticisms that can be made here: one relating to Butler's own logic, the other applying a broader analytical context. The Report notes how, since the 1960s, the initial JIC membership of intelligence producers and users (the MoD and the Foreign Office) has been expanded to include the Treasury (1968), the Department of Trade and Industry (1997) and the Home Office (2000).[86] While this reflects the shifting parameters of national intelligence over the period, Butler acknowledges the possibility that 'the presence of more policy heavy-weights than in the past' may have compromised JIC objectivity.[87] Furthermore, even some of the producers on the JIC had no analytical background. Hence, the possibility of JIC *judgements* being influenced by policy concerns seems strong indeed. Yet, despite the evidence throughout the Report of the distance between the actual information being collected and the judgements based upon it, the limited scope of seconded assessments staff to mount challenges to 'prevailing wisdom',[88] and the pressures of time and events to search for and validate intelligence[89] that has subsequently proved to be groundless, Butler declares that this objectivity had not been threatened. And why? Because 'we have been assured by all witnesses that the tradition of the JIC has prevented policy imperatives from dominating objective assessment in the JIC's deliberations'.[90]

If this reference is to all witnesses who were serving on the JIC between 1998 and 2002, then one might respond that 'they would say that, wouldn't they'. If the reference is to all witnesses including previous JIC members and officials, then we are entitled to doubt that this statement is true: among those interviewed by Butler were former JIC Chair Roderic Braithwaite and Michael Herman, both of whom have made strong public criticisms of JIC performance over Iraq. In Braithwaite's view, the JIC

> stepped outside its traditional role. It entered the Prime Minister's magic circle. It was engulfed in the atmosphere of excitement which surrounds decision-making in a crisis. Whether they realised it or not, its members went beyond assessment to become part of the process of making and advocating policy. That inevitably undermined their objectivity.[91]

For his part, Michael Herman came to consider that the JIC 'got too close to the problem in a sense or too sucked in to the Whitehall consensus that something had to be done about Iraq. I suspect that if the JIC gets too close to the issues then there is this temptation of providing intelligence to please.'[92] In a broader context, the problem with Butler's conclusion is that it assumes that political power operates only overtly. Even Lord Hutton, a judge, had grasped the possibility of more 'subconscious' operations of power and influence in his discussion of the relationship between Scarlett and the head of the Downing Street media machine, Alistair Campbell.[93] But the Butler Report provides inadequate analysis of the extent to which prior assumptions regarding Iraqi behaviour, including worst-case scenarios of the possession and deployment of chemical and biological weapons and deception, when combined with political imperatives emanating from the political core of both US and UK administrations, contributed to the production of 'assessments' that were barely supportable at the time and subsequently proved to be highly inaccurate. The dominant consciousness meant that the JIC never asked the questions it should have. As Michael Herman has pointed out, the question that should have been asked in the absence of any firm information after 1998 was: 'Could it be because there are no WMD at all?'[94] When concern was expressed by analysts, it was overridden by the very political 'heavyweights' by whom Butler was reassured as to the JIC's objectivity.

Australian Inquiries

Largely overlooked amongst the avalanche of documentation arising out of multiple investigations in the USA and the UK and other writing on the Iraq intelligence failure, two Australian reports shed considerable light on the nature and quality of intelligence on Iraq. The two agencies most centrally involved in Australian assessments of Iraq's weapons capability were the Office of National Assessments (ONA), with responsibility to report to the Prime Minister on matters of international political, strategic and economic significance to Australia, and the Defence Intelligence Organisation (DIO), a provider of all-source intelligence in support of defence decision making and the planning and conduct of Australian Defence Force operations abroad.

Australia had relied overwhelmingly on intelligence supplied by the USA and the UK in shaping its analysis of Iraq's WMD. As this intelligence became increasingly controversial – particularly in the case of the UK, where one controversial dossier (in September 2002) was followed by another (the February 2003 plagiarized dossier) – the Senate asked the Joint Parliamentary Committee on the Australian Security Intelligence Organisation (ASIO), Australian Secret Intelligence Service (ASIS) and Defence Signals Directorate (DSD) to look into 'the nature, accuracy and independence of the intelligence used by the Australian government' and the accuracy of its presentation of the case for war.[95] As elsewhere, it was not an inquiry welcomed by the executive branch. It was also an inquiry beset by even more restrictions than those that took place in the USA and the UK,[96] but nevertheless adds importantly to our understanding of the nature of the intelligence failure. One of its recommendations was to establish the Flood Inquiry, which reported on the state of Australia's intelligence agencies in the light of their poor performance with regard to Iraq.

The parliamentary report confirms that a 'substantial proportion' of Western intelligence on Iraq was derived from the efforts of UNSCOM and UNMOVIC.[97] Additionally, 'as a direct consequence of the events of 11 September 2001, both the US and UK intelligence agencies . . . had applied a substantial intelligence gathering effort on the broader Middle East and more latterly Iraq'.[98] As a result, four issues in particular, which 'were to become important supporting evidence to the decision to go to war', emerged – and all of which would in time prove to be bogus:

- The attempt to acquire uranium from Niger.
- The acquisition of high-strength aluminium tubes, allegedly for use in centrifuge enrichment.

- The use of mobile BW laboratories.
- The development of unmanned aerial vehicles to deliver CW and BW agents.

As in the USA and the UK, in the period up to the summer of 2002, the assessments of the Australian intelligence agencies were measured. While acknowledging the possibility that Iraq could revive its WMD programmes, their analyses included as many qualifications as certainties. Based largely on intelligence from the USA and the UK, Australian intelligence reports in the period recognized that

- intelligence on Iraq was 'slight on the scope and location of Iraq's WMD activities';
- 'scarce, patchy and inconclusive' in relation to its nuclear programme;
- quantities of chemical agent held were 'small' or 'unknown', or with anthrax 'likely sizeable';
- Iraq's military capability was 'limited';
- its infrastructure was 'in decline'.[99]

In March 2001, the ONA concluded that 'the scale of threat from Iraq WMD is less than it was a decade ago'. A February 2002 ONA assessment, drawing on US intelligence, noted that 'US agencies differ on whether aluminium pipes . . . were meant for gas centrifuges', and while assessing that Iraq was 'likely to have a nuclear programme', believed that 'it is unlikely to be far advanced'.[100] As late as two weeks before the British September 2002 dossier was released, on 6 September 2002, the ONA reported that 'Iraq is highly unlikely to have nuclear weapons, though intelligence on its nuclear programme is scarce. It has the expertise to make nuclear weapons, but almost certainly lacks the necessary plutonium or highly-enriched uranium.'[101]

From this point, which also marked the publication of the British dossier and the imminent publication of the CIA NIE, based on essentially the same pool of intelligence that informed Australian estimates, two significant things happened. Firstly, the number of intelligence reports being received on Iraq's WMD from US and UK intelligence sources 'increased exponentially',[102] necessitating an increased amount of reporting and faster rate of analysis on the part of the Australian agencies, resulting in less time in which to analyse the incoming intelligence. Secondly, in analysing the new intelligence, the opinions of the ONA and DIO, hitherto marked by their similarity, began to diverge.

The ONA seemingly responded to the new intelligence by firming up its earlier qualified judgements. For example, whereas earlier it had reported that evidence on Iraq's nuclear weapons was 'patchy and inconclusive', by 13 September 2003 it was asserting that 'there is no reason to believe that Saddam Hussein has abandoned his ambition to acquire nuclear weapons'.[103] Despite remaining cautious over claims in the British dossier relating to aluminium tubes and attempts to procure uranium from Niger, the language of the assessments displays a new certainty which the report suggests was influenced by the more assertive claims being made in the USA and the UK. Between October and December 2002, six further reports were produced by the ONA, and while they still contained qualifiers about the inconclusive nature of the available evidence, the parliamentary report notes that 'the subsequent statements are in the indicative rather than the subjunctive mood, thereby denoting greater culpability on Iraq's part and certainty on the part of the analyst'.[104] Specifically, these reports claimed that:

- Iraq had been taking further steps to hide its WMD capability.
- Iraq was moving chemical and biological weapons away from storage depots.
- Iraq was adept at hiding its WMD capabilities, including moving equipment frequently and using mobile laboratories.
- Saddam remained intent on concealing his WMD.
- Many of Iraq's WMD activities were hidden within civilian industry or in mobile or underground facilities.

The shift in emphasis to focus on the centrality of concealment for Saddam's regime is significant, as it mirrored a similar shift in the CIA's focus. At a stroke, this shift both explained remaining caveats about the certainty of intelligence and the shift from uncertainty that WMD existed to an assumption that they did. It also explained in advance why Hans Blix's UN team was unlikely to uncover hard evidence of these programmes. By the end of January 2003, with war looming, the ONA's assessments were unrecognizable from the qualified assessments of a year earlier, despite implicitly acknowledging the lack of evidence to prove key claims. By this time, ONA was reporting that 'there is a wealth of intelligence on Saddam's WMD activities, but it paints a circumstantial picture that is conclusive overall rather than resting on a single piece of irrefutable evidence. [However] so far no intelligence has accurately pointed to the location of WMD.'[105] Despite the lack of specific intelligence, the impact of the continuous flow of intelligence from the USA and the UK reinforcing what had become the dominant assumption in the ONA left its analysts without the confidence to challenge it. Instead, unjustified leaps in analysis occurred – for example, that

> [A]n Iraqi artillery unit was ordered to ensure that UN inspectors would not find chemical residues on their equipment . . . . Such intelligence leaves little room for doubt that Saddam must have something to hide – he must have WMD – and confirms his deception efforts are so systematic that inspectors could not find all his WMD even if given years to do so.[106]

During this period, the reports emanating from the DIO remained more critical of the incoming intelligence. It reported that Iraq probably had a limited stockpile of chemical weapons, that because of problems of storage and degradation, it was uncertain whether these could be deployed usefully, and that although

Iraq had the capacity to undertake chemical weapons production, there was no evidence that any was actually taking place. On biological weapons, its reporting was sceptical of CIA claims of mobile laboratories, and in December 2002 even noted that there had been 'no known BW production since 1991 and no known BW testing or evaluation since 1991' – judgements that would subsequently prove correct.[107]

This picture of divergence, coupled with the extent to which Australia relied on shared intelligence from the USA and the UK, raises the question of the independence of Australian intelligence analysis in this case. A wider question, which also relates to the UK, is to what extent foreign policy on key issues is shaped in advance by alliance patterns and the interests of the dominant partner or partners in those alliances?

The ONA's errors of analysis were the same as those in the USA and the UK – again, unsurprising, since they were based on essentially the same pooled intelligence. How did they come about? One reason, suggested by former ONA analyst Andrew Wilkie, was that

> The raw intelligence we were receiving seldom arrived with adequate notes on the sources of that material or its reliability. More problematic, I think, was the way in which Australia's relatively tiny agencies needed to rely heavily on the sometimes weak and sometimes skewed views that were contained in the assessments coming out of Washington in particular.[108]

This problem would have been compounded by both the sheer scale of Australian reliance on US and UK intelligence and the limited size of the Australian intelligence agencies in question. In short, they were over-reliant on intelligence sharing and under-resourced. In the eight months between 1 January and 31 August 2002, and the almost identical period between 1 September 2002 and the outbreak of war, the large increase in incoming intelligence resulted in a tenfold increase in the number of reports being produced. Of this intelligence, 97 per cent came from the USA and the UK.[109] Moreover, a high proportion of it was coming from 'untested' sources. In the first of these two periods, only 11 per cent of intelligence was based on tested sources, rising to just 22 per cent in the months leading to war.[110] Not only was Australia relying almost completely on foreign intelligence, it was relying on these agencies' untested sources.

In an environment dominated by incoming intelligence, the character of intelligence partners is clearly of central importance. While the DIO's primary US relationship was with the DIA, the ONA's was with the CIA. It had not looked beyond its US and UK providers to cross-check on the intelligence it was receiving. The inquiry was told that the 'ONA had some access to French and German intelligence; however, the relationship was not as close "with our regular allies". On the matter of Iraq, they had not received material.' Indeed, they had no formalized intelligence-sharing arrangement with these countries.[111]

A further explanation of the failure may lie in the perception that the route to promotion lay in analysis fitting what the analyst perceived to be desired policy outcome, especially where objectivity and the desired outcome conflicted.[112] More important, though, was the fact that the Australian agencies were ill equipped to deal adequately with such a volume of intelligence. This was particularly true of the ONA, which had just sixty staff at the time, of whom thirty-six were analysts. Iraq was covered by the Middle East and strategic analysis sections, which between them could boast only three analysts. Moreover, Iraq was not their only focus.[113] Of the DIO's 142 analysts, thirty-five normally worked on the Middle East, South Asia and terrorism and other transnational issues. A further forty-nine analysed WMD and weapons systems.[114] As the Flood Report noted: 'Australia's focus on its nearer region meant there was limited analytical capacity in relation to Iraq and, while there was better capability in relation to WMD issues, it was still limited when compared to the capacity of US and UK counterparts.'[115] Flood found that 'assessments staff were working extended hours over long periods and operating under significant time pressures'.[116] While ONA managers 'judged the resources to be adequate at the time', they also accepted that 'a higher level of resourcing might have enabled analysts and their managers more time to stand back and consider alternative assessments'.[117]

The lack of time contributed to one of the key shortcomings identified in the Flood Report, one common to the USA and the UK as well. Flood found

> a failure rigorously to challenge preconceptions or assumptions about the Iraqi regime's intentions. It is natural that analysts approach an issue with a set of expectations and contextual understanding. . . . But on an issue with such potentially serious policy implications as Iraq's WMD capabilities and the threat posed by Saddam, more rigorous challenging of the assumptions underlying their assessments should have been carried out. While individual analysts almost certainly traveled the ground in their own minds, and managers challenged the bases for particular judgements, there is little evidence that systematic and contestable challenging was applied in a sustained way to analysts' starting assumptions.[118]

Flood concluded unambiguously that there 'has been a failure of intelligence on Iraq WMD. Intelligence was thin, ambiguous and incomplete.'[119] As Flood rightly noted, this failure was shared by the USA and the UK. Surprisingly, then, he went on to conclude that, 'On the critical issue of independence, the Inquiry's investigations showed that, despite a heavy reliance on foreign-sourced intelligence collection, both agencies had formulated assessments independent of those of the US and the UK.' This is a bizarre conclusion, in that the timing of the ONA shift can be explained only in terms of the shift in the partner agency to which it was most closely linked – the CIA. While his conclusion that there was 'no evidence to suggest policy or political influence on assessments made on Iraq WMD'[120] has been the subject of debate in Australia, in a sense there was not the same need for the Howard Government to make the kind of political running that the Bush and Blair governments did. The skewed intelligence that the ONA accepted largely at face value, based on intelligence analysis at least partly influenced by political pressure from the USA and the UK, gave him an alibi that effectively shielded him from the degree of controversy that has attached to Bush and Blair.

Conclusion

In terms of Betts's hypothesis and its utility in explaining where to look in locating intelligence failure, it should be noted that his analysis did not deal explicitly with the impact of intelligence failure on international partners. In the Australian case, the failure was largely one of analysis, but it was an inescapable consequence of such a near-total reliance on intelligence partners whose own analysis was being affected by the political environment created by policymakers. In short, it was to a significant degree an inherited failure with its roots in the same US and UK policymaker failures. It represents the flip side of the argument in favour of intelligence sharing.

More generally, the case of Iraqi WMD highlights two facts. First, it reminds us of the need to distinguish clearly between *policy* failure and *intelligence* failure. The fact that these can both be present in any given case complicates the task. Nevertheless, it is important to ask how far the failure over Iraq's WMD was an intelligence failure and how far a failure of policy. There is certainly ample evidence of decisions on war being arrived at in advance of the intelligence-based case being constructed.[121]

Second, this case also highlights the fact that locating the source of intelligence failure is a complex task. The concept of the intelligence cycle, implying sequential processes rather than concurrent activity at various levels, can encourage commentators to locate intelligence failure at one particular stage of the cycle. However, as this case demonstrates, the distinction between the stages is not always as clear-cut in practice as the model might suggest. As this case also suggests, intelligence failure can be multi- rather than mono-causal. With regard to Iraq's WMD, the failure can be located at various, at times overlapping, points – in collection, analysis, dissemination, within management, in the structure of the intelligence community, and beyond.

The Silberman–Robb Commission rejected the idea that the failure over Iraqi WMD represented a 'perfect storm' – a one-time coming together of a combination of factors unique to a particular time and place and, as such, unlikely to be replicated anywhere else. Yet policy and intelligence failure were joined in this case to an extent beyond any previously known case. As Senator Ron Wyden put it, 'bad intelligence and bad policy decisions are not mutually exclusive. It is clear that the Administration compounded the failures of the intelligence community by exaggerating and manipulating the Community's conclusions to the public.'[122]

Where does this leave Betts's hypothesis? Betts does not discount the possibility of failures in collection and analysis. Nor does he discount the possibility that failure can be multi-causal. In essence, his hypothesis suggests that the sources of intelligence failure can be considered as being pyramidical. From the investigations considered here, we know of significant failures of collection, even more significant failures in analysis, serious failures of management, and have suggestions of politicization, or something closely related to it. Without an equivalent investigation of policymakers' use of intelligence, there is no equivalent official judgement on their role in the failure. Nevertheless, the case of Iraq suggests that, while framed in the very different circumstances of 1978, Betts's hypothesis still holds good in alerting us as to where to look in locating the sources of intelligence failure.

8

Can Intelligence be Democratic?

No assassination instructions should ever be recorded.

CIA Manual, c.1954, in Lathrop, *The Literary Spy*

Introduction

ARGUABLY, the idea of 'democratic intelligence' is as oxymoronic as 'military music'. While the central tenets of democratic governance are transparent decision making and the acceptance of responsibility by those making decisions, the secrecy that is all-pervasive in security intelligence – indeed, is a necessary condition for it according to our definition in chapter 1 – means that taking responsibility for intelligence failure can frequently be avoided. Since there is no immediate prospect of the abolition of the agencies, we need to consider the conditions under which secret agencies might be better controlled in the interests of democracy, so as to reduce any tendencies towards illegal activities, increase the efficiency with which they warn and protect against genuine security threats, and reduce the likelihood of intelligence being politically abused, as in the case of Iraq.

As the previous chapters have shown, this task raises major challenges, which have only become greater in the wake of the post-9/11 security panic.[1] To use this phrase is not to deny that there are real security threats, but to note that they may become exaggerated. States vary widely in the extent of the commitments they make to their populations. Some promise very little – indeed, authoritarian regimes are more parasitic on, than servants of, their populations – while others understand that they are expected to provide widespread economic, social and political security. Yet, according to social contract theory, the core task of the state is to provide a basic element of personal and collective security against threats to life and well-being. Governments view 'security intelligence' as a key element in the fulfilment of that task, and therefore guard jealously their ability to carry it out, which necessarily involves some degree of secrecy. The greater the *perception* of threats, the more intensely this view is held. This is not necessarily a problem for democratic governance if governments are trusted not to abuse the rights of citizens and others in their pursuit of information and conduct of security policy. But the historical record suggests that officials should not be allowed to work away in complete secrecy, not because they are necessarily dishonest or corrupt (though they may be both), but because it is wrong in principle, and, as the historical record shows, a combination of security fetishism and secrecy can quickly lead even the most upright of officials to abuse the rights of others.

'Who guards the guardians?' is the question to be answered. Just as intelligence agencies engage in surveillance to carry out their security and safety tasks, so overseers must carry out surveillance in order to ensure that the agencies do not themselves threaten the security and safety of citizens. So what is needed is some structure for oversight or surveillance of secret state officials. Thirty years ago the very idea would have been rejected as naïve and dangerous, even within countries with otherwise liberal democratic systems. But then a series of scandals, often involving the abuse of human rights by security intelligence agencies, gave rise to governmental inquiries that resulted in various innovative oversight structures. Further, the democratization of governments in Latin America since the late 1970s and in Eastern European countries since 1989 has been accompanied by serious efforts to get to grips with the challenges of overseeing intelligence. The precise arrangements adopted have varied, in line with different political histories and cultures, and some have brought about more genuine change than others; but all these efforts have sought to deal with a common set of challenges.[2]

The character of these challenges can be gauged from previous chapters. First, we recall that surveillance is central to contemporary governance. Our concern with security intelligence – the generation of knowledge and application of power in secret – places a very high premium on oversight to counter the risks. Second, there are a number of organizational issues. Political executives have normally established state security intelligence agencies without seeking parliamentary approval, and therefore the precise mix of agencies has reflected what executives wanted at the time. These structures have not always been especially efficient, or may have been entirely inimical to a democratic culture, and therefore a task for oversight bodies everywhere is to consider the appropriate mix and number of agencies. Overseeing state agencies can be challenge enough, but as long as they operate in the normal manner of bureaucracies, at least we understand the basic principles on which oversight can proceed: clear lines of authority and responsibility, auditing and inspection. A contemporary challenge for oversight is the development of security networks, as examined in chapter 3. These not only cross jurisdictional boundaries within nations, but may also involve foreign agencies and organizations from private and NGO sectors. How can the resulting complexity be overseen?

Third, there are issues in relation to the gathering of information and the ability of agencies to turn this into intelligence via a process of analysis. The former covers issues both of efficacy and propriety: do agencies have adequate resources to gather the information they require, and in doing so, do they pay proper heed to the rights of those from whom information is sought? By definition, some of the covert techniques used by agencies go beyond those normally deployed by states for the purposes of governance. Indeed, many of these techniques would normally be illegal, so any oversight regime presupposes some legal regime for the authorization of such techniques; otherwise there is the danger of 'plausible deniability' in which agencies and their political masters simply deny their use of illegal techniques and there is no real check on possible abuses at all. The need for oversight has been further reinforced with the post-9/11 shift in doctrine towards collectors as active 'hunters' rather than passive 'gatherers' of information, as we discussed at the end of chapter 4. In this context, overseers must consider carefully how to do their job: to wait for issues to erupt and then deal with them (a reactive or firefighting approach) or to adopt a more pro-active, 'police patrol' approach.[3]

The concern with covert techniques normally concentrates on technical forms of gathering information – telephone tapping, bugging and so on. The threat they pose to privacy is aggravated by, for example, the large 'data warehouses' being constructed from multiple public and private sources that apparently overthrow principles of data protection. But events since 9/11 have returned the relatively neglected area of human sources or informers to the centre of controversy. Technical means certainly raise issues of rights in connection with the invasion of privacy, but the ethical issues are relatively straightforward compared with those raised by the search for human sources. To take one example, the recruitment of informers can involve blackmail, and their motivations can compromise entirely the value of information they provide. To take another, interrogation techniques amounting to torture have been used against those captured or kidnapped as terrorist suspects since 9/11. In a number of cases, detainees have died as a result. Although some soldiers have been tried, the ability to check systematic abuses has been seriously hindered by the unilateral declaration by the USA that it is not bound by various conventions on the treatment of prisoners.[4]

Fourth, as we saw in chapter 5, issues arise concerning what agencies do with the information gathered. How successful are they in interpreting the meaning of the information correctly, and how is the *absence* of information interpreted? How efficient or otherwise are they in sharing intelligence with others who are in a position to act on it? When it comes to action being taken, are there adequate arrangements in place for ensuring that this is in accordance with the law? If secret actions are to be taken against those perceived to constitute threats, then what checks exist to ensure that the actions are proportionate? Finally, how can we inhibit the politicization of intelligence? We use the term 'inhibit' rather than 'prevent', since intelligence is so central to government and state activities that it is idle to suppose that it can be completely insulated from the political process. Indeed, in democratic regimes it should *not* be completely insulated, because a corps of Platonic Security Guardians would themselves constitute a security threat – this is the central paradox of security.[5] There is no neat solution to the oversight problem – there will always be tensions within democratic states between security professionals and their overseers. If there are no tensions, then the oversight system is simply not working.

Defining Control, Review and Oversight

Some of these tensions are reflected in debates as to the terminology used to describe the functions of overseers. These are not semantic debates, but reflect the contest for access to information about and influence over security intelligence agencies. The clearest and least controversial distinction is between 'control' and 'oversight'. It is generally acknowledged that the head of an agency requires adequate powers to manage and direct its operations – this is what we shall call 'control'. 'Oversight',[6] by comparison, refers to a process of superintendence of the agencies that is concerned not with day-to-day management but with ensuring that the overall policies of the agency are consistent with its legal mandate. The key political debates involve the nature and extent of this 'superintendence'.

Should oversight cover current operations or, in the interests of security, be restricted to *post hoc* review? On the principle that stable doors should be shut before horses can bolt, it is argued that the former is required, so as to prevent agencies from doing things that are illegal, improper or just stupid; but there are risks for overseers. The US congressional committees provide the clearest manifestation of this arrangement, so that, for example, presidents wishing to authorize covert actions have to notify congressional overseers in advance. While this maximizes the opportunity for overseers to exert influence, it also raises the danger of attempts to 'micro manage' the agencies from afar. This will not always make sense in terms of effectiveness, and insiders will always fear leaks, but prior knowledge may also compromise the ability of overseers to criticize if and when things go wrong.

There was a brief but lively debate on this issue in Canada when the CSIS Act not only separated the Security Service from the RCMP but also established a novel structure for oversight that involved a committee of privy councillors outside Parliament, supported by a research staff. The initial Security Intelligence Review Committee (SIRC) adopted a highly activist stance towards the new CSIS, and was criticized by some for exceeding its (implicity *post hoc*) review mandate in stretching for a role similar to that found in the US Congress. SIRC members certainly adopted the term 'oversight' in their early reports, basing this, in part, on the word *surveiller* in the French-language version of their title: *Comité de Surveillance des Activités de Renseignement de Sécurité*.[7] Subsequently SIRC has accepted a more limited role in reviewing CSIS performance, 'on a retrospective basis to assure itself – and by extension Parliament and the people of Canada – that the Service has acted appropriately and within the law'.[8]

The Legal and Ethical Bases for Oversight

One of the ever-present dangers inherent in the shift towards the democratiza-tion of intelligence in the last thirty years has been that legal reform might be more symbolic than real, that behind new governmental architectures of legal-ity and accountability, largely unreconstructed subcultures of political policing and denial of human rights may survive. Written reports can be constructed in such a way that agency operations appear to be compliant with whatever mini-mal legal standards have been adopted. Lawyers are, after all, 'hired guns'. Within the Bush Administration, for example, much legal energy was put into the task of finding ways in which techniques commonly assumed to be torture might be 'legalized'.[9] Thus, a legal framework for security intelligence is a necessary, but not a sufficient, condition for democratic oversight. Therefore, as SIRC indicates above, the standards to be established for oversight must include not just the legality but also the broader issue of propriety involving considera-tion of ethical and rights' issues.

Although executives may consider that they have very good reason for mini-mizing external oversight of intelligence agencies, for example, if they doubt the loyalty of political or other minorities, they understand that it may make their life easier if there is some legal framework. For example, they are less likely to fall foul of human rights conventions, and in Europe, such a framework will help them to negotiate access to favoured organizations such as NATO and the EU. Certainly, in Europe, in particular, much work has gone into advice and discussion with newly democratized regimes as to how intelligence services might best be controlled. This has resulted in the publication of a handbook of best legal practice that provides an excellent summary of current thinking.[10] All international bodies – the UN, the EU, the Summit of Americas, the Organization for Economic Co-operation and Development (OECD), and others – have in the last decade identified the need for legislation of clear legal stan-dards for the establishment of agencies and their possession of special powers.

Broadly speaking, there are two main senses in which special powers may restrict rights. First, the ECHR allows restrictions on privacy, freedom of thought, expression and association (Articles 8–11) if 'prescribed by law' and as 'necessary in a democratic society', and are proportionate to the protection of national security, the protection of morals, the rights of others and public safety. Second, derogation from most rights can be made 'in time of war or other public emergency threatening the life of the nation' (Article 15(1)), though there can be no derogation from the Article 3 prohibition of torture or inhuman or degrading treatment. This is especially significant in the light of the use of torture in post-9/11 interrogations. Of course, precisely what consti-tutes a 'threat to the life of the nation' is debatable, but it should be imminent and exceptional.[11]

The basic intelligence statute needs to identify clearly the specific threats to national security that the agency is to address, and what powers it will have. For example, is the agency a 'passive' gatherer and analyst of information, or is it empowered to act by such methods as disruption or arrest powers? How is the director to be appointed, including safeguards against improper pressure from ministers? What special powers for information gathering does the agency possess, and who may authorize their use? Hans Born and Ian Leigh deploy the principles generated in 1980 by the McDonald Commission in its investigation of abuses by the RCMP:[12] that the rule of law should be strictly observed, that investigative techniques should be deployed in proportion to the security threat and weighed against the possible damage to rights, that less intrusive alternatives should be used if possible, and that the greater the invasion of privacy involved, the higher the necessary level of authorization.[13] Rules must be established limiting the purposes for which information may be gathered, retained and disseminated, and any exemption of the agency from normal freedom of information and access legislation should be restricted only in so far as is necessary in relation to the national security mandate. Finally, agency employees must be trained to appropriate ethical standards, and, as the first line of defence against abuse of agency powers, be protected if they feel obliged to 'blow the whistle'.

A legal framework is required for the relationship between ministers and agencies. This requires a delicate system for checking, since two different sets of problems result if there is either too much or too little ministerial control of intelligence agencies, especially those with internal security mandates. If there is too much, then the problem may be just one of inefficiency, as security professionals are directed by an enthusiastic but ignorant minister, but, more likely, ministers may fall into the temptation to deploy security agencies for their own partisan ends – for example, spying on and disrupting opposition parties or dissenters. Certainly, in many Eastern European countries, even after the end of the Cold War, agencies were used in this way, or government opponents believed that they were, which largely amounted to the same thing.[14] Alternatively, if ministers adopt the position that they would prefer not to know what agencies are doing, since it may be messy and illegal, then the problem will be that of agencies as 'rogue elephants', in which the agency acts primarily on the political and ideological preferences of its own employees. Imbued as they may well be by a strong belief in their own wisdom as to the national security needs of a nation, the chances of them riding roughshod over the rights and freedoms of others are indeed high. So, while elected ministers clearly have to be responsible for establishing the main targets and operational guidelines for agencies, they must not have direct managerial responsibility. The issue of covert action, discussed in chapter 5, represents the very sharpest end of the issue of executive knowledge and/or authorization, especially if states wish to maintain 'deniability'. Since the actions envisaged will be, by definition, illegal in the state in which they take place, it is highly tempting for ministers to find a way of 'plausibly denying' knowledge of them should they become public. However, this is to invite serious abuses.

Security intelligence is 'low visibility' work and there is extensive scope for discretion. This is particularly the case for those operating 'in the field', handling informers and deploying other information-gathering techniques. Therefore, before we go on to examine external oversight by parliamentary and other bodies, we discuss the ethical issues that provide the important counterweight to legal standards. If the question posed in this chapter – can intelligence be democratic? – struck some readers as odd, even more may laugh at the idea of discussing intelligence and ethics. Yet, as noted earlier, intelligence exists and cannot be disinvented. So, perhaps we should seek to develop it in progressive ways to become a servant of the collective good, as in supporting public safety and peacekeeping, rather than treat it as just a necessary evil until we can work out a way of doing away with it, like WMD.[15]

The answers to these questions cannot be found simply by 'reading off' from any particular set of ethical principles. Toni Erskine provides an illuminating summary of how three main approaches – realist, consequentialist and deontological – might be applied to intelligence activities.[16] She discusses Hobbesian realism, pointing out that this is not amoral, by definition; rather, it rests on the moral duty of the sovereign to protect her subjects. The resulting argument that intelligence activities are justified if they serve the well-being of the state and the nation lends legitimacy to intelligence collection as currently practised. The second approach judges actions by the value of their consequences and, compared with realism, may extend consideration to the interests of those outside the immediate national political community. Here, intelligence activities will be acceptable if they maximize the good through balancing the benefits of increased knowledge against the costs of how it might have been acquired, in a way similar to that in which the principle of 'double effect' operates in the field of just war theory.[17] The difficulty resides in the highly complex computations of goods and harms required in order to draw up Michael Herman's 'ethical balance sheet'.[18] There is no need for such calculations with the deontological approach, based on the work of Kant, where some actions are simply prohibited. The key principles guiding one's action are that it might become universally adopted by all other agents, and that other people are treated as ends in themselves, not as tools. Clearly, many intelligence methods fail to meet such standards, including any deployment of deception and coercion.[19]

These three different positions provide us with clear choices to be made: for example, recruiting and running informers or human sources requires various mixtures of manipulation and deception. For the realist these will be utilized as long as to do so is in the national interest; for the consequentialist, these will be utilized as long as the benefits of the knowledge outweigh the costs of acquiring it – although Herman does draw the line at gross violations of human rights.[20] For the deontologist, such methods should not be utilized. But it is not only the collectors who will face ethical dilemmas; if intelligence is to be defined in some sense as seeking knowledge so that it is 'telling truth to power', then analysts may have to make some very tricky judgements if their product conflicts with the conventional wisdom of policymakers. This was seen at the time of the Vietnam War, both in respect of CIA intelligence as to the course of the war itself and the issue of whether or not Communists were orchestrating the anti-war movement in the USA.[21] The same issue has re-emerged in the controversies around the intelligence regarding Iraqi WMD that were discussed in chapter 7.

There are clear implications here for oversight: not just individual security officials are 'moral agents'; so are the agencies and governments of which they are part,[22] so statutes, guidelines and codes of practice must all be drawn up within the context of ethical agreements. But again, final resolutions of ethical dilemmas will not be found in statutes or even in declarations of human rights. As we saw above, the latter deploy a deontological prohibition of activities such as murder and torture, but are consequentialist in other respects – for example, permitting the breach of rights in order to safeguard the nation in times of emergency. Since intelligence cannot be disinvented, and current practice is dominated by realist ethics, perhaps the most we can strive for is harm minimization: we need to regulate the 'second oldest profession'[23] in such a way as to minimize the harm it does to producers, consumers and citizens.

One way in which this can be done is to resist the frequently used, but ultimately inappropriate, metaphor of *balancing* security and rights.[24] We can see how, over the past thirty years, intelligence scandals have often been followed by inquiries and increases in oversight, sometimes accompanied by restrictions on agency powers. And we have seen clearly how the perceived intelligence failure represented by 9/11 has been followed by increases in agencies' legal powers, thus suggesting a pendulum swing between the poles of, first, rights and then, security. Yet the idea of balance is misplaced, since, ultimately, rights and security cannot simply be traded off against each other. There is actually little evidence that increased security can be achieved by reducing the legality and propriety with which security intelligence is conducted. Rather, there are two broad justifications for placing human rights and freedoms at the centre of security intelligence: it is right *in principle*, as enshrined in the UN Charter and ECHR. Also, it is right on a *pragmatic* level: states cannot achieve long-term democratic legitimacy unless they respect human rights and freedoms. Of course, in the short term, this raises difficulties for police and security officials who may feel overwhelmed by the extent of, for example, organized trafficking of arms, drugs and people. There *is* tension between security and rights: in the short run, the ability to conduct surveillance of an individual or a group may be reduced by the requirement to follow procedures that seek to protect privacy, but in the longer term, such procedures are required if a state is to gain democratic legitimacy from its citizens. Procedures should be designed in order that, even in the short term, the invasion of rights is *proportionate* to the alleged threat, but also to prevent surveillance being directed at the wrong person or conducted in such a way as to amount to intimidation. Thus legal rules and ethical codes themselves will contribute to the effectiveness of security as much as to propriety.[25] Equally, the very denial of rights may trigger insecurity and political violence, as happened in Northern Ireland in the late 1960s.

Organizing External Oversight

Four 'levels' of control and oversight are required. We have already discussed aspects of the first two: the agency and the executive. So, for example, the immediate 'control' of an agency is conducted by its director, but within the parameters of ministerial directions, which are, in turn, required by the relevant statute passed by the legislature. The statute will, in turn, reflect the preferences of the governing party or coalition and, possibly, the contribution of NGOs or other groups. Similarly, oversight should begin within the agency, but this must be reinforced by officials in the executive branch, a parliamentary committee and, whenever appropriate, judges. Finally, the media, citizens and NGOs will also provide oversight, albeit sporadically.

This overall framework is represented in figure 8.1. This inevitably oversimplifies what can be quite complex institutional arrangements within particular nation-states, but shows the basic relationship between control and oversight. The forms of control that we have already discussed – statutes, codes, etc. – are drawn up by the institution at the appropriate 'level' – agency director, minister, Parliament. Historically, if there was any 'oversight' of intelligence agencies, it was carried out by the same offices: for example, parliamentary

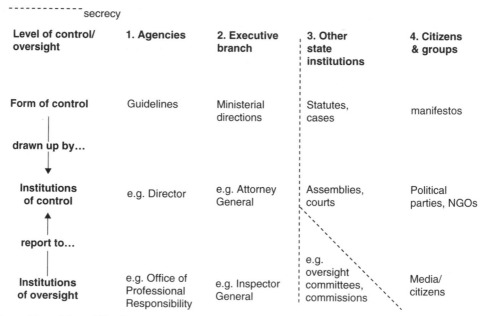

secrecy				
Level of control/ oversight	**1. Agencies**	**2. Executive branch**	**3. Other state institutions**	**4. Citizens & groups**
Form of control	Guidelines	Ministerial directions	Statutes, cases	manifestos
↓ drawn up by...				
Institutions of control	e.g. Director	e.g. Attorney General	Assemblies, courts	Political parties, NGOs
↑ report to...				
Institutions of oversight	e.g. Office of Professional Responsibility	e.g. Inspector General	e.g. oversight committees, commissions	Media/ citizens

Source: Adapted from Gill, *Policing Policies*, p. 252

Figure 8.1 Control and oversight of security intelligence agencies

systems rely on a general notion of ministerial responsibility to Parliament for the actions of their departments, so, theoretically, if it emerged that an intelligence agency had acted illegally or improperly, the minister with overall responsibility for the agency would be held to account. Of course, there were several problems with this: ministers preferred not to know about most agency operations, there was no independent mechanism by which ministers could find out about agency operations if they wanted to, and their normal response to parliamentary questions would be to refuse comment on matters of national security. Parliaments were similarly ill equipped to oversee intelligence agencies; even in presidential systems, in which their powers did not depend entirely on the executive, legislators often chose not to exercise the powers they did have. Famously, during Hoover's long tenure of the FBI, the Bureau was alone in receiving what it requested and, unlike other agencies, in a lump sum to be expended at Hoover's discretion.[26] The patent inadequacy of traditional ministerial and parliamentary mechanisms has now led to the development of separate oversight institutions at each level.

Logically, given its indispensability to our original definition of intelligence, secrecy is a central issue in the relationship of different intelligence oversight institutions. There are a number of different ways in which secrecy breaks up the flow of security intelligence information – both between and within the levels depicted in figure 8.1. The ostensible motive for this is to retain the security of operations so that they are not exposed in ways that would destroy their effectiveness and, possibly, endanger sources. For example, even those within agencies may not have access to information regarding operations into which they have not been indoctrinated and therefore have no 'need to know'. But the most significant in terms of oversight is the barrier of secrecy between those who have received security clearance[27] in order to do their agency or ministerial jobs and those who have not – the public at large, parliamentarians, judges, etc. Clearly, if those with oversight responsibilities are to be able to do their job, they must have access to information in the possession of the agencies, and therefore must be inside the 'ring' of secrecy. Their problem is that, having been granted this privileged access, they are then compromised by their inability to speak publicly about what they have seen! This can be a problem especially for parliamentarians whose *raison d'être* is that of public, not private, representative. On the principle that they should retain their independence from the executive, parliamentarians may resist the idea of being security-cleared in order to do their job, in which case some other mechanism will have to be found whereby agencies can be reassured of their loyalty and discretion. There is some variation in the extent to which parliamentarians are or are not granted full access to agency information – this ambiguity is reflected in the figure by the barrier of secrecy marking them off from both the executive and the public.

Having identified the need for legal and ethical codes to be promulgated, the responsibility for ensuring that these are incorporated into agency training and working practices rests primarily with agency directors. Legal and ethical standards have to be taken seriously if they are to become part of the organizational culture, rather than just window dressing. Changing the culture within intelligence agencies is a more difficult task than providing them with a more democratic legal charter.[28] If pressure for cultural change comes only from external oversight bodies, there is a danger that it will be viewed by officials and insiders as meddling, and mainly about public relations. Therefore, there is increasing recognition of the need for some internal oversight mechanism to reinforce changes made to operational guidelines and training. The work of such offices, often with titles such as Office of Professional Responsibility, treads a fine line: on the one hand, there is a danger that they too might be seen as carrying out a tokenistic role for the sake of appearances; on the other, if they are too enthusiastic, they may face criticism from insiders that they are hamstringing operators and leading to a culture of fear and low morale. Arguably, the people most likely to become aware of inefficiency or impropriety by security agents are those most familiar with agency operations and *modus operandi* – that is, those within the agency. What they will do with that information is another matter. Here, personnel in such offices face the dilemma present in any organization: if they define their role as purely a disciplinary one, then they will be viewed with contempt and fear much as 'rat squads' (internal affairs departments) are within police forces. Therefore, their role must be at least in part an educational one.

Their work must also be linked into the next, ministerial level so that whoever has oversight responsibility there receives information as to problems that require resolution by authorities outside the agency itself. It is very likely that ministers will have responsibilities for more than just the security intelligence agency or agencies, and it may well be considered appropriate for them to have some assistance in ensuring that agencies act in accord not only with established legal standards but also with ministerial directions. Yet it will also be desirable to provide some insulation from ministers, in order to avoid political misuse of the agency. One mechanism that has been developed to perform this role is the office of Inspector General. Around a dozen inspectors general can be found in the US intelligence community, and others in Canada, Australia, South Africa and, most recently, Bosnia–Herzegovina. Their roles and reporting relationships vary – some also report to Parliament – but their primary function is to strengthen executive oversight.[29]

When we consider oversight from outside the executive, a range of new issues arise. Should external overseers be located in Parliament or in some other body? What should be their mandate, or over what, precisely, should they have oversight? How are they to be chosen, and by whom? Must they be vetted? What powers will they have to obtain access to intelligence personnel and files? To whom do they report? World-wide we are now faced with a variety of institutional structures that have been developed as different countries have confronted these questions, but it is possible to detect some patterns. For example, the idea of Parliament itself providing the core of oversight structures, if not the only one, is more or less universal.[30] As the first steps were made to external oversight, there were fears that parliaments would not be appropriate, for example, because of their tendency to partisanship and to leak information for political advantage. There were exceptions: for example, the Bundestag was central to oversight in what was then West Germany from the 1950s, although this developed in the unusual circumstances of post-war reconstruction and a determination to avoid the secret police nightmare of Nazism. In the USA, too, the post-Watergate reforms centred on Congress, but countries such as Canada, the UK and Australia created external review bodies outside Parliament: SIRC in Canada (1984), a combination of Commissioner and Tribunal in the UK (1985 and 1989), and an Inspector General in Australia (1986). But now all these have or plan parliamentary committees, though to supplement rather than replace these other bodies.[31] Parliamentary committees are now to be found in most of the post-Communist states of Europe, and in Western Europe, only France stubbornly resists parliamentary (or any other form of) intelligence oversight. South Africa and several large Latin American states also established committees in the 1990s.

The historical source of parliamentary assertion of power over executives is the 'power of the purse' – that is, budgetary control. Historically, intelligence budgets have been regarded as closely kept secrets, on the grounds that, by adding to the 'jigsaw' of information available, knowing the size of the budget makes it easier for target states to work out the extent of intelligence operations against them. This would clearly be true of line-by-line budgets, but is highly unlikely if single-line intelligence budgets are published, and this is becoming the norm. For example, the Single Intelligence Account (SIA) for MI5, MI6 and GCHQ for 2004–5 was £1,295 million.[32] Much other intelligence effort occurs within the military budget, and so computing the total size of intelligence budgets is difficult everywhere. In the US Congress, the intelligence committees have a very direct impact on the size and distribution of agency budgets, but parliamentary intelligence committees tend to oversee and report on the adequacy, efficiency and efficacy with which the money is spent. For example, the mandate for the UK ISC is the 'expenditure, administration and policy' of the agencies. The other potential area of parliamentary oversight will concern the legality, propriety and rights implications of agency activities. Given the general tension between issues of 'security efficiency' and 'propriety', it can be difficult for committees to pay adequate attention to both. It may be the case that parliamentary committees are drawn too much into management issues and forget their important role in checking for rights abuses.

How is a parliamentary committee to be constituted? The critical issue is the extent of the independence of the committee from the executive. This independence will be clearest if the members are chosen by the assembly itself, as, for example, in Argentina and Germany, rather than by the Prime Minister, as in the UK. A significant number of committees have been established jointly between both houses of bicameral parliaments – for example, in Argentina and the UK. Given the fear that intelligence services may be used by governments for their own partisan purposes, committees must have cross-party membership, and requiring the chairperson to be from an opposition party, as, for example, in Hungary, will reinforce at least the appearance of independence. Whoever the members, and however they are chosen, if they are to have full access to materials that are otherwise secret, are they to be subject to security vetting? For parliamentarians anxious to maintain their autonomy, this is a delicate issue, as they are understandably reluctant to submit themselves to vetting by the very agencies over whom they are to exercise oversight. Informal political processes will ensure that those deemed unsuitable will probably not be appointed in the first place, but where there are formal processes of vetting, then there should be an independent mechanism for resolving disputes arising from a negative report against a parliamentarian.[33]

At the heart of the issue as to whether oversight is to be real and effective, rather than tokenistic, is the issue of access to information. Clearly, parliamentarians require a degree of access that enables them to fulfil their mandate, but the extent of their formal powers is only part of the answer. Parliamentary committees may be privileged in many ways, but at root, they face the same problems of negotiating gatekeepers as do all researchers into powerful organizations. Legislation varies. For example, not only do US congressional committees have a right to all the information regarding covert action that they ask for, but agency heads have a legal obligation to keep the committees 'fully and currently informed' of all such actions, though 'to the extent consistent with due regard for the protection from unauthorised disclosure of classified information relating to sensitive intelligence sources and methods'. Legislation in Australia and the UK deploys the term 'sensitive' in a similar way, to describe information that ministers may prevent committees from accessing.[34] But even where legislation formally enables untrammelled access, committees will still need to deploy skill in negotiating with informal gatekeepers in ministries and agencies.

The secrecy of intelligence work means that it is relatively easy for insiders to mislead external visitors, especially if their visits are sporadic, predictable and limited to interviews with selected officials and files. Security and intelligence personnel are skilled at answering precisely the question that is asked, and no more. Therefore the first task for any committee is to discover what the right questions are. This, in turn, depends on the expertise and experience available to members and the staff that they have. For example, the extent of the legislative inquiries into 9/11 was largely, but not entirely, determined by the availability of staff. The US Congressional Joint Inquiry team had twenty-four researchers divided into five investigative teams that interviewed officials, reviewed documents and submitted questionnaires not only to the FBI, CIA and NSA, but also to other departments.[35] Staff reviewed almost 500,000 pages of documents, conducted 300 interviews, and participated in briefings and panel discussions involving 600 officials from the intelligence agencies and elsewhere.[36] Most parliamentarians can only gawp in envy at the staff resources available to members of the US Congress, yet the effectiveness of oversight is never determined by resources alone. The UK effort, by comparison, was hampered from the start by the fact that half of the nine-person ISC (including the Chair) was newly appointed after the 2001 election. The members themselves 'took evidence' over the year from thirty-seven witnesses (ministers, heads of services and other officials) and made 'visits' to the agencies. But what might properly be described as 'investigative' work fell to the single investigator who was assigned to carry out five investigations during the year, none of which appear to have concerned 9/11.[37] The conclusions drawn by the ISC appear to have been based entirely on briefings from agency heads; at least, there is nothing in its Report to lead one to suppose otherwise.

The final factor for parliamentarians is their reporting relationship with their parent assembly. The privileged position inside the 'barrier of secrecy' requires that there be some mechanism for ensuring that their public reports do not include compromising material, but, again, the precise procedures vary. Ideally, the committee itself will make this decision, after consultation with the agencies has produced agreement as to what, if anything, should be omitted; but in some cases, the executive retains a firmer grip. For example, the UK ISC reports to the Prime Minister, who then presents the report to Parliament and the public. Even though security and intelligence issues have had a much higher profile since 9/11, they are still not ones on which members of parliaments are likely to gain great popularity. Yet they always pose the risk for politicians that they become regarded as some kind of political risk if they are seen as connected with the spooks, or, if they are critical, they may find themselves portrayed as 'irresponsible' or 'unpatriotic'. On the other hand, agencies may well succeed in co-opting critics.[38] So, to be effective, parliamentarians require a strong commitment of time, given all the other demands on it, and energy, given the relatively difficult areas into which they are enquiring; and, at the end of the day, should not expect too many thanks.

Parliamentary Oversight: The Case of the UK Intelligence and Security Committee

Although there is insufficient space here to conduct a full evaluation of the first decade of the ISC, it can be said that it has probably exceeded the expectations of some, including one of us, in terms of access to information and establishing itself as a serious critic of the agencies. Yet it might also be criticized for timidity, perhaps as a result of seeing itself more as part of the Whitehall machine for the *management* of the security intelligence community than as its *overseer*. To be sure, there is a fine line between these concepts, but ISC reports read more like those from management consultants than parliamentary critics. Two early commentaries on the ISC, though different in a number of ways, make similar points regarding the government's intentions in establishing the ISC in the first place. For one of us, this was about reasserting executive control of information regarding intelligence activities, because the traditional technique of insisting on complete secrecy had become untenable – for example, because of challenges under the ECHR.[39] For Ken Robertson, similarly, changes in the functions of the agencies, such as being drawn into countering organized crime, required a statutory mandate because, if cases ended up in court, then deniability would no longer be adequate protection for mistakes. So the ISA and the Committee were about 'risk management'.[40]

In quantitative terms, the ISC has certainly steadily increased its output: in 1995–7 its four published reports averaged twenty-nine paragraphs; in 1997–2001 the six reports averaged sixty-seven paragraphs; and in 2001–5 the seven reports averaged 110 paragraphs. In 1998 the government started to publish its response to ISC reports, and annual parliamentary debates commenced.

The Committee's first two 'terms' have been systematically analysed by Marc Davies. He concluded that during 1995–7 the Committee developed, as it gained familiarity with the area, but remained relatively deferential to the agencies and offered no substantive criticism.[41] During 1997–2001 he finds it 'immediately apparent that the ISC had grown significantly in confidence and that it was no longer deferential to the intelligence agencies. The committee offered stinging criticism of the agencies on a number of issues, most notably in the Mitrokhin report.'[42] Thus, Davies concludes:

> Despite being initially cautious and reluctant to criticise, the Committee had developed and shown itself willing to criticise both the intelligence agencies and the government. The overall record of the Committee suggests that despite a slow start, it eventually gathered pace and became increasingly credible as an oversight body.[43]

In the 2001–5 term, of course, the context within which the ISC operated shifted rapidly, first, because of 9/11, and then because of the intelligence controversies around the invasion of Iraq. Although the 9/11 attacks were not on the UK, by comparison with the extensive congressional inquiries in the USA, that in the UK was minuscule. The 2001–2 ISC *Annual Report* identified some resource pressures in MI5, MI6 and DIS, referred to a JIC July 2001 assessment that al-Qaeda attacks were in the final planning stages but that timings, targets and methods were unknown; noted the redeployment of staff post-9/11 and increased MI5 resources in collection and dissemination, but, significantly, said nothing about analytical deficiencies. Finally, it noted the lack of linguists.[44]

The three ISC reports other than annual reports during this period concerned the Bali bombings in October 2002, the assessments regarding Iraqi WMD published in September 2003, and the treatment of detainees by intelligence personnel in Afghanistan, Guantánamo Bay and Iraq, published in March 2005. Each of them contain criticisms, but they are very limited, and hardly challenge the government's own agendas for improving intelligence performance. Regarding Bali, the Foreign Office took advantage of the coincident arrival of the ISC in Canberra to ask it to investigate. The ISC concluded

Table 8.1 Intelligence and Security Committee reports (ex-annual), 1995–2005			
Cm number	**Title**	**Date of publication**	**No. of paragraphs**
2873	Interim	May 1995	11
3065	Security Service Work Against Organized Crime	December 1995	9
?	***	Spring 1996 (unpublished)	?
?	Agencies' work 'in the interests of the economic well-being of the UK'	November 1996 (unpublished)	?
4309	Sierra Leone	April 1999	17
4764	Agencies' handling of the information provided by Mr Mitrokhin	June 2000	79
5724	Inquiry into Intelligence Assessments and Advice Prior to the Terrorist Bombings on Bali 12 October 2002	December 2002	50
5972	Iraq Weapons of Mass Destruction – Intelligence and Assessments	September 2003	145
6469	Handling of Detainees by UK Intelligence Personnel in Afghanistan, Guantánamo Bay and Iraq	March 2005	131

Note: *** is the device by which ISC reports indicate redacted material. In this case, the very subject of the report remains classified.

that, on the available intelligence, there was no action that could have been taken to prevent the attacks, but, in the light of incidents earlier in the year in Indonesia, criticized MI5 for a 'serious misjudgement' in not raising the threat level from SIGNIFICANT to HIGH. More generally, they suggested that the threat assessment system needed another level between SIGNIFICANT and HIGH,[45] though it is very unclear why this would make much difference to the behaviour of those reading the assessments. In February 2003 the government's response included the announcement that the multi-agency Counter-Terrorist Analysis Centre established after 9/11 was to be expanded into JTAC (see discussion in chapter 3), located in Thames House under the MI5 Director General.[46] The time-scale here and the lack of any ISC reference to a JTAC suggests a degree of orchestration to legitimate changes already in train – MI5 was proud of the innovation of JTAC, yet did not accept the ISC criticism of its threat assessments.[47]

Before the political controversy over the 'sexing-up' or otherwise of the pre-war case for the invasion of Iraq arose, the ISC had already flagged the issue when it transmitted its *Annual Report for 2002–3* to the Prime Minister on 8 May 2003.[48] Accordingly, the ISC sought 'to examine whether the available intelligence, which informed the decision to invade Iraq, was adequate and properly assessed and whether it was accurately reflected in Government publications'.[49] It reported four months later that, based on the intelligence it had seen, 'there was convincing intelligence that Iraq had active chemical, biological and nuclear programmes and the capability to produce chemical and biological weapons'.[50] With respect to the 24 September 2002 dossier, the ISC said that it was 'founded on the assessments then available', and had not been ' "sexed up" by Alistair Campbell or anyone else'. It reported that the JIC had not been subjected to political pressures, and that its independence and impartiality had not been compromised.[51]

In an earlier draft of Blair's Foreword to the dossier, he had acknowledged that there was no threat of nuclear attack on the UK, but this was excluded from the published version, an omission described by the ISC as 'unfortunate'.[52] The government was also rebuked over the presentation of the 45-minute claim in the dossier.[53] The ISC concluded:

> The dossier was for public consumption and not for experienced readers of intelligence material. . . . The fact that it was assessed to refer to battlefield chemical and biological munitions and their movement on the battlefield, not to any other form of chemical or biological attack, should have been highlighted in the dossier. *This was unhelpful to an understanding of the issue.*[54]

In its response, the Government took no responsibility for the *silences* in the dossier. It was content that the ISC recognized that the dossier did *not* say that Iraq posed a 'current and imminent' threat to the UK mainland,[55] but made no response to the criticism of the exclusion of the UK attack caveat in the Foreword. Similarly, regarding the ISC criticism that the 45-minute claim was 'unhelpful', the government merely noted 'that the dossier did *not* say that Iraq could deliver chemical or biological weapons by ballistic missiles within 45 minutes'.[56] No, it did not; but it was *precisely* this failure to make clear just what the assessments were that amounted to serious misrepresentation of the nature of the threat from Iraq.

There is one footnote to this issue that raises questions as to who is overseeing what, and in whose interests. In July 2003 MI6 withdrew the intelligence relating the accelerated production of biological and chemical agents that had been crucially withheld from DIS experts and was seen as reinforcing the 45-minute claim shortly before the publication of the September dossier.[57] Sir Richard Dearlove, chief of MI6, told the ISC of this when he gave evidence to their inquiry the same month. The Foreign Secretary, Jack Straw, was only told about the withdrawal of this report on 8 September 2003 because he had to authorize ISC access to the reporting. But when, on 9 September, the ISC sent its WMD report to the Prime Minister, no mention was made of this very significant fact, and Blair was informed only when Butler reported in July 2004.[58] A junior Foreign Office minister told the House of Lords that the MI6 chief had given this information to the ISC on condition that it did not include it in its report, because it involved sensitive operational matters.[59] But that provision is to protect information from damaging parliamentary or public disclosure, not to prevent it going to the Prime Minister with his overriding responsibility for national security!

Read in the context of the steady spread of democratic oversight of intelligence in the last thirty years, one thing is very striking about all ISC reports published before 2005 – namely, the complete absence of any explicit reference to human rights. In 2005, however, the ISC reported on an issue at the heart of the 'global war on terror': the treatment of those detained in Afghanistan, Guantánamo Bay and Iraq. As with the question of WMD assessments, the ISC appears to have been ahead of the game, since it says that it 'raised the matter of detainees' with the Prime Minister in June 2003, several months before the controversies broke with the publication of pictures of abuses at Abu Ghraib prison in Baghdad.[60] Paying careful attention to its own boundaries, the ISC investigated any involvement in or witnessing of abuse by intelligence personnel, the adequacy of training as to what to do if it was witnessed, and when ministers were informed of any concerns. Their report rehearsed the relevant conventions on treatment of prisoners, noting that the USA does not regard those detained in Afghanistan as covered by them.[61] The ISC also noted the post-1972 ban on the deployment of the 'five techniques'[62] of interrogation used during internment in Northern Ireland. The substance of the report is taken up with some cases in which intelligence personnel did report their concerns at the treatment of detainees by US personnel, finds that these were relatively few (fewer than fifteen out of over 2000 interviews witnessed), criticized the lack of training of staff in Convention matters before deployment to Afghanistan, Guantánamo and Iraq, and noted that when concerns were expressed to US authorities, these were inadequately followed up.

Yet, the ISC demonstrated its keen awareness of the political realities of the issue by noting the 'very difficult and unusual operating conditions'[63] and the junior status of UK personnel in the 'coalition of the willing':

> The UK intelligence community has a duty to obtain intelligence for the purpose of protecting the UK from terrorist threats and the Agencies saw access to the detainees as a source of such intelligence. The Agencies told us that this access and the additional intelligence offered by the US authorities were provided on a privileged basis, which could have been withdrawn.[64]

In places, the Report really does not provide adequate oversight; certainly the actions of UK soldiers lies within the remit of the Defence Select Committee, and the ISC noted that a number were court-martialled, but the Committee did not even explore the issue that soldiers might have 'prepared' detainees for interrogation, as US evidence shows.[65] The ISC noted the widespread concern about the use of information obtained under torture, and noted briefly the pragmatic and principled arguments, but '[did] not attempt to answer these difficult questions'. Instead, it quoted at some length the Foreign Secretary's utilitarian justification for using such information if necessary.[66] We might have expected a parliamentary oversight committee to discuss this more critically; after all, the minister can speak for himself.

There is no doubt that the pattern of ISC reports (annual and otherwise) and, since 1998, government responses and annual parliamentary debates marks a significant improvement on the pre-1994 situation. But if we take the notion of oversight to incorporate issues of both efficacy and propriety, then one would have to conclude that the ISC has so far paid far greater attention to the former than the latter, and, thus, the mode of its establishment and functioning has seen it join the Whitehall framework for the management of the security intelligence agencies, rather than a Westminster-based mechanism for holding the agencies to account. Given the nature of the executive-dominated parliamentary system in the UK and the historical shyness of the agencies, this is hardly surprising, but it needs to be addressed by future committees, especially as the law and doctrine of counter-terrorist policy are toughened in the wake of the 7 July 2005 London bombings.

It is understandable that the ISC has sought to gain the trust of agencies and government, rather than grandstanding, but it must not allow itself to be sucked into the warm embrace of Whitehall consensus. Its reports are for Parliament and the public, and therefore need to be phrased in a way that the latter will understand. For example, its report on WMD may have said only that there was intelligence regarding weapons *programmes*, not weapons *as such*; but if they saw no intelligence regarding weapons, it would have been very helpful to the public if they had said so! Similarly, to describe the government's September 2002 dossier as 'unhelpful to an understanding of the issue' was an extraordinary understatement – the ISC's performance over the WMD controversy has so far fuelled the criticism of it as too much the creature of Downing Street.[67]

Extra-Parliamentary Oversight

There are a variety of other external oversight institutions that we need to consider, some permanent, others set up on an *ad hoc* basis. As we noted above, in the early days of increasing oversight, there was some suspicion of parliaments both by agencies and by ministers. For example, in Canada the McDonald Commission recommended an oversight structure for the new CSIS that would culminate in a parliamentary committee, but the government instead established in 1984 the SIRC, to which between three and five people would be appointed with the tasks of reviewing CSIS policies and investigating public complaints – for example, against refusals of security clearance. SIRC would report at least annually to the minister, who would lay the reports before Parliament. Parliament itself was not entirely happy with having only this indirect role in oversight, and established a national security subcommittee in the 1990s; but it always struggled without government blessing, since it could not access the information such committees require if they are to do a serious job. SIRC also raised parliamentary ire by being less forthcoming on its work than parliamentarians thought was their due; for their part, SIRC members took the view that they could not say anything publicly to members that had not been authorized by the minister to go to Parliament. It is fair to say that, in its early days, SIRC produced informative reports, established that it was serious about oversight, and accelerated the transition from the old RCMP Security Service to the civilianized CSIS. During the 1990s, a less activist leadership and a smaller membership that resulted in part from the electoral upheaval in 1993, when the previous governing party was virtually wiped out in the Commons, reduced the legitimacy and impact of the Committee.[68] In 1996 the Government responded to (or took advantage of) publicity concerning Canada's SIGINT agency, the Communications Security Establishment (CSE), by appointing a commissioner with similar powers to SIRC, to review CSE activities to ensure compliance with law, to respond to public complaints, and to report at least annually to the Minister of National Defence, who tables the report in Parliament.

The general shift towards legislative oversight of intelligence has not, paradoxically, reduced the establishment of *ad hoc* commissions of inquiry by governments in the face of scandal or controversy. Chapter 7 examined a number of commissions set up to look at Iraq. Canada set up a judicial commission, which, when it reports, will hopefully shed light on the operation of security networks that have developed so rapidly since 9/11. Maher Arar, a dual Syrian and Canadian citizen, was returning to Canada from the Middle East in autumn 2002 when he was detained at JFK airport and, after a few days, sent to Syria by means of the process of 'extraordinary rendition' discussed in chapter 5. He was imprisoned there for eleven months and tortured before being released without charge and returning to Canada. As a general rule, Canadians do not take kindly to their citizens being kidnapped by officials south of the border, and the anger at this case only intensified when it became clear that the information on which Arar was initially detained at JFK had derived from Canadian security officials, either the RCMP or the CSIS or both. In February 2004 the government established a commission of inquiry, headed by Justice Dennis O'Connor, with two mandates: first, to investigate and report on the actions of Canadian officials with respect to Arar's detention and treatment, and second, to consider the advisability of some independent review mechanism for the RCMP with respect to its national security functions.[69] Judging by the thoroughness with which the inquiry is being conducted, it has the potential to impact on the oversight architecture as much as McDonald did in the 1980s.

In the USA, the frustration of senior members of the joint congressional inquiry into 9/11 at inadequate co-operation from the executive branch led them to endorse the establishment of a separate commission of inquiry.[70] This idea had been growing in strength for some months, and was supported by the families of victims of 9/11. Although the White House insisted initially that this would distract the agencies from their primary tasks, it subsequently changed its mind.[71] However, it was only after further wrangling between the White House and Congress that agreement was reached in the last session before Congress adjourned in 2002, and the 9/11 Commission, whose report was discussed in chapter 6, was created.[72] Like the congressional inquiry, the Commission struggled against persistent obstruction from the executive failing to provide access to documents and key personnel for testimony.[73] When it did hold public hearings, however, with, *inter alia*, Attorney General John Ashcroft, former FBI director Louis Freeh, CIA director George Tenet and national security adviser Condoleeza Rice in mid-April 2004, they were questioned vigorously on the basis of the Commission's initial findings itemizing the lack of preparedness throughout the US counter-terrorism architecture.[74]

In recent years the UK has had a veritable 'season of inquiry'[75] into security intelligence and related matters. In addition to inquiries concerned with Iraq, and Bichard with respect to the Soham murders,[76] there have been others regarding Northern Ireland, specifically in relation to collusion between the security forces and loyalist paramilitaries in the killings of suspected Republican activists and sympathizers. As we saw in chapter 5, after many years of official denials, inquiries by a Canadian judge and a senior British police officer indicated that state agencies colluded with loyalist paramilitaries in the killing of lawyers and other Republican targets.

As a result of these findings, a public inquiry into the murder of Rosemary Nelson, a Catholic solicitor, started in April 2005. But the process proved painful for the authorities in more ways than one; as part of the ongoing peace process in Northern Ireland, Lord Saville was appointed to re-visit the events of 30 January 1972 – 'Bloody Sunday' – in Londonderry, when fourteen demonstrators were killed by paratroopers. The report made at the time by Lord Widgery[77] had been long discredited, and the subsequent inquiry by Saville was certainly more thorough; it was expected to report late in 2005. But whatever its conclusions, the government has been so horrified by the costs that it has passed a new Inquiries Act that, in essence, seeks to give the government greater control, not just over costs, but also over the ability of inquiries to obtain information. This measure to reassert control over inquiries has proved controversial: not only has it been criticized by the Commons' Public Administration Select Committee, but it has also led the family of Pat Finucane to write to judges asking them not to agree to sit under the terms of the new Act should the public inquiry for which the family has been campaigning actually be established.[78]

Media, NGOs and Citizens

Space permits only a few examples of oversight taking place at the fourth level. First, there have been challenges to the detention of terrorist suspects without trial and to other provisions of the new counter-terrorist legislation such as the USA PATRIOT Act and the UK ATCSA 2001, undertaken by civil liberty groups such as the American Civil Liberties Union and Liberty in the UK. Second, there have been efforts at more wide-ranging critiques of executive initiatives: for example, Electronic Privacy Information Center (EPIC) and Privacy International produced a joint report regarding the impact of current and proposed laws in fifty countries since 9/11. It identifies four main trends:

swift erosion of pro-privacy laws; greater data sharing between corporations, police and security agencies (see chapter 3); greater eavesdropping (see chapter 4); and sharply increased interest in people-tracking technologies.[79] In the UK, *Statewatch* provides a running critical commentary on the impact of new counter-terrorist laws, specially within Europe, including a 'scoreboard' on the extent to which EU measures taken since the Madrid bombing in March 2004 relate specifically to terrorism, or more generally to crime and disorder issues.

The media in general remain significant, if inconsistent, contributors to oversight.[80] Certainly, the heightened public concern with security in the wake of 9/11 has increased greatly media attention to intelligence matters, and the media have played an important role in alerting the public to concerns among intelligence professionals at the politicization of their product.[81] However, bitter battles over information control have resulted – witness the bare knuckle fight between Downing Street and the BBC over Gilligan's '45-minute' report in May 2003 – and their long-term impact on the relationship between democratic governments, intelligence agencies and the public could be problematic.

Conclusion

Oversight of intelligence, whoever carries it out, is inescapably political. Overseers must remember that they are engaged in contests of power in which the stakes are high. They must avoid paranoia as they traverse the wilderness of mirrors, but must remain alert to the possibility of being misled. For example, a central part of Stevens's inquiry into collusion in Northern Ireland was the role of Brian Nelson, a member of the UDA and an informer. Stevens reports that as soon as he embarked on his inquiry, the security agencies set out to obstruct him:

- The fact of Nelson's possession of FRU documents was concealed from Stevens.
- The army provided written statements to Stevens that documents he requested did not exist, but they were later obtained.
- When Stevens started his inquiry, the FRU trained Nelson in counter-interrogation techniques in case he was arrested.
- The initial Stevens operation to arrest Nelson was aborted when the FRU warned Nelson and he fled to the UK.
- On the night before the next operation to arrest Nelson, Stevens's incident room was destroyed by fire: fire alarms and intruder alarms in the offices had been disabled, and Stevens himself concluded: 'I believe it was a deliberate act of arson.'[82]

Judges may well be appointed in the hope that their findings will be accepted more readily than those of parliamentarians, but, as Lord Hutton's experience indicates, this is not always so, and the reputation of judges may be damaged. The way in which terms of reference are defined, the resources of staff and time allocated, and the provision of information are all critical issues in determining the thoroughness with which inquiries may be conducted; but politics is always just below the surface. Inquiries, even if entirely independent, also make crucial decisions as to how they will tell a story – what was remarkable about Hutton's inquiry was his decision to publish almost all the evidence on the inquiry website[83] so that the private communications between senior officials of just weeks earlier were available for public scrutiny. What was far less remarkable was that Hutton ultimately put the most limited construction on his terms of reference.

Periodic and *ad hoc* inquiries will always have their place when the government wheels come off, but urgent attention is still required to address the problem of maintaining oversight in the new age of security intelligence networks. We have a fairly clear grasp of the mechanisms of accountability as they operate (or not) within the bureaucratic structures of the state: for all their failings as efficient means of service delivery, hierarchies did have the advantage that lines of accountability were clear. To be sure, they could also be highly secretive, but, with appropriate access to persons and papers, the possibility of holding people to account was real. We have barely started on the problem of working out means of oversight that are appropriate to rapidly developing and proliferating networks. The answer to the question 'Who is to monitor and police informal networks?'[84] is extremely elusive.

There are ideas about how to secure accountability while maintaining the flexibility of private–public networks delivering services, but these tend to emphasize financial and efficiency issues more than the propriety issues that concern us with respect to security intelligence networks.[85] For participants in the latter, convinced (sometimes with justification, sometimes not) that public safety and national security are in their hands, the very lack of transparency that is afforded by informal networks is their great advantage. People might well decide that the professional risks inherent in security intelligence work are just not worth taking if there is a clearly documented audit trail leading back to their desk. There is often great scepticism that managers (not all of whom in the military and the police will necessarily have intelligence experience) will protect operatives and analysts if a wrong judgement is made. Power flows are yet more subtle in fluid networks, and traditional forms of inquiry may simply not be appropriate once decisions and knowledge are generated within networks, rather than in traditional bureaucracies. Addressing this problem, Sheptycki suggests that networked intelligence 'cells' must be organized so that the inefficiencies of hierarchy can be avoided and intelligence shared with the assurance that flows can be audited for compliance with human rights standards such as proportionality.[86] Clearly, this is an admirable goal, but immensely difficult to achieve. We agree with Bayley and Shearing that if the 'public interest' is to be safeguarded, then government must retain the functions of regulation, auditing and facilitation of security networks.[87] At a minimum, the problem can only be tackled at each of the levels of oversight identified here: training in ethical guidelines within agencies, ministerial oversight via an institution such as an inspector general, parliamentary oversight and, finally, public vigilance.

Conclusion: Intelligence for a More Secure World?

> The state never has any use for truth as such, but only for truth which is useful to it, more precisely for anything useful to it, whether it be truth, half-truth, or error.
>
> Friedrich Nietzsche, in Lathrop, *The Literary Spy*

W E argued at the beginning of this book that the study of intelligence must strive to become more self-consciously analytical and theoretical than hitherto, because it is so significant for both domestic and international security. At the domestic level, intelligence may help to save lives; internationally, it can provide, or be used to provide, the basis for decisions to go to war, and hence cost lives. The events of the past few years – 9/11, Iraq and, most recently, the 7/7 bombings in London – indicate that a systematic analysis of intelligence structures and processes is long overdue. Historically, intelligence has been the exclusive province of insiders, and there is no denying that much intelligence work must take place in secret if it is to be of value. However, it is clear from both the regularity and costs of intelligence failures that intelligence is too important to be left to the spooks.

Citizens have been excluded for too long from any knowledge of intelligence policies and practices, but now live in societies in which security fears apparently increase relentlessly. In one sense this is highly ironic given the lifting of the Cold War fear of mutual annihilation, as none of the current threats are on that scale. But in another sense it is not: the multiplicity of potential security threats, the regularity of serious incidents, the rapid growth in the market for security products and services, and the actions of governments seeking to demonstrate that they are still 'in control' through pronouncement and legislation, all combine to create an occasionally febrile atmosphere in which a 'politics of fear' can thrive. One important task for researchers is to make sense of and communicate the extent to which fears are well founded and how far they are manufactured. An essential part of this process is to educate publics as to the realistic possibilities of what intelligence can deliver. Another is to explain the limits of intelligence – what intelligence cannot realistically be expected to do – and that some events may be better explained in terms of a combination of policy and intelligence failure rather than as resulting solely from failures of intelligence. In the context of post-9/11 fears, it is also important not to lose sight of the dangers inherent in state and corporate intelligence-related activities that can damage both individual rights and the broader democratic process. A full and nuanced understanding of the nature of intelligence failure is essential in a post-9/11 context, but the question of democratic accountability remains a central concern of intelligence studies. 'Defending democracy' in this world has involved significant erosions of liberal-democratic norms, and the subject needs to address the risk outlined by Bernard Porter in 1989: 'that the medicine can, if not administered under the very strictest and widest supervision, have effects which are as damaging as the disease'.[1]

In the early chapters we discussed core definitional issues, and identified the point that, historically, security intelligence has been associated with the operation of states and governments. All maintain intelligence agencies whose function is *surveillance* – the monitoring of populations in order to generate *knowledge* that can inform security policies and thus the exercise of governmental *power*, as well as enhance the relative security of the state in relation to potential adversaries. However, in some countries these functions are conducted under such different political conditions that fundamental distinctions must be made. All states, whether liberal-democratic or authoritarian, maintain agencies whose function is to gather information about internal threats to the regime, but in some states this function is so significant that it might actually define the regime, for example, as a 'counter-intelligence' or 'national security' state. Some states enjoy such little legitimacy and/or perceive themselves to be so threatened by foreign interests that surveillance for the purposes of state security is almost the only meaningful state activity. However, change is possible, and, therefore, the 'research map' we proposed in chapter 2 can be used by researchers to compare agencies across different types of regime and to chart shifts, whether progressive or regressive, over time.

But states, wherever located on a spectrum between 'national security' and 'liberal-democratic' are not the only players. In chapter 3 we discussed the development of security networks involving both corporate and community sectors. Since 9/11, states have reasserted their primacy as security actors in a plethora of new counter-terrorism laws, new doctrines regarding prevention and pre-emption, and increased resources poured into state intelligence agencies. So was our analysis in chapter 3 premature in emphasizing the diverse nature of contemporary security intelligence? We do not think so; we did not use the globalization concept in order to suggest that states were less significant but, rather, to point to the increasing plurality of security intelligence actors. Corporations and communities have always provided for their own security to some extent, but states have *chosen* to empower them further in order to increase the potential for surveillance via a greater number of eyes and ears, while restricting their own expenditures. Yet, these other actors are not just incorporated smoothly into state security systems; their own priorities may lead them to act differently on occasion. Thus security networks are not simply a vehicle through which states extend their capacity for security governance; we must analyse carefully the interrelationships of the agencies involved and the security policies and practices they develop.

One central question is how we should characterize the role of the United States within the contemporary global intelligence network. Reg Whitaker has described the USA as a 'global Leviathan'[2] in the post-9/11 world, raising the intriguing possibility that it is the first 'transnational security state'. There is nothing new in the USA seeing itself as the 'world policeman' – its insistence on its right and duty to act in this way can be traced back to 1898 – but the current situation is qualitatively different. Since 1991 the USA has been the sole super-power – the only state with sufficient economic and military resources to give it the capacity to take independent action almost anywhere on the planet. Beyond this, the possibility of collective international action can depend heavily on US willingness to lend political and/or material support – as, for example, in Kosovo, Rwanda and Sudan. The idea of the USA as Leviathan should not be taken literally, in so far as other states have not given up their own mechanisms for the maintenance of *internal* security; but the global 'War on Terror' was declared and defined in Washington, and its primary emphases are those established by the Bush Administration. There has been resistance by some states to some elements of it, but the international community has essentially danced to a tune called by Washington, either willingly or after some cajoling. Shifts in domestic laws aimed at facilitating information gathering and sharing, increased efforts to enhance cross-national intelligence co-operation, and war in Afghanistan and Iraq all reflect this US dominance, and where international law has stood in the way, the USA has been willing to either side-step or ignore it. However, looking ahead, the situation in Iraq, the ballooning US budget deficit, the controversies around the use of intelligence in the lead-up to the invasion of Iraq, and public disquiet over the war, all suggest that it would be premature to predict longevity for such an approach to international relations.

In chapters 6 and 7 we discussed the nature of intelligence failure, and showed that intelligence failures are inevitable. In discussing failure, it is necessary to distinguish, broadly, between intelligence (or knowledge) failures and policy (or power) failures; that is, two sets of people are involved here – intelligence professionals and policy-making executives. We identified key 'pressure points' where 'knowledge' failures are most likely to occur. For example, targets may be misidentified or the wrong targets chosen; gathering may fail for many reasons – many states just do not have adequate resources to indulge in sophisticated technical gathering, or targets' counter-intelligence may be very effective. But even if relevant information can be gathered on the right targets, analysis may fail. As we saw in the case of Iraq's WMD, for all the information gathered by the sophisticated intelligence apparatus of the world's most powerful nations, supplemented by the work of specialist UN weapons inspectors, the lack of evidence of WMD was continually evaluated as indicating that the regime continued to conceal them, rather than as indicating that they had been destroyed. As Tony Blair repeatedly asked, if Saddam Hussein had destroyed his WMD, why didn't he just come clean to the inspectors? Certainly, regime concealment efforts did continue throughout the 1990s for various political and security reasons – Iraq, after all, existed in a hostile regional environment – but there was a distinct lack of analytical imagination which was then used by policymakers to help sustain their case.

Policy or political failure can occur for a variety of reasons, some of them unanticipated. However, it also arises where policy is based on conviction or ideology rather than solely on *knowledge*. We argued in chapter 7 that, though there were failures of intelligence collection, analysis and management in the case of (the non-existent) Iraqi WMD, by far the greater failure was political. The decision to displace the regime of Saddam Hussein was not rooted firmly or solely in intelligence. Intelligence was used to justify a policy decision that was arrived at for different reasons. In particular, the Butler Inquiry in the UK exposed as false the idea that intelligence in 2002 showed Iraq to represent any greater risk to the countries that went to war than it had in the immediately preceding years. A combination of 'cherry picking', failures across the intelligence–policymaker fault line and policymaker exaggeration meant that power determined 'knowledge'.

Other sources of failure may be found at the stage of dissemination – intelligence may not reach the people who can do something with it, or it may simply be too imprecise for any specific action to be taken. In the last few years, the problem of warning intelligence has vexed agencies and governments. What is the point of issuing vague warnings about a general possibility of future terrorist attack, unspecific as to time or place, since the benefit of some general increase in 'vigilance' might be far outweighed by increased levels of fear and insecurity? Further, the more these occur, the higher the risk that security fatigue will set in, bringing with it the consequential risk of 'boy who cried wolf' syndrome. On the other hand, if governments disseminate exaggerated versions of intelligence to the public in order to bolster support for unpopular policies, as happened in 2002–3, then, again, the failure is far more political than professional.

The costs of failure can be very high, whether it is in the sense that intelligence does not provide adequate forewarning of some 'surprise' attack, as on 9/11 or 7/7, warns us of a 'threat' that does not actually exist, as in the case of Iraq's WMD, or threatens the integrity of the political process. This might be seen at an international level; for example, the use of covert information gathering against members of the UN Security Council and Secretary of State Powell's February 2003 presentation at the UN of contentious material as 'fact' in order to secure a resolution specifically authorizing the use of force against Iraq, both constituted an abuse of UN processes.

Within nations, also, the abuse of intelligence can be highly damaging to democratic structures and processes. This may lead some to argue that there is a complete incompatibility between democracy and secret intelligence activities.

We do not agree with this, since all states face *some* covertly organized threats to the safety and security of their populations, and governments have a primary obligation to provide protection against those threats. The trick is, of course, to ensure that security intelligence is properly directed at genuine threats to public safety and security, rather than at the opponents of the government of the day or some minority group who can be scapegoated as a distraction from intractable social problems. Security intelligence must remain a limited means of governance, and not become an end in itself.[3]

Whatever the cause, 'failures' generate demands for reform. One of the reasons why we must take care in analysing the causes – political and/or professional – of failure is that if we mis-diagnose the problem, then the chances of any reforms improving security in the future will be remote indeed. We must also beware of the possibility that reforms are more about giving concerned publics (i.e. electorates) the impression of action and change than actually bringing it about. This will be even more the case where governments seek to disguise political failure (a characteristic of liberal democracies) by blaming the professionals – something we saw in the Iraq débâcle. To the political pressures we might add economic pressures. An important element in the growth of security intelligence networks is the profitability of selling technological solutions to security problems. Each needs to be evaluated on its merits, but, in general, we must be aware that technological 'fixes' to otherwise intractable political and social issues rarely exist. Just as, almost half a century ago, President Eisenhower warned against the accumulation of unwarranted influence over policy making by the 'military-industrial complex', so we must beware the accumulation of excessive power by a 'security-industrial complex' growing fat on fears of terrorism.

There are many reasons why intelligence reform rarely works. Reassuring publics as to competence on security issues is crucial to state legitimacy, and failure increases politicians' dependence on intelligence officials. Of course, these may be the very people who are either responsible for the failure (or *held* responsible for it, a different thing), and their expertise and positions, enhanced by secrecy, may enable them to resist reforms. Security intelligence failures normally produce demands and resources for more of the same. Since surveillance itself tends to be defined narrowly as information gathering, rather than in our broader sense of developing knowledge and exercising power, failures can be held to result from inadequate collection, with the remedy being to legislate for yet more intrusive gathering techniques at home and more resources for technical and human foreign intelligence. Issues of analysis and the translation of intelligence into policy often receive less attention. We have seen that the 9/11 and Iraq inquiries did identify analytical deficiencies, but, though real, they cannot be understood outside the context of the political failures ducked by the inquiries.

Another typical government response to policy failure is reorganization. A central aspect of democratization in Eastern Europe has been the reform of authoritarian, often military, Soviet-style agencies, whose primary, if not sole, concern was domestic counter-intelligence, into civilianized, law-based agencies with a broader recipe of targets, including transnational crime and terrorism. This process has been very uneven; in some countries progress has been real, while in others apparent changes disguise essentially unreconstructed practices. The former include those who convinced the EU that reforms were adequate to justify accession – for example, Poland and Hungary – while the Russian FSB is a good example of the latter tendency.

Less dramatically, we have seen how the USA has sought to reorganize its intelligence community in the wake, first, of 9/11 and second, the Iraq failure. Clearly, governmental reorganization is inextricably bound up with politics, and just as in former Central and East European countries, intelligence reform was a central symbol of the democratization process, so, in the United States, intelligence reform has been symbolic of governmental determination to place security at the heart of US politics. Ironically, even before 9/11, more was probably written on the subject of intelligence reform in the USA than in the rest of the world combined. Throughout the 1990s a series of inquiries and commissions deliberated on the subject of 'fixing' the US intelligence structure, but precious little happened. Now, two main shifts are under way: first, the creation of the Department of Homeland Security by the amalgamation of various former domestic departments covering borders, immigration, secret service, coastguard and emergency management. The resulting gargantuan bureaucracy may well provide a potent *symbol* of the new concern with security, but it is far from clear that it will actually enhance the domestic security of Americans. One major criticism of the lamentable performance of FEMA in the wake of the devastation that Hurricane Katrina inflicted on New Orleans was that its focus and resources had been disproportionately diverted towards counter-terrorism.[4]

The second main reorganization has been the establishment of the Director of National Intelligence (DNI), with greater authority over the ill-named federal 'intelligence community' than that enjoyed previously by the DCI.[5] On paper, the DNI certainly has greater authority, but whether he or she is actually able to make it stick when the Department of Defense still consumes 80 per cent of the intelligence budget remains to be seen. However, thinking more generally about the prospects for intelligence reform, we should not take the USA as a template. Although issues relating to co-ordination and intelligence sharing affect all national intelligence structures, the relatively small number and scale of intelligence agencies in most states means that there is some reasonable prospect of alleviating problems. In the USA the problems are qualitatively different, deriving from the fragmented federal system of government and, paradoxically, such wealth that agencies proliferate at all levels of government. The result is an intelligence 'community' that is so large and so fragmented that the prudent answer to the question of how it should be reformed for better performance is: 'I wouldn't start from here.'

If one were starting afresh, then one would begin with strategy and doctrine in the light of the threat environment, and only then consider how agencies might be best organized to gather information about and counter those threats. However, the reality of day-to-day government is that these issues are viewed from the perspective of existing agencies, and necessary changes may simply be impossible. As it is, a common reaction to the co-ordination problem is to establish new task forces or agencies that are meant to overcome organizational fragmentation but which, in the longer term, may simply compound it. A related organizational issue is that much greater flexibility is required on the part of agencies as they seek to comprehend the apparent fluidity of extremist networks. Perhaps what is needed is a reversal of 'mirror-imaging': instead of analysts making culture-bound assumptions about how others organize, what is needed is imitation of the flexibility of target organizations and networks. For example, the 9/11 Commission recommended that 'need to know', so central to the development of state intelligence agencies as a means of securing operational information about sources and methods, be replaced by 'need to share' in order to maximize the potential for intelligence to learn about and counter threats.[6] It remains far from clear how this is to be achieved. As we suggested in chapter 3, even assuming that formidable technical issues can be surmounted, there remains the learnt reluctance of officials and analysts to share information for a variety of sound reasons.[7]

It is clear that the challenges facing intelligence officials and practitioners are enormous. Can they adapt time-honoured organizations, policies and practices to a world in which threats appear to be more diverse, fluid and complex? The pressure on them to perform, coming from governments and publics alike in the context of a world of heightened sensitivities that sometimes border on paranoia, alerts us to the clear danger that they may be drawn into illegal, improper and even counter-productive methods. This is by no means inevitable, but we already have enough evidence from the history of counter-terrorism policies in, for example, Northern Ireland and the post-9/11 statement by the US government that the President considers himself not to be bound by various international agreements such as the Geneva conventions on the treatment of detainees. The torture and ill-treatment of detainees in Afghanistan, Iraq, Guantánamo Bay and, it is assumed, at the various CIA-run 'black sites' intended to put al-Qaeda suspects beyond the reach of any national or international organization, make clear the urgent need to reiterate the importance of democratic control of intelligence in order to enhance both effectiveness and propriety.

The performance of the official legislative overseers of intelligence in the USA and the UK has been weak. These overseers have made some appropriate criticisms of the extent of professional intelligence failures in relation to 9/11 and Iraq, but have fought shy of explicitly identifying the extent to which failure has been political rather than professional. In this crucial respect they cannot be said to have dealt effectively with the question of intelligence failure – here, half an answer cannot be an accurate answer. As we have argued, intelligence is an inescapably political activity. Intelligence oversight is, therefore, also inherently political. Overseers have a democratic duty to look beyond the political welfare of current presidents and prime ministers in order to address the longer-term needs not only for public security but also for public education. Just as surveillance defines what intelligence agencies do in respect of their societies, so publics need robust and reliable surveillance of the agencies that operate in their name. The lesson of the recent past is that it does not yet exist.

Notes

Chapter 1 What is Intelligence?

1 Kitson and Kelso, 'England hunt rugby spies'. In a further incident, in November 2005, two men were caught while covertly filming the All Blacks rugby team during a training session: Kitson, 'All Blacks discover spies in the bushes'.

2 Throughout the book we use 'MI5' and 'MI6' when referring to the UK Security Service and Secret Intelligence Service respectively, as a widely recognized shorthand (as, indeed, the agencies themselves do with their website addresses), but recognize the essentially historical nature of these titles. On this, see <http://www.mi6.gov.uk/output/Page50.html>.

3 <http://www.mi5.gov.uk/output/Page7.html>.

4 Butler, *Review of Intelligence on Weapons of Mass Destruction* (henceforth Butler Report), para. 52.

5 P. Flood, *Report of the Inquiry into Australian Intelligence Agencies* (henceforth Flood Report), p. 8.

6 Moynihan, *Secrecy*, p. 202.

7 As Sherman Kent pointed out, 'intelligence' can, in fact, refer to any of three things: a kind of *knowledge*; the type of *organization* that produces the knowledge; or the *activity* pursued by the organization. Kent, *Strategic Intelligence*, p. ix.

8 The funnel of causality is used as a framework in Kegley and Wittkopf, *American Foreign Policy*, ch. 2.

9 <http://www.odci.gov/cia/publications/facttell/intelligence_cycle.html>.

10 Cited in Senate Select Committee on Intelligence, *Report on the US Intelligence Community's Prewar Intelligence Assessments on Iraq* (henceforth SSCI Report), p. 5.

11 Ibid., p. 4.

12 Ibid., p. 16.

13 For example, see Godson, 'Intelligence for the 1990s', p. 4.

14 Herman, *Intelligence Power*, pp. 54–6.

15 Herman, 'Ethics and intelligence', p. 342.

16 For example, in the Pinochet era the extent of recourse to 'high end' covert actions was a reflection of the nature of the regime and the prevailing security culture. See Dinges, *The Condor Years*, and O'Shaughnessy, *Pinochet*, chs 3 and 4.

17 L. K. Johnson, 'On drawing a bright line', p. 286. This question is discussed further in ch. 8.

18 *MI5: The Security Service*, at <www.mi5.gov.uk/how_we_operate/how_we_operate_1.htm>.

19 <www.fbi.gov/intelligence/intell.htm>, accessed 16 Nov. 2005.

20 Warner, 'Wanted: a definition of "intelligence"'.

21 Ibid.

22 Cited in ibid.

23 L.K. Johnson, 'Intelligence', p. 365.
24 Warner, 'Wanted'.
25 Richard Betts has argued that 'The comparative advantage of the intelligence community over outside analysts is in bringing together secret information with knowledge from open sources. The more far-seeing a project, the less likely secret information is to play a role in the assessment': Betts, 'Fixing intelligence', p. 50. This suggests that intelligence services' comparative advantage over bodies using exclusively open source material lies in particular in short-term analysis, and that in medium and long-term analysis the relative advantage that secret information bestows on intelligence agencies is progressively eroded, increasing the likelihood that the projections of open source analysts will be similarly valid.
26 With regard to Vietnam, e.g., Daniel Ellsberg has written of how 'I had never questioned the assumption of many students of presidential power that secrecy is vital to preserve a president's range of options. But I now saw how the system of secrecy and lying could give him options he would be better off without': Ellsberg, *Secrets*, p. 205.
27 Kahn, 'An historical theory of intelligence', p. 79.
28 See, e.g., Laqueur, *Terrorism*, pp. 18–20.
29 Thucydides, *The Peloponnesian War*, pp. 172–3.
30 For example, see ibid., ch. 24.
31 On the distinction between 'threats' and 'vulnerabilities', see Buzan, *People, States and Fear*, ch. 3.
32 See L. K. Johnson, 'Bricks and mortar', pp. 3–4.
33 Gill, *Policing Politics*, p. 163.
34 Knott, *Secret and Sanctioned*, ch. 3.
35 Porter, *The Origins of the Vigilant State*; Allason, *The Branch*.
36 See Porter, *Plots and Paranoia*. More generally, see Mazower, *Policing of Politics*. On McKinley's assassination, see Fine, 'Anarchism and the assassination of McKinley'.
37 Andrew and Gordievsky, *KGB*, ch. 2; Andrew, *Secret Service*, ch. 6; Porter, *Plots and Paranoia*, chs. 7–8.
38 See Krivitsky's autobiography, *I Was Stalin's Agent*. The full record of his MI5 debriefing was released at the National Archives in 2003, in files KV2/802–5. See also Kern, *A Death in Washington*; Callaghan and Phythian, 'State surveillance of the CPGB leadership'.
39 Andrew, *Secret Service*, pp. 260–1.
40 Ibid., p. 298.
41 Sillitoe, *Cloak Without Dagger*, pp. 196–8.
42 For an account of his role in publicizing the existence of the D-Notice system, see Watkins, *A Short Walk Down Fleet Street*, ch. 4.
43 See Chapman, *Licence to Thrill*.
44 J. Black, 'The geopolitics of James Bond', p. 302. There are similar examples of fiction feeding reality from US intelligence. To take one example, actress Barbara Feldon, Agent 99 in the 1960s television spy spoof *Get Smart*, has recalled how she was 'invited to visit the CIA for an exhibit they had of gadgets from "Get Smart", "I Spy", "The Man from U.N.C.L.E.", the Bond movies, and so forth. And they said that during those years, the CIA actually did watch those shows and made some of those devices actually work.' Cited in Lathrop, *The Literary Spy*, p. 153.
45 E. P. Thompson, 'The secret state within the state', p. 612.
46 Pincher, *Their Trade Is Treachery*.
47 For example, *Too Secret Too Long*, and *The Spycatcher Affair*.
48 The revelations from ex-MI5 officers Miranda Ingram and Cathy Massiter were significant here. See the excerpts in West (ed.), *The Faber Book of Espionage*, ch. 11.
49 See Geraghty, *The Irish War*; and Foot, *Who Framed Colin Wallace?*
50 See Milne, *The Enemy Within*; and Hitchens, 'Who runs Britain?'

51 Wright, *Spycatcher*. See also Dorril and Ramsay, *Smear!*; Leigh, *The Wilson Plot*; and Benn, 'The case for dismantling the secret state'.
52 Dearlove and Saunders, *Introduction to British Politics*, p. 545.
53 Hollingsworth and Fielding, *Defending the Realm*; and Tomlinson, *The Big Breach*.
54 Porter, *Plots and Paranoia*, p. viii.
55 Aldrich, "Grow your own", p. 148.
56 For a national security typology identifying three types of national security (Outward-Oriented, National Securitism, and Inward-Oriented), see Tapia-Valdés, 'A typology of national security policies'. More generally, see Rouquie, *The Military and the State in Latin America*.
57 The classic exposé, demonstrating the siege mentality of the apartheid state, is Winter, *Inside BOSS*.
58 Dziak, *Chekisty*.
59 See Black and Morris, *Israel's Secret Wars*, ch. 9. The available intelligence allegedly included a personal warning from King Hussein of Jordan to Prime Minister Golda Meir: see p. 321. See also Raviv and Melman, *Every Spy a Prince*, ch. 10. Interestingly, intelligence does not figure centrally in Michael B. Oren's acclaimed account of the 1967 war: Oren, *Six Days of War*.
60 The flavour of the debate can be seen in Draper, 'Is the CIA necessary?' For the debate in a UK context see Gill, "Sack the spooks".
61 See Rogers, *Losing Control*, ch. 4.
62 Schweizer, 'The growth of economic espionage', pp. 11–12.
63 Cited in L. K. Johnson, 'Spies', p. 20.
64 Treverton, 'Intelligence and the "market state"'.
65 Ibid., p. 73.
66 Ibid., p. 76 n. 5.
67 See ch. 4.
68 Edelman, *The Symbolic Uses of Politics*, pp. 69–72; Keller, *The Liberals and J. Edgar Hoover*, pp. 23–7; and R.G. Powers, *Secrecy and Power*, ch. 9.
69 MacEachin, 'Predicting the Soviet invasion of Afghanistan'.
70 This is in essence the argument of former National Co-ordinator for Security, Infrastructure Protection, and Counterterrorism, Richard Clarke, in *Against All Enemies*. See also Mann, *Rise of the Vulcans*.
71 Miller and van Natta, 'In years of plots and clues, scope of Qaeda eluded US'.
72 Aldrich, 'Grow your own', pp. 136–8.
73 Hogan, *Cross of Iron*; Leffler, *A Preponderance of Power*.
74 Keegan, *Intelligence in War*, pp. 383–4.
75 Knightley, *The Second Oldest Profession*; Dorril, *MI6*; and Jeffreys-Jones, *Cloak and Dollar*.
76 For example, as articulated in Dr Julius Mader's introduction to the 1968 East German publication *Who's Who in CIA*: 'We know, it is true, that the extensive intelligence machinery of imperialist USA was not, is not, and never will be, in a position to turn back the wheel of history. The destinies of the nations cannot be fixed in the offices of the CIA': p. 14.
77 For a sense of the scope of the KGB's overseas operations, see Andrew and Mitrokhin, *The Mitrokhin Archive II*.
78 Herman, *Intelligence Services in the Information Age*, p. ix.
79 Herman, 'The Cold War: did intelligence make a difference?', in ibid., p. 159.
80 Winks, *Cloak and Gown*, p. 63.
81 Gaddis, 'Intelligence, espionage, and Cold War history', p. 104.
82 Quoted in Kegley and Wittkopf, *American Foreign Policy*, p. 132.
83 For example, with regard to the 1956 Suez crisis, see Lucas and Morey, 'The hidden "alliance"'.

84 Aldrich, "Grow your own", p. 144.

85 Betts, 'Analysis, war, and decision', p. 62.

86 Shlaim, 'Failures in national intelligence estimates', p. 378.

87 Kessler, *The CIA at War*, p. 261. In a UK context, former MI5 officer Annie Machon offers the example of the reluctance of managers in F Branch, the counter-subversion section, to acknowledge that the threat from groups such as the Militant Tendency had receded: Machon, *Spies, Lies and Whistleblowers*, pp. 37–53.

88 The phrase comes from the 1920 T. S. Eliot poem 'Gerontion', and was used by David Martin as the title of his study of US counter-intelligence and Cold War paranoia: Martin, *Wilderness of Mirrors*.

Chapter 2   How Do We Understand Intelligence?

1   Scott and Jackson, 'The study of intelligence in theory and practice,' p. 147.

2   Andrew and Dilks, *The Missing Dimension*; Hoare (ed.), *British Intelligence in the Twentieth Century*; Andrew, 'Intelligence, international relations and "under-theorisation"', p. 172.

3   Fry and Hochstein, 'Epistemic communities', pp. 17–18. For a restatement of the neo-realist case and the primacy of security in an anarchic world system, see Mearsheimer, *The Tragedy of Great Power Politics*.

4   For example, Hulnick, *Fixing the Spy Machine*; Lowenthal, *Intelligence*; Odom, *Fixing Intelligence*. Two recent articles by Loch Johnson represent exceptions: 'Bricks and mortar for a theory of intelligence'; 'Preface to a theory of strategic intelligence'.

5   Kahn, 'An historical theory of intelligence'.

6   Hay, *Political Analysis*, pp. 10–13; Sanders, 'Behaviouralism'.

7   Cf. Marsh and Furlong, 'A skin not a sweater'; Bottoms, 'The relationship between theory and research in criminology'.

8   Sheila Kerr noted that Roger Hilsman's 1958 critique of US strategic intelligence 'found that contemporary US doctrine put too much emphasis on the accumulation of descriptive facts as the essence of knowledge': 'Turning knowledge into wisdom', p. 9.

9   Allison and Zelikow, *Essence of Decision*, p. 4.

10 Norton-Taylor, *Truth is a Difficult Concept*, p. 86.

11 Terriff et al., *Security Studies Today*, pp. 99–114; Morrow with Brown, *Critical Theory and Methodology*, pp. 62–82; Marsh and Furlong, 'A skin not a sweater', pp. 25-6.

12 For example, Randall, 'Feminism'.

13 A partial exception is Enloe, *Bananas, Beaches and Bases*.

14 Pettman, *Worlding Women*, p. 4.

15 Ibid., p. 105.

16 Der Derian, *Antidiplomacy*, p. 27.

17 Ibid., p. 46.

18 Rathmell, 'Towards postmodern intelligence,' pp. 95–6.

19 Ibid., p. 97.

20 Ibid., pp. 97–8. For a specific argument on this fifth factor, see Ferris, 'Netcentric warfare, C4ISR and information operations', pp. 203–4.

21 Rathmell, 'Towards postmodern intelligence,' p. 101. Cf. also Barger, *Toward a Revolution in Intelligence Affairs*, p. 99. David Lyon puts it more strongly in his discussion of postmodernists 'embracing chaos': *Postmodernity*, pp. 74–8.

22 'Objectivity' is not possible in social and behavioural sciences, but intersubjectivity is its pragmatic surrogate, and ensures that an observation could have been made by any other observer in the same situation: Kaplan, *The Conduct of Inquiry*, pp. 127–8. Similarly, Bevir and Rhodes argue that the quality of narratives produced by interpretist work can be evaluated by comparisons of comprehensiveness, consistency and heuristic value: 'Interpretive theory', p. 142.

23 Eyre, 'Ballot-box blues'. See also Brooks, 'The art of intelligence'.
24 Discussing the writing of his novel, *Absolute Friends*, John Le Carré said: 'you have got to write a novel to tell the truth': BBC *Front Row*, 1 Jan. 2004. More generally, West, 'Fiction, faction and intelligence'.
25 Lyon, *Postmodernity*, pp. 48–52. Also Walsh (ed.), *The Gulf War Did Not Happen*.
26 Der Derian, *Antidiplomacy*, p. 59.
27 Lyon, *Postmodernity*, pp. 6–7; Rathmell, 'Towards postmodern intelligence', p. 93.
28 On the role of deception, e.g., see Epstein, *Deception*.
29 For example, Lyon, *Surveillance after September 11*, pp. 40–55.
30 Cf. Evans's objections to postmodernism in both *In Defence of History* and *Lying about Hitler*.
31 Hay, *Political Analysis*, p. 47.
32 Danermark et al., *Explaining Society*, pp. 91–3. For example, L. K. Johnson, 'Bricks and mortar', p. 1; Marrin and Clemente, 'Improving intelligence analysis'.
33 Fry and Hochstein, 'Epistemic communities', p. 25.
34 Morrow with Brown, *Critical Theory*, p. 78.
35 Marsh and Furlong, 'A skin not a sweater', pp. 30–1.
36 Wrong, *Power*, ch. 1.
37 Hay, *Political Analysis*, p. 94.
38 Ibid., ch. 3 for a summary; see also McAnulla, 'Structure and agency'.
39 Allison and Zelikow, *Essence of Decision*.
40 Jessop, 'Interpretive sociology'. This is an equivalent approach to role theory in foreign policy analysis: Kegley and Wittkopf, *American Foreign Policy*, pp. 464–5.
41 Hay, *Political Analysis*, pp. 126–34.
42 Cerny makes the point that the structural dominance of the nation-state is reflected throughout social science: 'Globalization and the disarticulation of political power'.
43 This might be compared with the approach in Holsti, *International Politics*, ch. 1. See also Buzan et al., *Security*, pp. 5–7.
44 Cf. levels are 'interwoven': Layder, *New Strategies in Social Research*, pp. 71–106.
45 Scott and Jackson, 'The study of intelligence', p. 150.
46 Dandeker, *Surveillance, Power and Modernity*; Giddens, *The Nation State and Violence*, pp. 181–92.
47 Foucault, 'Governmentality'.
48 Bozeman, 'Knowledge and comparative method'. Der Derian, 'Anti-diplomacy: intelligence theory and surveillance practice', pp. 34–5.
49 Lyon, *Surveillance Society*, 2001, p. 103. Cf. also der Derian, *Antidiplomacy*, p. 46; Whitaker, *The End of Privacy*.
50 Lyon, *Surveillance after September 11*.
51 Of course, 'weak' states may be compared with 'strong' states in terms of the former's greater concern with *internal* security. Buzan, *People, States and Fear*, esp. pp. 96–107.
52 Kent, *Strategic Intelligence*, p. 3.
53 Müller-Wille, *For Our Eyes Only?*
54 For example, Richelson and Ball, *The Ties that Bind*, on the UK–USA agreement.
55 For example, Nomikos, 'Intelligence requirements'.
56 Eysenck and Keane, *Cognitive Psychology*, p. 54.
57 Ibid., *passim*. For consideration of these issues in the specific context of intelligence, see Kent Center, *Making Sense of Transnational Threats*, pp. 3–5.
58 Mayntz, 'Governing failures and the problem of governability'.
59 Edwards and Gill, 'After transnational organised crime?'.
60 Kent Center, *Making Sense of Transnational Threats*, pp. 6–8.
61 Hulnick suggests that in reality it is best to see 'the intelligence process as a matrix of interconnected, mostly autonomous functions': 'Controlling intelligence estimates'.
62 Scott, *Power*, pp. 6–12. Also Clegg, *Frameworks of Power*.

63 Wilsnack, 'Information control'. Cf. J. Scott, *Power*, pp. 16–25.

64 Friedrich, *Man and His Government*, pp. 201–2.

65 For a summary of this debate, see M. Hill, *The Policy Process in the Modern State*, pp. 98–126.

66 Fry and Hochstein, 'Epistemic communities', p. 20.

67 Bok, *Secrets*, pp. 6–7.

68 For example, C. Johnson, *Blowback*; C. Simpson, *Blowback*.

69 Cf. Giddens, *The Nation State and Violence*, pp. 10–11, regarding the 'dialectic of control' in social systems. See also Clegg, 'Power and authority'.

70 Halliday, 'The end of the Cold War and international relations', p. 38.

71 Danermark, et al., *Explaining Society*, pp. 60–1; cf. also Jervis, *System Effects*, pp. 15–16; Layder, *New Strategies*, pp. 102–3.

72 Kegley suggested four: describe, explain, predict and prescribe: *Controversies in International Relations Theory*, p. 8.

73 L. K. Johnson uses this approach in 'Bricks and mortar', though the general applicability of the propositions there could, we suggest, be enhanced by being rephrased more generally in terms of information and power.

74 For example, P. H. J. Davies, 'Intelligence culture'.

75 Although, as Scott and Jackson rightly surmise, there is no guarantee that they will be listened to!: 'The study of intelligence', pp. 152–3. Cf. also L. K. Johnson, 'Preface', pp. 653–4.

Chapter 3   Who Does Intelligence?

1 Fry and Hochstein, 'Epistemic communities', p. 22.

2 Johnston and Shearing, *Governing Security*, pp. 144–8.

3 Buzan et al., *Security*, pp. 11–12.

4 Andrew and Dilks, *The Missing Dimension*; Hoare (ed.), *British Intelligence in the Twentieth Century*.

5 Frances et al., 'Introduction'.

6 Castells, *The Rise of the Network Society*, p. 445.

7 Cf. L. K. Johnson, 'Bricks and mortar'.

8 Thompson et al. (eds), *Markets, Hierarchies and Networks*.

9 Leishman, 'Policing in Japan', pp. 121–2.

10 Cf. Frances et al., 'Introduction', pp. 16–18.

11 For example, Sheptycki, *Review of the Influence of Strategic Intelligence*, pp. 23–4.

12 Knoke and Kuklinski, 'Network analysis', p. 173.

13 Manning, 'Policing new social spaces'.

14 Cf. Dowding, 'Model or metaphor?'; Brodeur and Dupont, 'Will the knowledge workers put their act together?'.

15 McGrew, 'Conceptualizing global politics'.

16 Gill, *Rounding up the Usual Suspects?*, pp. 77–91; B. Flood, 'Strategic aspects of the UK national intelligence model'.

17 Gill, *Rounding up the Usual Suspects?*, pp. 98–128; Woodiwiss, *Organized Crime*, esp. pp. 362–89.

18 Home Office, *Guidelines on Special Branch work*, para. 3.

19 Ibid., para. 13.

20 Ibid., para. 15.

21 HMIC, *A Need to Know*.

22 Home Office, 'Anti-terrorist legislation'.

23 Muir, 'End of the road for Special Branch'.

24 For a general discussion, see Cameron, 'Beyond the nation state'.

25 Security Service Act 1989, sect. 1 (2–3).

26 Home Office, 'Anti-terrorist legislation'.
27 Poveda, *Lawlessness and Reform*.
28 Kean & Hamilton, *9/11 Commission Report: Final Report of the National Commission on Terrorist Attacks upon the United States* (hereafter, *9/11 Commission Report*), pp. 209–10.
29 Office of the Inspector General, *The FBI's Efforts to Improve the Sharing of Intelligence and Other Information*. See also Cumming and Masse, *FBI Intelligence Reform since September 11, 2001*.
30 *9/11 Commission Report*, p. 275.
31 D. C. McDonald, *Commission of Enquiry*.
32 *9/11 Commission Report*, pp. 423–8.
33 Testimony of Robert S. Muller III, FBI director, before the Congressional Joint Inquiry, 17 Oct. 2002.
34 Bumiller and Sanger, 'Bush, as terror inquiry swirls, seeks cabinet post on security'.
35 Jordan, 'Homeland security faces massive overhaul'.
36 For example, Jeffreys-Jones, *The CIA and American Democracy*; Ranelagh, *The Agency*; Westerfield (ed.), *Inside the CIA's Private World*.
37 For example, P. H. J. Davies, *MI6 and the Machinery of Spying*; Dorril, *MI6*.
38 For example, Andrew and Gordievsky, *KGB*.
39 Dziak, *Chekisty*.
40 Ranelagh, *The Agency*, pp. 385–90.
41 <http//www.gwu.edu/~nsarchiv/news/20001113/>.
42 Cited in Kornbluh, *The Pinochet File*, pp. 1–2, 36.
43 In addition to meetings with the *coup* plotters, the CIA smuggled in guns required for the kidnap operation, while the CIA station authorized the payment of the US $50,000 to the unidentified abduction team. Ibid., p. 28.
44 Ibid., pp. 29, 73.
45 Indeed, elements within the CIA station in Santiago even argued against covert support for opposition political parties in favour of a focus on developing 'the conditions which would be conducive to military actions', including support of extremist groups such as Patria y Libertad, so as to 'promote economic chaos, escalate political tensions and induce a climate of desperation in which . . . the people generally come to desire military intervention': ibid., p. 107.
46 See <www.sis.gov.uk>.
47 <www.cia.gov>.
48 <www.nsa.gov>. See also Bamford, *Body of Secrets*.
49 <www.gchq.gov.uk>.
50 Ritter, *Iraq Confidential*, pp. 133–43.
51 Jensen, *Army Surveillance in America, 1775–1980*.
52 Cepik, 'The Brazilian intelligence system'.
53 See discussion below in ch. 5. Also, more generally, Dycus, 'The role of military intelligence in homeland security'; Haggerty and Ericson, 'The militarization of policing'.
54 A comparison of these systems is provided by Herman, *Intelligence Power*, pp. 257–79. See also P. H. J. Davies, 'Intelligence culture'.
55 Butler Report, para. 43.
56 Scarlett evidence to Hutton Inquiry, 26 Aug. 2003, at 92–6; <www.the-hutton-inquiry.org.uk>.
57 Ibid., 23 Sept. 2003, at 78–9; <www.the-hutton-inquiry.org.uk>.
58 HMG, *Central Intelligence Machinery*, p. 12. Later versions were titled *National Intelligence Machinery*.
59 Prime Minister, *Government Response to the Intelligence and Security Committee Inquiry into Intelligence, Assessments and Advice prior to the Terrorist Bombings on Bali 12 October 2002*, para. 11.

60 Personal information to PG.
61 ISC, *Annual Report 2003–2004*, paras 92–9.
62 Letter to Senators Susan Collins and Carl Levin, 13 Apr. 2004; accessed at <www.fas.org/irp>, Apr. 2004.
63 A snapshot of these in the USA is provided in Gill, *Rounding up the Usual Suspects?*, pp. 40–54.
64 *9/11 Commission Report*, pp. 407–16.
65 Ignatius, 'Can the spy agencies dig out?'; Pincus, 'Negroponte steps into loop'.
66 Schreier and Caparini, *Privatizing Security*, p. 39.
67 O'Reilly and Ellison, ' "Eye spy private high" '; Mackay, *Allan Pinkerton*, pp. 137–60.
68 For example, Shearing and Stenning (eds), *Private Policing*; Johnston, *The Rebirth of Private Policing*; *idem*, *Policing Britain*; Button, *Private Policing*.
69 Hulnick, *Fixing the Spy Machine*, pp. 151–71 provides a general survey of 'spying for profit' in the USA; see also Marx, *Undercover*.
70 <www.group4securicor.com>, accessed 15 Feb. 2005.
71 <www.ci-wackenhut.com>, accessed 15 Feb. 2005.
72 <www.securitas.com>, accessed 15 Feb. 2005; Johnston, 'Transnational private policing', pp. 28–9.
73 <www.pinkertonagency.com/global/services.html>, accessed 15 Feb. 2005.
74 Johnston, 'Transnational private policing', p. 34; Singer, *Corporate Warriors*, pp. 124–30; <www.mpri.com/site/about.html>, accessed 15 Feb. 2005.
75 <www.crg.com/html/service_level 3.php?id=362>, accessed 15 Feb. 2005.
76 Ibid.
77 Singer, 'The private military industry and Iraq'.
78 <www.crg.com/html/service_level3.php?id=588>, accessed 15 Feb. 2005.
79 BBC, 'Concern over Iraq security firms'.
80 Deibert, 'Deep probe'.
81 Bayley and Shearing, *The New Structure of Policing*, pp. 7–9.
82 Gill, *Rounding up the Usual Suspects?*, pp. 188–9.
83 Steele, *The New Craft of Intelligence*, esp. pp. xiii–xviii.
84 Strohm, 'Homeland Security to expand biometric visitor tracking system'.
85 Klerks, 'The network paradigm'; Sparrow, 'Network vulnerabilities'.
86 McClintock, *The American Connection: State Terror and Popular Resistance in El Salvador*; idem, *The American Connection, State Terror and Popular Resistance in Guatemala*.
87 <www.fas.org/irp/world/para/scope.htm>, accessed 15 Feb. 2005.
88 Bayley and Shearing, *The New Structure of Policing*, pp. 6–7.
89 For example, Cox, 'The covert world'.
90 Johnston, 'Transnational private policing'.
91 Deibert, 'Deep probe', p. 189.
92 For example, Gimenez-Salinas, 'New approaches regarding private/public security'; Johnston, *Policing Britain*, pp. 167–75; Jones and Newburn, *Private Security and Public Policing*.
93 Philips, 'Up to 200 Italian police ran parallel anti-terror force'.
94 Cf. Dorn, 'Proteiform criminalities'.
95 Gill, *Rounding up the Usual Suspects?*, pp. 54–7, 246–9.
96 Kickert and Koppenjaan, 'Public management and network management'.
97 Aldrich, 'Transatlantic intelligence and security cooperation', p. 732; Brodeur and Dupont, 'Will the knowledge workers put their act together?'
98 Manningham-Buller, 'The international terrorist threat and the dilemmas in countering it'.
99 Archick, *US–EU Cooperation against Terrorism*.
100 Bigo talks similarly of 'police archipelagos' in 'Liaison officers in Europe'.

101   Ibid., p. 85

102   For example, see Brodeur, 'Cops and spooks', on the implications of co-operation between police and security.

103   For example, see *9/11 Commission Report*, pp. 416–19.

104   Seifert, *Data Mining*, p. 1.

105   Markle Foundation, *Creating a Trusted Information Network for Homeland Security*.

106   Ferris, 'Netcentric warfare', pp. 205–9.

107   Travers, 'The coming intelligence failure'.

108   Carter, *Law Enforcement Intelligence*.

109   <http//www.opsi.gov.uk/acts/acts2005/50015–b.htm#2>, accessed 5 Nov. 2005.

110   Aldrich 'Transatlantic intelligence and security cooperation', pp. 738–9.

111   Cf. O'Reilly and Ellison, ' "Eye spy private high" '.

Chapter 4   How Do They Gather Information?

1   For example, Born and Leigh, *Making Intelligence Accountable*, pp. 55–63.

2   Gill, *Rounding up the Usual Suspects?*, pp. 92–3, 145; Grieve, 'Developments in UK criminal intelligence', p. 34.

3   Ransom, *The Intelligence Establishment*, p. 81.

4   L. K. Johnson, *Bombs, Bugs, Drugs and Thugs*, pp. 185–6.

5   Flood Report, p. 16.

6   L. K. Johnson, *America as a World Power*, p. 273.

7   For example, Penkovsky, *The Penkovsky Papers*; Schechter and Deriabin, *The Spy Who Saved the World*; and Mangold, *Cold Warrior*.

8   Herman has suggested a hierarchy of intelligence value by HUMINT source, beginning with casual travellers and experts and ascending through refugees, business contacts, occasional secret informants, political opponents and exiles, defectors and agents/ informers in place. However, this does not take full account of the possible political agenda of defectors, or of cases where, because of the limitations on other types of intelligence, businessmen may provide a highly valuable entrée, as with Iraq in the 1980s. Herman, *Intelligence Power*, pp. 62–3.

9   Paul Henderson, managing director of Matrix Churchill, recalls his MI5 contact telling him: 'We have a Cold War situation. . . . It is very important for this country to monitor what is happening in Eastern Europe and the Soviet Union, particularly since those countries are so close to home': Henderson, *The Unlikely Spy*, p. 26.

10   See Phythian, *Arming Iraq*, ch. 6; Cowley, *Guns, Lies and Spies*.

11   R. Scott, *Appendices*, Mr O: Statement, 8 Nov. 1993.

12   For example, see the account in Hoy and Ostrovsky, *By Way of Deception*.

13   Copeland, *Beyond Cloak and* Dagger, p. 151.

14   Ibid., pp. 151–2.

15   Kessler, *The CIA at War*, p. 142.

16   Cited in Kliem, 'The spy who loved her'.

17   Wolf, *Memoirs of a Spymaster*, p. 149.

18   Host governments are obviously alert to the practice. For an example, see Walsh, 'Russia accuses "spies" working in foreign NGOs'.

19   Miller, 'Shades of cover'.

20   Tomlinson, *The Big Breach*, p. 176.

21   Goshko, 'Annan: US spying charge could hurt disarmament'.

22   BBC, 'Secrets, spies & videotape'.

23   Ibid. See also the case of the CIA's 'Moe Dobbs' in Ritter, *Endgame*, ch. 10, expanded in idem, *Iraq Confidential*, esp. chs 6 and 13.

24 Gellman, 'Annan suspicious of UNSCOM role'. The *Washington Post* had known of this since October, but had withheld it at the request of the US government. See also Gellman, 'Arms inspectors "shake the tree" '.

25 Williams, 'UNSCOM suffers a terminal blow'.

26 Russell, 'CIA's strategic intelligence in Iraq', p. 206.

27 On the links between sport and intelligence in the GDR, see Dennis, *The Stasi*, ch. 9.

28 For example, see Wolf, *Memoirs of a Spymaster*, p. 134.

29 *Economist* , 'Can spies be made better?'.

30 Sulick, 'Al Qaeda answers CIA's hiring call'. The requirement raises the question posed by Betts, which applies equally to other Western national agencies: 'Should US intelligence trust recent, poorly educated immigrants for these jobs if they involve highly sensitive intercepts? How much will it matter if there are errors in translation, or wilful mistranslations, that cannot be caught because there are no resources to cross-check the translators?': Betts, 'Fixing intelligence', p. 47.

31 Kessler, *The CIA at War*, p. 140.

32 There is also the question of trust. For example, in relation to 9/11 and the post-9/11 'War on Terror', Richard Perle thought that 'one of the reasons why we're in trouble is we have depended too much on intelligence coming from friendly countries, some of whom are not entirely friendly and some of whom, even if they are friendly, have their own reasons for failing to share certain intelligence with us': BBC, *Spies R Us*. In this respect, the question of trust in intelligence sharing has similarities with trust in the context of extended deterrence. For a recent account, see Morgan, *Deterrence Now*.

33 Risen and Rohde, 'A hostile land foils the quest for bin Laden'.

34 Gellman, 'Secret unit expands Rumsfeld's domain'.

35 BBC, 'Subversive my arse'. On being informed that a former close colleague was a spy, one of the targets, Tariq Ali, commented: 'It is a bit distressing, especially as he must have been liked, he must have made friends. That is a form of fundamentalism for you, if you are prepared to subordinate everything else to what is your political aim or work aim. And I guess that's what spies are.'

36 Machon, *Spies, Lies & Whistleblowers*, p. 52.

37 Cory, *Cory Collusion Inquiry Report: Patrick Finucane*.

38 Ware, 'Torture, murder, mayhem'.

39 Ingram and Harkin, *Stakeknife*, p. 64.

40 Ibid., p. 81.

41 Walzer, *Just and Unjust Wars*, pp. 152–9.

42 Cowan, 'Unmasking leaves Provos seething with mutual suspicion'; Morrison, 'The story of Stakeknife is full of holes'.

43 See, e.g., H. McDonald, 'Revealed: five British spies inside IRA'.

44 Chesterton, *The Man Who Was Thursday*.

45 Dorril, *MI6*, p. 789.

46 For example, see Andrew, 'Conclusion', p. 228.

47 Interview with JIC official.

48 As far back as 1966, Senator Milton Young claimed: 'As far as foreign policy is concerned, I think the National Security Agency and the intelligence it develops has far more to do with foreign policy than does the intelligence developed by the CIA': cited in Aid and Wiebes, 'The importance of signals intelligence in the Cold War', p. 7.

49 Ibid., p. 5.

50 A CIA officer, cited in ibid., p. 6.

51 Rogers, *Losing Control*, p. 32.

52 Richelson, *A Century of Spies*, pp. 385–7; Gordievsky, *Next Stop Execution*, p. 272. It is also worth noting that two 1984 NIEs concluded that the alert was intended to intimidate the West rather than represent a genuine scare. See Richelson, *Century of spies*, p. 386. It

is worth noting because it appears to be wrong; see Rogers, *Losing Control*, p. 32. See also Gates, *From the Shadows*, pp. 270–3.

53 Aid and Wiebes, 'The importance of signals intelligence', p. 15.

54 L. K. Johnson, *America's Secret Power*, pp. 64–6.

55 On Echelon, see <http://www.fas.org/irp/program/process/echelon.htm>.

56 Reportedly, by the mid-1990s, the NSA 'was capable of intercepting the equivalent of the entire collection of the US Library of Congress (1 quadrillion Bits of information) every three hours': Aid, 'The time of troubles', p. 17.

57 Kessler, *The CIA at War*, p. 73.

58 Ranelagh, *The Agency*, pp. 207–8.

59 Kessler, *The CIA at War*, p. 74.

60 Bright and Beaumont, 'Britain spied on UN allies over war vote'.

61 Short, *An Honourable Deception?*, pp. 242–3.

62 Regulation of Investigatory Powers Act, 2000, Part II.

63 Chief Surveillance Commissioner, *Annual Report 2004–2005*, Annexes A and C; <www.surveillancecommissioners.gov.uk>, accessed 1 Dec. 2005.

64 Intelligence Services Commissioner, *Report for 2004*, para. 31; <www.statewatch.org/news/2005/nov/int-rep-2004.pdf>, accessed 1 Dec. 2005.

65 Interception of Communications Commissioner, *Report for 2004*, Nov. 2005, paras 20–3; <www.statewatch.org/news/2005/nov/teltap-2004.pdf>, accessed 1 Dec. 2005.

66 Ibid., annex and paras 33–5.

67 *Statewatch*, 12 (3–4) 2002, p. 1.

68 <www.aclu.org/SafeandFree>, accessed 24 Mar. 2003. In the UK the Regulation of Investigatory Powers Act (RIPA) 2000 already included similar powers in Part III. In readiness for this, the government has established a National Technical Assistance Centre that is located in MI5's headquarters, which enables real-time monitoring of selected internet traffic. Also, it is reported that the use of encryption by terrorist and criminal suspects has not been as widespread as had been predicted when RIPA was passed: Intelligence Services Commissioner, *Report for 2004*, para. 7.

69 Kessler, *The CIA at War*, p. 70.

70 Richelson, *The Wizards of Langley*, pp. 198–202, 276.

71 For an example, see Sanger, 'What are Koreans up to?'

72 Baer, *See No Evil*, p. xvii.

73 L. K. Johnson, 'Spymaster Richard Helms' p. 32.

74 Gormley, 'The limits of intelligence', pp. 11–13.

75 This section is drawn from the Federation of American Scientists, 'Signals intelligence in the Gulf War'. See also Richelson, *The Wizards of Langley*, pp. 247–50.

76 Woodward, *The Commanders*, pp. 219–20.

77 Ibid., pp. 220–1.

78 Ibid.

79 Simpson, *From the House of War*, p. 41.

80 During the 1990s Baer had been involved in planning a *coup* to remove Saddam Hussein from power. Using the name Robert Pope, he was also thought to be planning an assassination attempt. For Clinton Administration National Security Adviser Anthony Lake, Baer's plan made the Bay of Pigs disaster 'look good' at a time when he 'did not want America to be blamed again for supporting a plan to topple Saddam and then backing out'. See Kessler, *The CIA at War*, p. 267.

81 See Hersh, *Chain of Command*; Greenberg and Dratel(eds), *The Torture Papers*.

82 Gow, 'Bush gives green light to CIA for assassination of named terrorists'.

83 Baer, *See No Evil*, p. xvii.

84 BBC, *Spies R Us*.

85 Cilluffo, Marks and Salmoiraghi, 'The use and limits of US intelligence', p. 63.

86 *9/11 Commission Report*, p. 415.
87 Cited in Jehl, 'New spy plan said to involve satellite system'. Similarly, John Pike of Globalsecurity.org thought that 'These days, you really have to assume that if there's anything we see in North Korea, it's something they intend for us to see': ibid.
88 Cogan, 'Hunters not gatherers', p. 304.
89 Kessler, *The CIA at War*, p. 127.
90 Cogan, 'Hunters not gatherers', p. 317.
91 Amnesty International, *Guantánamo and Beyond*.
92 On the origins and evolution of the practice, see Jane Mayer, 'Outsourcing torture'.
93 Cobain et al., 'Destination Cairo'; Goldenberg, 'More than 80,000 held by US since 9/11 attacks'. In Nov. 2005 Spain launched a judicial inquiry into claims that its airports had been used for this purpose. Nash, 'Madrid begins inquiry into CIA "torture" flights'.
94 Amnesty International, *Guantánamo and Beyond*.
95 Ibid.
96 Priest, 'Help from France key in covert operations'.
97 Hooper, 'Kidnap probe reveals CIA modus operandi'.
98 Hooper, 'Italy demands US explanation over kidnapped cleric'; Wilkinson and Miller, 'Italy says it didn't know of CIA plan'.
99 Wilkinson, 'Italy seeks former US diplomat in kidnapping'.
100 Priest, 'CIA holds terror suspects in secret prisons'; McGrory and Reid, 'CIA accused of running secret jails in Europe for terrorists'.
101 Senate Majority Leader Bill Frist said: 'If accurate, such an egregious disclosure could have long-term and far-reaching damaging and dangerous consequences, and will imperil our efforts to protect the American people and our homeland from terrorist attack': Weisman, 'GOP leaders urge probe in prisons leak'.
102 Human Rights Watch, 'Statement on US secret detention facilities in Europe'.
103 See Applebaum, 'The torture myth'. For a less negative assessment of the utility of torture, see the *Economist*, 'Torture: ends, means and barbarity'.

Chapter 5   What Do They Do with the Information Gathered?

1 For example, Warner, 'Transnational organised crime and the secret agencies', pp. 147–9; Gill, *Rounding up the Usual Suspects?*, pp. 234–6.
2 *9/11 Commission Report*, p.77.
3 See discussion in ch. 3.
4 Hibbert, 'Intelligence and policy'.
5 Mandel similarly discusses (i) the personality and proficiency of officials; (ii) the complexity of intelligence performance; (iii) internal bureaucratic obstacles; and (iv) the external policy environment: 'Distortions'.
6 Kent Center, *Making Sense*, p. 4.
7 Lowenthal, *Intelligence*, pp. 92–3.
8 Cf. Sheptycki, 'Organizational pathologies', pp. 316–17.
9 *9/11 Commission Report*, p. 355.
10 Wohlstetter, *Pearl Harbor*, p. 392; cf. also Sheptycki, 'Organizational pathologies', pp. 315–16.
11 Bond, 'Methods and issues in risk and threat assessment', p. 120.
12 Klerks, 'The network paradigm'.
13 Mandel, 'Distortions', p. 70.
14 *9/11 Commission Report*, p. 92.
15 This term was created by Irving Janis: 'The more amiability and esprit de corps among the members of policy-making in-group, the greater is the danger that independent critical

thinking will be replaced by groupthink, which is likely to result in irrational and dehumanising actions directed against out-groups': *Victims of Groupthink*, p. 13.
16 Mandel, 'Distortions', p. 73.
17 Cf. the 'digital divide' in Sheptycki, 'Organizational pathologies', pp. 313–14.
18 *9/11 Commission Report*, pp. 78–80. For discussion of the impact of 'the wall' in the *USS Cole* investigations, see ibid., pp. 266–72.
19 Gill, *Rounding up the Usual Suspects?*, p. 213.
20 Sheptycki, 'Organizational pathologies', p. 317; Gill, *Rounding up the Usual Suspects?*, pp. 212–15.
21 Mandel, 'Distortions', p. 76.
22 Heldon, 'Exploratory analysis tools'; cf. also the 'alternative analysis' recommended by the Kent Center, *Making Sense*.
23 Bruce, 'Dynamic adaptation'.
24 *9/11 Commission Report*, pp. 344–8.
25 Foreign and Commonwealth Secretary, *Review of Intelligence on Weapons of Mass Destruction*.
26 Stella Rimington on whether she would, as MI5 director general, have resisted Blair's request for a dossier: 'I can't say, as I don't know the circumstances . . . but I expect I would have thought: no good will come of this': Grice, 'Dossier a mistake – Rimington'.
27 Gill, *Rounding up the Usual Suspects?*, p. 226; Herman, *Intelligence Power*, p. 45.
28 Herman, *Intelligence Power*, p. 45.
29 Kent, *Strategic Intelligence*, pp. 7–8.
30 Shulsky and Schmitt, *Silent Warfare*, pp. 57–8; *9/11 Commission Report*, pp. 90–1.
31 Herman, *Intelligence Power*, p. 235; Shulsky and Schmitt, *Silent Warfare*, p. 59.
32 *9/11 Commission Report*, pp. 344–8.
33 Shulsky and Schmitt, *Silent Warfare*, pp. 60–1.
34 *9/11 Commission Report*, p. 342.
35 Ibid.
36 Herman, *Intelligence Power*, p. 46.
37 Berkowitz and Goodman, *Best Truth*, p. 64.
38 Coll, *Ghost Wars*, pp. 149–50.
39 Herman, *Intelligence Power*, p. 326; see also Wilensky, *Organizational Intelligence*, pp. 42–8.
40 Berkowitz and Goodman, *Best Truth*, pp. 72–3.
41 Ibid., pp. 96–8. In a similar vein, Herman argues that intelligence managers must convey entrepreneurial values as well as public service and scholarly ones: *Intelligence Power*, pp. 336–8.
42 *9/11 Commission Report*, p. 417.
43 Richelson and Ball, e.g., discuss the history of intelligence co-operation between the UKUSA countries: UK, US, Canada, Australia and New Zealand: *The Ties that Bind*, esp. pp. 239–61.
44 *9/11 Commission Report*, pp. 353–60.
45 For example, see *9/11 Commission Report*, p. 143. See also Lowenthal, *Intelligence*, pp. 100–1.
46 Butler Report, para. 45.
47 Ibid., para. 603.
48 Ibid., para. 45, fn. 13.
49 Ibid., para. 604.
50 Foreign and Commonwealth Secretary, *Review of Intelligence on Weapons of Mass Destruction*, paras 29–30.
51 For example, see Leigh, 'Britain's security services and journalists'.
52 Sweeney, *Trading with the Enemy*, pp. 169–71.
53 Hutton, *Report of the Inquiry into the Circumstances Surrounding the Death of Dr. David Kelly CMG*, para. 255 (hereafter Hutton Report).

54 Ibid., para. 112.
55 TV interview with Amy Goodman, 30 Dec. 2003, transcript in *Security and Intelligence Digest*, Intel Research, PO Box 550, London SW3 2YQ.
56 Butler Report, p. 90.
57 For example, <www.cia.gov/>, <www.fbi.gov/>, <www.csis-scrs.gc.ca/eng/>, <www.mi5.gov.uk>, <www.ncis.co.uk>.
58 *9/11 Commission Report*, p. 265.
59 'Influence' is often used in the literature as a more general term than 'power' to discuss the social and political phenomenon in which we are interested – an early exponent was Dahl, *Modern Political Analysis*, esp. pp. 12–48.
60 J. Scott, *Power*, pp. 12–16. Wrong uses a similar classification of force, manipulation and persuasion in *Power*, pp. 21–34.
61 Lowenthal provides just such a 'ladder' of covert action: *Intelligence*, p. 130.
62 Ch. 4 of the *9/11 Commission Report*, entitled 'Responses to Al Qaeda's Initial Assaults', provides a detailed account that illustrates these combinations in practice, pp. 108–43.
63 An obvious exception to this is Israel, whose policies of targeted assassinations and settlement construction are carried out entirely openly but contrary to successive UN resolutions and other prohibitions.
64 L. Scott, 'Secret intelligence, covert action and clandestine diplomacy'.
65 A good example is Godson, *Dirty Tricks or Trump Cards*.
66 Lowenthal, *Intelligence*, p. 131.
67 CSIS Act 1984, sect. 12.
68 Security Service Act 1989, sect. 1 (2).
69 Intelligence Services Act, 1994, sect. 7.
70 One form of action that police may take is to arrest people; this power is not available to MI5. The debate as to whether security agencies such as MI5 should or should not possess arrest powers forms an important part of the whole debate around the democratic control of security policing. The combination of special information-gathering powers and powers of arrest are often seen as the ingredients for repressive forms of 'political policing'.
71 Holt, *The Deceivers*, p. 2.
72 Herman, *Intelligence Power*, p. 55.
73 One of the earliest CIA covert actions was providing financial and propaganda support to Christian Democrats in Italy after World War II, in order to prevent the Communist Party taking power. Ranelagh, *The Agency*, pp. 176–7.
74 For example, see *9/11 Commission Report*, pp. 185–6, for details of measures to disrupt al-Qaeda financing after 1998.
75 Berkowitz and Goodman, *Best Truth*, pp. 143–5.
76 Coll, *Ghost Wars*, pp. 534–5.
77 Foreign Affairs Committee, *Sierra Leone*, para. 26.
78 See Spicer, *An Unorthodox Soldier*; and the report of the official inquiry, Legg and Ibbs, *Report of the Sierra Leone Arms Investigation*.
79 Singer, *Corporate Warriors*, pp. 114–15.
80 Cory, *Cory Collusion Inquiry Report*, para. 1.293.
81 Stevens, *Stevens Enquiry*, para. 44.7. Also idem, *Not for the Faint-Hearted*, pp. 171–6.
82 Examples of documents are included in Perkus (ed.), *COINTELPRO*.
83 Poveda, *Lawlessness and Reform*, provides a good account of this shift.
84 For example, Eggen, 'FBI taps campus police in anti-terror operations'.
85 Gill, *Rounding up the Usual Suspects?*, pp. 232–6.
86 Cited in *9/11 Commission Report*, p. 189.
87 For example, Coll, *Ghost Wars*.

Chapter 6   Why Does Intelligence Fail?

1   See, e.g., the 'Checklist of what can go wrong' in the intelligence cycle, in Berkowitz and Goodman, *Strategic Intelligence*, pp. 195–202.

2   Jeffreys-Jones, *The CIA and American Democracy*, p. 8. On the origins of the CIA, see also Rudgers, *Creating the Secret State*.

3   Central Intelligence Agency, *A Consumer's Guide to Intelligence*, p. 42.

4   *Economist*, 'Can spies be made better?', p. 29.

5   Jay (ed.), *The Oxford Dictionary of Political Quotations*, p. 297.

6   Betts, 'Analysis, war, and decision', p. 61. For Andrew, 'The historical record suggests . . . that the points at which the intelligence cycle most frequently breaks down are in the assessment process and the policy interface rather than in collection. How and why that breakdown occurs require far more research – and research, first and foremost, in archives': 'Intelligence, international relations and "under-theorisation"', p. 172.

7   Betts, 'Analysis, war, and decision', p. 61.

8   Betts notes that 'A common reaction to traumatic surprise is the recommendation to cope with ambiguity and ambivalence by acting on the most threatening possible inter-pretations. If there is *any* evidence of threat, assume it is valid, even if the *apparent* weight of contrary indicators is greater': ibid., p. 73. On the question of surprise more generally, see Handel, 'Surprise in diplomacy'; and Shulsky and Schmitt, *Silent Warfare*, pp. 62–73.

9   Gormley, 'The limits of intelligence', p. 15.

10   *9/11 Commission Report*, sect. 11.1. The other three were policy, capabilities and manage-ment.

11   Freedman, 'The CIA and the Soviet threat', p. 136. See also, Cahn, 'Team B'.

12   Stack, 'Competitive intelligence', p. 201.

13   Woodward, *Plan of Attack*, p. 197.

14   Lichtblau, 'Flight groundings lead allies to query Washington'.

15   I. Black, 'EU agrees to give air passenger data to US'.

16   Webster and Bowcott, 'Terror suspect turned out to be Welsh insurance agent'; Bremner, 'FBI admits error over Air France'.

17   Goo, 'List of foiled plots puzzling to some'.

18   Younge and Dodd, 'CIA blunder on al-Jazeera "terror messages"'.

19   BBC, *Spies R Us*.

20   Ibid.

21   On the case of North Korea, see Pinkston and Saunders, 'Seeing North Korea clearly'.

22   Drum, 'Political animal'.

23   Gordon, 'Poor intelligence misled troops about risk of drawn-out war'.

24   Ibid.

25   It concluded that 'The JIC may, in some assessments, also have misread the nature of Iraqi governmental and social structures. The absence of intelligence in this area may also have hampered planning for the post-war phase. . . . We note that the collection of intelligence on Iraq's prohibited weapons programmes was designated as being a JIC First Order of Priority whereas intelligence on Iraqi political issues was designated as being Third Order': Butler Report, para. 459.

26   Robarge, 'CIA analysis of the 1967 Arab–Israeli war'.

27   Regarded as essentially an analytical failure. See MacEachin, *US Intelligence and the Confrontation in Poland, 1980–1981*.

28   Steury, 'How the CIA missed Stalin's bomb'. Steury cites explanations for the failure that 'it was not the overall intelligence *process* – with its focus on collection – that had failed to warn of the Soviet atomic bomb, but intelligence *analysis* – the ability to assem-ble, integrate, and derive meaning from the full range of information collected'.

29 Marrin, 'Preventing intelligence failures by learning from the past', p. 660.
30 Letter from Sir A. Gascoigne to Foreign Office, 5 July 1950, in Yasamee and Hamilton (eds) *Documents on British Policy Overseas*, pp. 31–2.
31 MacEachin, 'Predicting the Soviet invasion of Afghanistan'. Later, in 1979, analysis suggested that the costs of an invasion would include 'the grave and open-ended task of holding down an Afghan insurgency in rugged terrain. The Soviets would also have to consider the likely prospect that they would be contending with an increasingly hostile and anti-Soviet population. The USSR would then have to consider the likelihood of an adverse reaction in the West, as well as further complications with Iran, India, and Pakistan. Moscow would also have to weigh the negative effects elsewhere in the Muslim world of a massive Soviet military presence in Afghanistan. . . . A conspicuous use of Soviet military force against an Asian population would also provide the Chinese considerable political capital.' Cited in ibid.
32 Davis, 'Tensions in analyst–policymaker relations', p. 9.
33 The full list of cases considered is as follows:

Case	Date
Likelihood of North Vietnam intervention in South Vietnam	1945–65
Likelihood of all-out Soviet support of Hanoi	1950–65
Cuba	1957
Sino–Soviet Split	1959
1st Chinese nuclear test	1964
Soviet ALFA-class submarine	1969
Libya	1969
OPEC price increase of December 1973	1973
Ethiopia	1973
Afghanistan	1978
Iran	1978
Nicaragua – The Nature of Somoza's Opposition	1978

See Westerfield (ed.) *Inside CIA's Private World*, pp. 238–54.

34 Ibid., p. 254.
35 MacEachin, 'CIA assessments of the Soviet Union'.
36 Thomas and Vistica, 'A troubled company'.
37 On the importance of Gorbachev to the events of 1989 and 1990, see Brown, 'Gorbachev and the end of the Cold War', and idem, *The Gorbachev Factor*.
38 Treverton, *Reshaping National Intelligence for an Age of Information*, pp. 1–8.
39 Perkovich, *India's Nuclear Bomb*, pp. 417–18; Kessler, *The CIA at War*, pp. 210–12.
40 Kessler, *The CIA at War*, p. 212.
41 Knightley, 'The biggest con-trick', p. 14. In a similar vein, see Preston, 'They miss so much it's spooky'.
42 Knightley, 'The biggest con-trick', p. 14.
43 Keegan, *Intelligence in War*.
44 For example, Gaddis, 'Intelligence, espionage, and Cold War origins'.
45 Knightley, *The Second Oldest Profession*, p. 6.
46 L. K. Johnson, *America's Secret Power*, ch. 4.
47 On the specific case of forewarning about Operation Barbarossa, see Murphy, *What Stalin Knew*.
48 Robarge, 'CIA analysis of the 1967 Arab–Israeli war'.
49 Cooper, 'The CIA and decision-making', p. 227.
50 On Phoenix, see Andradé, *Ashes to Ashes*.

51   Ford, 'Unpopular pessimism'.
52   Ibid.
53   Ibid.
54   Ford, 'Revisiting Vietnam'.
55   Ibid.
56   Woodward, *Plan of Attack*, p. 249. In April 2005, Tenet told an audience: 'Those were the two dumbest words I ever said': Goldenberg, 'Ex-CIA chief eats humble pie'.
57   See Sick, *All Fall Down*, pp. 33–6.
58   BBC, *Spies R Us*. Nevertheless, there were inherent difficulties involved in estimating the likelihood of an uprising against the Shah. As a senior CIA analyst put it: 'We knew the Shah was widely unpopular, and we knew there would be mass demonstration, even riots. But how many shopkeepers would resort to violence, and how long would Army officers remain loyal to the Shah? Perhaps the Army would shoot down 10,000 rioters, maybe 20,000. If the ranks of the insurgents swelled further, though, how far would the Army be willing to go before it decided the Shah was a losing proposition? All this we duly reported; but no one could predict with confidence the number of dissidents who would actually take up arms, or the "tipping point" for Army loyalty.' Cited in L. K. Johnson, *America as a World Power*, p. 277.
59   Ford, 'The US government's experience with intelligence analysis'.
60   BBC, *Spies R Us*.
61   Ibid. See also Sick, *All Fall Down*, pp. 106–8; and Bill, *The Eagle and the Lion*, ch. 10.
62   Donovan, 'National intelligence and the Iranian revolution', p. 159.
63   Cited in ibid., p. 160.
64   Robarge, 'CIA analysis of the 1967 Arab–Israeli war'.
65   On the qualities required of intelligence leaders, see Gardiner, 'Dealing with intelligence–policy disconnects'.
66   Petersen, 'The challenge for the political analyst'.
67   Ibid.
68   Herman, 'Threat assessments and the legitimation of policy', p. 177.
69   Exemplifying the tension at the heart of this question, on succeeding George Tenet as DCI in 2004, Porter Goss sent out an internal memorandum which told CIA personnel that their job was to 'support the administration and its policies in our work'. The memo continued: 'As agency employees we do not identify with, support or champion opposition to the administration or its policies.' At the same time, it noted that 'We provide the intelligence as we see it – and let the facts alone speak to the policymaker': Jehl, 'New CIA chief tells workers to back Administration policies'.
70   L. K. Johnson, 'Spymaster Richard Helms', pp. 34–5.
71   Cited in Davis, 'Tensions in analyst–policymaker relations', p. 4.
72   Ibid., p. 7.
73   Hersh, *Chain of Command*, p. 223.
74   Linzer, 'Two detail Bolton's efforts to punish dissent'.
75   For example, a survey of scientists employed by the US Fish and Wildlife Service revealed pressure to alter findings to suit either external customers or government policy preferences: Cart, 'US scientists say they are told to alter findings'.
76   Shlaim, 'Failures in national intelligence estimates'.
77   Herman, 'Threat assessments', p. 177.
78   Hersh, 'Behind the "mushroom cloud" '.
79   Hersh, *Chain of Command*, pp. 218–19.
80   Pollack, *The Threatening Storm*, pp. 248–80.
81   For example, Cilluffo, Marks and Salmoiraghi, 'The use and limits of US intelligence'.
82   Drew, 'Pinning the blame', p. 6.
83   Clarke, *Against All Enemies*.

84 *9/11 Commission Report*, p. 260.
85 Ibid.
86 Ibid.
87 Ibid., p. 263.
88 Ibid., p. 262.
89 Ibid.
90 Ibid., p. 277.
91 Benetto, 'Predicted bomb attacks reveal intelligence gaps on al-Qa'ida'.
92 Norton-Taylor, 'Security services face worst scenario'.
93 Gregory and Wilkinson, 'Riding pillion for tackling terrorism is a high risk policy'.
94 ISC, *Annual Report 2001–2002*, p. 24.
95 ISC, *Annual Report 2003–2004*, pp. 11–12.
96 Cited in Meacher, 'Britain now faces its own blowback'.
97 Ibid.
98 Sciolino and Van Natta, 'June report led Britain to lower its terror alert'.
99 C. Black, 'Intelligence got it wrong'.
100 The extent to which Khan featured in surveillance operations remains unclear. See, e.g., Dodd, 'Officials missed clues to trap July 7 bomber'; Barnett and Townsend, 'July bomber in link to foiled London terror plot'.
101 Harnden and Ansari, 'Pakistan: the incubator for al-Qaeda's attacks on London'.
102 Herbert and Sengupta, 'Revealed: how Aldgate bomber became a single-minded jihadist killer'.
103 For example, see Cowan, 'CCTV captures July 7 terrorists staging a dry run before attacks'.
104 In the context of 7/7, see Norton-Taylor, 'There's no such thing as total security'.
105 For a discussion, see Freedman, *The Official History of the Falklands Campaign*, i.

Chapter 7   Intelligence on Iraqi WMD: What Kind of Intelligence Failure?

1 Commission on the Intelligence Capabilities of the United States Regarding Weapons of Mass Destruction, *Report* (henceforth 'Silberman–Robb'), p. 3.
2 SSCI Report, p. 1.
3 Ibid., p. 2. Only the first of these was planned to be dealt with exclusively in the phase 2 report. In practice, none is treated in detail in the June 2004 report.
4 Ibid., p. 3.
5 Ibid., p. 8.
6 Ibid., p. 5.
7 Ibid., p. 11.
8 Kent, *The Law and Custom of the National Security Estimate*.
9 SSCI Report, p. 13.
10 Ibid., p. 302.
11 Ibid., p. 14.
12 Ibid., p. 15.
13 Ibid., p. 25.
14 Ibid., p. 260.
15 Ibid., p. 25. The CIA had cited budgetary constraints as a factor: ibid., p. 261.
16 Ibid., p. 14.
17 Ibid.
18 Ibid., p. 188.
19 Ibid., p. 187.
20 Central Intelligence Agency, *Iraq's Weapons of Mass Destruction Programs*, p. 2; see also p. 17.

21   SSCI Report, p. 188.
22   Ibid., p. 211.
23   Ibid., pp. 212–13. On 'layering', see ibid., pp. 22–3.
24   Ibid., p. 75.
25   Ibid., pp. 77, 80–1.
26   Ibid., p. 17.
27   For example, the NIE stated that 'we judge that we are seeing only a portion of Iraq's WMD efforts, owing to Baghdad's vigorous denial and deception efforts. Revelations after the Gulf War starkly demonstrate the extensive efforts undertaken by Iraq to deny information': ibid.
28   Ibid., p. 18.
29   Ibid., p. 20.
30   Scott Ritter, *Iraq Confidential, passim.*
31   SSCI Report, pp. 163–4, 462.
32   Ibid., pp. 230, 235.
33   Ibid., pp. 226, 236.
34   Woodward claims that there were just four as late as 2002, and that these were located in ministries such as foreign affairs and oil that did not allow them access to the kinds of military intelligence most needed. Ironically, given the Butler Inquiry's subsequent discovery of the limited nature of UK HUMINT sources in Iraq at this time, DCI Tenet regarded UK sources as being superior to those of the USA: Woodward, *Plan of Attack*, p. 107.
35   SSCI Report, p. 21.
36   Similarly, the UK Butler Inquiry concluded that there was a 'tendency for assessments to be coloured by over-reaction to previous errors': Butler Report, para. 458.
37   SSCI Report, p. 24.
38   Ibid., p. 23.
39   Ibid., p. 26.
40   Ibid., pp. 27–8.
41   Ibid., pp. 128–9.
42   Ibid., p. 129.
43   Ibid., pp. 160–1.
44   Ibid., p. 149. At p. 246, the number of these reports is put at ninety-five.
45   Ibid., p. 149.
46   Ibid., p. 248.
47   Ibid., p. 249.
48   Ibid., p. 28. On this, see also Betts, 'Fixing intelligence', p. 55.
49   SSCI Report, p. 29.
50   Ibid. See also ibid., p. 139.
51   Ibid.
52   Ibid., p. 16.
53   Ibid.
54   Ibid., p. 18.
55   Ibid., pp. 275–6, 285.
56   Ibid., p. 272.
57   Burrough et al., 'The path to war', p. 116.
58   SSCI Report, p. 456.
59   Ibid.
60   Ibid., p. 449.
61   See the examples of Administration pronouncements to this effect, ibid., pp. 453–4, and those provided in Senator Richard Durbin's additional views, p. 502.
62   See the examples, ibid., pp. 503–5.

63 Ibid., pp. 489–90.
64 Ibid., p. 505.
65 Clarke, *Against All Enemies*, p. 31.
66 SSCI Report, p. 505.
67 The meeting was held in Downing Street on 23 July 2002. The text is available at <http://www.downingstreetmemo.com/>. See also Doig and Phythian, 'The national interest and politics of threat exaggeration'.
68 SSCI Report, p. 464.
69 T. Powers, 'The failure', p. 6.
70 Silberman-Robb, p. 4, see also p. 9.
71 Ibid., p. 10.
72 Ibid., pp. 5, 3.
73 Ibid., p. 11.
74 Foreign Affairs Committee, *The Decision to Go to War in Iraq*.
75 ISC, *Iraqi Weapons of Mass Destruction*.
76 On the Hutton Inquiry, see Phythian, 'Hutton and Scott'.
77 See Kampfner, *Blair's Wars*, pp. 369–72.
78 See Nye, 'Peering into the future'.
79 Butler Report, para. 51.
80 Ibid., para. 52.
81 Ibid., para. 436.
82 Ibid., para. 466.
83 Ibid., para. 58.
84 Ibid., para. 63. Blair's subsequent appointment of William Ehrman as chairman of the JIC failed to meet this requirement. See Norton-Taylor and White, 'New intelligence chief fails to meet Butler guidelines'.
85 See Oborne, 'Butler has found Scarlett guilty', p. 10.
86 Butler Report, para. 42.
87 Ibid., para. 592.
88 Ibid., paras 598–9.
89 Ibid., paras 441–2.
90 Ibid., para. 596.
91 BBC, 'The Hutton Inquiry'.
92 BBC, 'A failure of intelligence'.
93 Hutton Report, para. 228.
94 BBC, 'A failure of intelligence'.
95 Parliamentary Joint Committee on ASIO, ASIS and DSD, *Intelligence on Iraq's Weapons of Mass Destruction*. p. vi.
96 On the restrictions, see ibid., p. vii.
97 Ibid., p. 14. UNMOVIC, the UN Monitoring, Verification and Inspection Commission, was established in December 1999 as *de facto* successor to UNSCOM.
98 Ibid.
99 Ibid., p. 29.
100 Ibid., p. 30.
101 Ibid.
102 Ibid., p. 31.
103 Ibid., p. 32.
104 Ibid., p. 33.
105 Ibid., p. 35.
106 Ibid.
107 Ibid., p. 37.
108 Ibid., p. 44.

109   Ibid., p. 46.
110   Ibid.
111   Ibid., pp. 49–50.
112   Ibid., p. 44.
113   Ibid., pp. 46–7.
114   Ibid., p. 47.
115   Flood Report, p. 24.
116   Ibid., p. 29.
117   Ibid., p. 30.
118   Ibid., p. 25.
119   Ibid., p. 34.
120   Ibid.
121   See the Downing Street memos from March to August 2002 at <http:// www.down-ingstreetmemo.com/>.
122   Wyden 'Wydens releases additional views'.

Chapter 8   Can Intelligence be Democratic?

1   Various authors have pointed to the risk of official exploitation of fear, including Robin, *Fear*; Bourke, *Fear*; Phythian, 'Still a matter of trust'; Curtis, 'Fear gives politicians a reason to be'; Shrimsley, 'The bogeyman'. The best-known articulation of this risk is Adam Curtis's three-part TV series, *The Power of Nightmares*, broadcast in the UK in Nov. 2004. See <http://news.bbc.co.uk/ 1/hi/programmes/3755686.stm>.

2   Throughout this chapter we are concerned with the general principles by which elected representatives may control permanent intelligence officials, rather than precise differences between, say, presidential and parliamentary systems. Therefore we use the terms 'legislative' and 'parliamentary' interchangeably.

3   Cf. L. K. Johnson, 'Law makers and Spies'.

4   The relevant government memos 2001–4 and reports concerning abuses at Abu Ghraib and Guantánamo are compiled in Greenberg and Dratel (eds), *The Torture Papers*.

5   Berki, *Security and Society*, pp. 1–43.

6   'Oversight' has another dictionary meaning: i.e. an omission or failure to notice. This may also be significant in the governance of intelligence, as it reflects the sentiment, that politicians may prefer not to know about the actions being taken in their name by security agencies.

7   Compare, e.g., the English and French versions of SIRC's *Annual Report 1985–86*, p. 3. The debate is recounted in more detail in Gill, 'Symbolic or real?'

8   SIRC, *Report 2001–2002*.

9   Greenberg and Dratel (eds), *The Torture Papers*, passim.

10   Born and Leigh, *Making Intelligence Accountable*. The following summary of legal principles draws on this except where otherwise stated.

11   Fenwick, *Civil Liberties*, pp. 78–82.

12   D. C. McDonald, *Commission of Inquiry*, esp. pp. 407–11.

13   Born and Leigh, *Making Intelligence Accountable*, pp. 37–42.

14   For example, Szikinger, 'National security in Hungary', pp. 85–8. Andrew suggests that the centrality of the intelligence community both to internal repression and to reinforcing misconceptions of the outside world are basic distinguishing features of authoritarianism: 'Intelligence, international relations and "under-theorisation"', pp. 177–80.

15   Herman, "Ethics and intelligence", p. 343.

16   Erskine, 'As rays of light to the human soul'.

17   See Walzer, *Just and Unjust Wars*, pp. 151–9.

18   Herman, *Intelligence Services in the Information Age*, p. 203.

19 Erskine, ' "As rays of light" ', pp. 371–2.
20 Herman, 'Ethics and intelligence', p. 346.
21 Godfrey, 'Ethics and intelligence'.
22 Erskine, 'As rays of light', p. 363.
23 Knightley, *The Second Oldest Profession*.
24 For example, Special Committee of the Senate on the CSIS, *Delicate Balance*.
25 This argument is developed in detail in Lustgarten and Leigh, *In from the Cold*, pp. 3–35.
26 Keller, *The Liberals and J. Edgar Hoover*, p. 111.
27 Clearances themselves exist in ascending order of access: e.g., from 'confidential' through to 'top secret'.
28 For example, Farson, 'Old Wine, new bottles and fancy labels'.
29 Born and Leigh, *Making Intelligence Accountable*, pp. 110–12.
30 Ibid., pp. 77–9 provides a useful comparison of arrangements in seven countries.
31 The Canadian government announced that it would establish a National Security Committee of Parliamentarians in December 2003, and introduced legislation to this effect in November 2005. 24 Nov. 2005, <www.pco-bcp.gc.ca>. The Bill did not pass because a general election was called in December 2005.
32 HMG, *National Intelligence Machinery*, 2005, p. 2.
33 Issues discussed in more detail by Born and Leigh, *Making Intelligence Accountable*, pp. 85–90.
34 United States Code, Title 50, sect. 413b; Intelligence Services Act 2001, sect. 30 (Australia); Intelligence Services Act 1994 (UK); Born and Leigh, *Making Intelligence Accountable*, 91–3; Gill, 'Reasserting Control'.
35 E. Hill, *Joint Inquiry Staff Statement*.
36 Senate Select Committee on Intelligence and House Permanent Select Committee on Intelligence, *Report of Joint Inquiry*, p. 2.
37 ISC, *Annual Report 2001–2002*, p. 5, paras. 29–31.
38 Cf. L. K. Johnson, 'Lawmakers and spies'.
39 Gill, 'Reasserting control'.
40 Robertson, 'Recent reform'.
41 M. Davies, *Guarding the Guardians*, pp. 117–18.
42 Ibid., p. 185.
43 Ibid., p. 246.
44 ISC, *Annual Report 2001–2002*.
45 ISC, *Inquiry into Intelligence Assessments and Advice*.
46 Prime Minister, *Government Response to the ISC Inquiry into Intelligence Assessments and Advice*, para. 11.
47 Personal communication to PG.
48 ISC, *Iraqi Weapons*, para. 12.
49 Ibid., para. 11.
50 Ibid., para. 66.
51 Ibid., paras. 107–8.
52 Ibid., para. 83.
53 Ibid., e.g. paras 83, 110–12.
54 Ibid., para. 86; emphasis added.
55 Prime Minister, *Government Response to ISC Report on Iraqi Weapons of Mass Destruction – Intelligence and Assessments*, para. 14, although Blair's Foreword described it as 'current and serious' (HMG, *Iraq's Weapons of Mass Destruction*, p. 3).
56 Prime Minister, ibid., para. 15.
57 Butler Report, paras 566–78.
58 ISC, *Annual Report, 2004–05*, para. 61.
59 Baroness Symons, *Hansard (Lords)*, 20 July 2004, col. 98.

60   ISC, *Handling of Detainees*, paras 3–4.

61   Ibid., para. 9.

62   Hooding, wall-standing, white noise, sleep and food deprivation.

63   ISC, *Handling of Detainees*, para. 111.

64   Ibid., para. 112.

65   The Taguba Report, Findings and Recommendations, Part One, para. 10, repr. in Greenberg and Dratel (eds), *The Torture Papers*, pp. 414–20.

66   ISC, *Handling of Detainees*, para. 33.

67   Gill, 'The politicisation of intelligence'; idem, 'Keeping in touch with "earthly awkwardness" '.

68   Whitaker , 'The Bristow affair'.

69   <www.ararcommission.ca>, accessed 15 May 2005.

70   Federation of American Scientists, *Secrecy News*, issue 91 (19 Sept. 2002), <www.fas.org/> accessed Oct. 2002.

71   Firestone and Risen, 'White House, in shift, backs inquiry on 9/11'.

72   Shenon, 'Bush names former New Jersey Governor to 9/11 panel.' Initially it was announced that the Commission would be headed by Henry Kissinger. He shortly declined, on the grounds that he was unwilling to disclose his international consulting clients, as required by federal law.

73   For example, 'Wrestling for the truth of 9/11', *New York Times*, 9 July 2003; 'The mystery deepens', *New York Times*, 3 Apr. 2004.

74   For example, Eggen and Pincus, 'Ashcroft's efforts on terrorism criticized'; Pincus and Eggen, 'Al Qaeda unchecked for years'. The staff reports and testimony are available at <www.9-11commission.gov>.

75   Cf. L. K. Johnson, *A Season of Inquiry*.

76   In December 2003, Ian Huntley, a school caretaker, was convicted of the murder of two young girls in Cambridgeshire. During his trial it became apparent that much 'intelligence' existed as to Huntley's sexual history that had not been appropriately recorded or disseminated by police. An inquiry by Sir Michael Bichard detailed the primitive state of police information management: *The Bichard Inquiry Report*. See also Gill, 'Policing in ignorance?'

77   Widgery, *Report of the Tribunal Appointed to Inquire into Events on Sunday 30th January 1972*.

78   Dyer, 'Finucane widow urges judges to shun inquiry'.

79   McCullagh, 'Report'. EPIC publishes regular reports on the impact of counter-terrorist laws in the US: <www.epic.org/reports>.

80   A systematic review of the impact of media in the security sector is provided by Caparini, *Media and Security Governance*.

81   One indicator of the unhappiness at the Iraq fiasco in parts of the Whitehall intelligence machinery is the number of documents leaked to the press since 2003 – press briefings were common before then, but leaked documents far less so, and certainly less than in the USA.

82   Stevens, *Enquiry*, para. 3.4.

83   <www.the-hutton-inquiry.org.uk>.

84   G. Thompson, *Between Hierarchies and Markets*, p. 176.

85   For example, Goldsmith and Eggers, *Governing by Network*, esp. pp. 121–56.

86   Sheptycki, *Review of the Influence of Strategic Intelligence*, pp. 24–5.

87   Bayley and Shearing, *The New Structure of Policing*, pp. 32–3; cf. Button, *Private Policing*, pp. 118–30; Schreier and Caparini, *Privatizing Security*, pp. 110–23. An interesting example is provided by Portland, Oregon, where the mayor and the municipal police commissioner insist that they be security-cleared to a level that will enable them to oversee the work of their officers involved in Joint Terrorism Task Forces: 'City sets March 30 showdown over Joint Terrorism Task Force', *Portland Communique*, 23 Mar. 2005.

Chapter 9   Conclusion: Intelligence for a More Secure World?

1   Porter, *Plots and Paranoia*, p. 234.
2   Whitaker, 'A Faustian bargain?'
3   On this risk, see Robin, *Fear*, esp. pp. 1–25.
4   Drum, 'Political animal'.
5   The initial proposal was made by the *9/11 Commission Report*, sect. 13.2.
6   Ibid., sect. 13.3.
7   Cf. also Barger, *Toward a Revolution in Intelligence Affairs*.

Bibliography

Aid, M. A., 'The time of troubles: The US National Security Agency in the twenty-first century', *Intelligence and National Security*, 15, 3 (2000), pp. 1–32.

Aid, M. A., and Wiebes, C., 'The importance of signals intelligence in the Cold War', *Intelligence and National Security*, 16, 1 (2001), pp. 1–26.

Aldrich, R. J., ' "Grow your own": Cold War intelligence and history supermarkets', *Intelligence and National Security*, 17,1 (2002), pp. 135–52.

Aldrich, R. J., 'Transatlantic intelligence and security cooperation', *International Affairs*, 80, 4 (2004), pp. 731–53.

Allason, R., *The Branch: A History of the Metropolitan Police Special Branch 1883–1983* (London, Secker & Warburg, 1983).

Allison, G., and Zelikow, P., *Essence of Decision*, 2nd edn (New York, Longman, 1999).

Amnesty International, *Guantánamo and Beyond: The Continuing Pursuit of Unchecked Executive Power* (Amnesty International, May 2005), <http://web.amnesty.org/library/Index/ENGAMR510632005?open&of=ENG-USA>, accessed on 1 Dec. 2005.

Andradé, D., *Ashes to Ashes: The Phoenix Program and the Vietnam War* (Lexington, MA, D. C. Heath, 1990).

Andrew, C., *Secret Service: The Making of the British Intelligence Community* (London, Heinemann, 1985).

Andrew, C., 'Conclusion: An agenda for future research', *Intelligence and National Security*, 12, 1 (1997), pp. 224–33.

Andrew, C., 'Intelligence, international relations and "under-theorisation" ', *Intelligence and National Security*, 19, 2 (2004), pp. 170–84.

Andrew, C., and Dilks, D., *The Missing Dimension: Governments and Intelligence Communities in the Twentieth Century* (London, Macmillan, 1984).

Andrew, C., and Gordievsky, O., *KGB: The Inside Story of its Foreign Operations from Lenin to Gorbachev* (New York, HarperCollins, 1991).

Andrew, C., and Mitrokhin, V., *The Mitrokhin Archive II: The KGB and the World* (London, Allen Lane/Penguin, 2005).

Applebaum, A., 'The torture myth', *Washington Post*, 12 Jan. 2005.

Archick, K., *US–EU Cooperation against Terrorism*, CRS Report (Washington, DC, Congressional Research Service, 2005), accessed at <www.fas.org/irp>, 1 Nov. 2005.

Baer, R., *See No Evil: The True Story of a Ground Soldier in the CIA's War on Terrorism* (New York, Crown, 2002).

Bamford, J., *Body of Secrets: How America's NSA and Britain's GCHQ Eavesdrop on the World* (London, Arrow Books, 2002).

Barger, D. G., *Toward a Revolution in Intelligence Affairs* (Santa Monica, CA, RAND, 2005), accessed at <www.rand.org/publications/TR/TR242/index.html>, 1 Dec. 2005.

Barnett, A., and Townsend, M., 'July bomber in link to foiled London terror plot', *Observer*, 13 Nov. 2005.

Bayley, D. H., and Shearing, C. D., *The New Structure of Policing: Description, Conceptualization, and Research Agenda*, National Institute of Justice Research Report 187083 (Washington, DC, Department of Justice, 2001), <www.ojp.usdoj.gov/nij>, accessed 10 Jan. 2005.

BBC, 'Secrets, spies & videotape', *Panorama*, BBC1, broadcast 23 Mar. 1999.

BBC, 'Subversive my arse', *True Spies*, BBC2, broadcast 27 Oct. 2002., <http://news.bbc.co.uk/1/hi/programmes/true_spies/default.stm>, accessed 1 Dec. 2005.

BBC, *Spies R Us*, Radio 4, broadcast 6, 13, 20 Feb. 2003, <http://www.bbc.co.uk/radio4/history/spies_cia.shtml>, accessed 1 Dec. 2005.

BBC, 'The Hutton Inquiry', *Panorama*, BBC1, broadcast 21 Jan. 2004.

BBC, 'Concern over Iraq security firms', *File on 4*, Radio 4, broadcast 25 May 2004.

BBC, 'A failure of intelligence', *Panorama*, BBC1, broadcast 11 July 2004.

Benetto, J., 'Predicted bomb attacks reveal intelligence gaps on al-Qa'ida', *The Independent*, 8 July 2005.

Benn, T., 'The case for dismantling the secret state', *New Left Review*, 190 (1991), pp. 127–30.

Berki, R. N., *Security and Society: Reflections on Law, Order and Politics* (London, Dent & Sons, 1986).

Berkowitz, B. D., and Goodman, A. E., *Strategic Intelligence for American National Security* (Princeton, Princeton University Press, 1991).

Berkowitz, B. D., and Goodman, A. E., *Best Truth: Intelligence in the Information Age* (New Haven, Yale University Press, 2000).

Betts, R. K., 'Analysis, war, and decision: why intelligence failures are inevitable', *World Politics*, 31, 1 (1978), pp. 61–89.

Betts, R. K., 'Fixing intelligence', *Foreign Affairs*, 81, 1 (2002), pp. 43–59.

Bevir, M., and Rhodes, R., 'Interpretive theory', in D. Marsh and G. Stoker (eds), *Theory and Methods in Political Science*, 2nd edn (Basingstoke, Palgrave, 2002), pp. 131–52.

Bichard, M., *The Bichard Inquiry Report*, HC653, 22 June 2004, <www.bichardinquiry.org.uk>, accessed 1 Dec. 2005.

Bigo, D., 'Liaison officers in Europe, new officers in the European security field', in J. Sheptycki (ed.), *Issues in Transnational Policing* (London, Routledge, 2000), pp. 67–99.

Bill, J. A., *The Eagle and the Lion: The Tragedy of American–Iranian Relations* (New Haven, Yale University Press, 1988).

Black, C., 'Intelligence got it wrong', *Guardian*, 8 July 2005.

Black, I., 'EU agrees to give air passenger data to US', *Guardian*, 18 Dec. 2003.

Black, I., and Morris, B., *Israel's Secret Wars: A History of Israel's Intelligence Services* (London, Warner Books, 1992).

Black, J., 'The geopolitics of James Bond', *Intelligence and National Security*, 19, 2 (2004), pp. 290–303.

Bok, S., *Secrets: On the Ethics of Concealment and Revelation* (Oxford, Oxford University Press, 1986).

Bond, R., 'Methods and issues in risk and threat assessment', in J. H. Ratcliffe (ed.), *Strategic Thinking in Criminal Intelligence* (Sydney, Federation Press, 2004), pp. 119–28.

Born, H., and Leigh, I., *Making Intelligence Accountable: Legal Standards and Best Practice for Oversight of Intelligence Agencies* (Oslo, Parliament of Norway, 2005).

Bottoms, A., 'The relationship between theory and research in criminology', in R. D. King and E. Wincup (eds), *Doing Research on Crime and Justice* (Oxford, Oxford University Press, 2000), pp. 15–60.

Bourke, J., *Fear: A Cultural History* (London, Virago, 2005).

Bozeman, A., 'Knowledge and comparative method in comparative intelligence studies', in A. Bozeman, *Strategic Intelligence and Statecraft* (Washington, DC, Brassey's Inc., 1992), pp. 198–205.

Bremner, C., 'FBI admits error over Air France', *Times*, 3 Jan. 2004.

Bright, M., and Beaumont, P., 'Britain spied on UN allies over war vote', *Observer*, 8 Feb. 2004.

Brodeur, J. P., 'Cops and spooks, the uneasy partnership', in T. Newburn (ed.), *Policing, Key Readings* (Cullompton, Willan, 2005), pp. 797–812.

Brodeur, J. P., and Dupont, B., 'Will the knowledge workers put their act together?', *Policing and Society*, 16, 1 (2006), pp. 7–26.

Brooks, D., 'The art of intelligence', *New York Times*, 2 Apr. 2005.

Brown, A., *The Gorbachev Factor* (Oxford, Oxford University Press, 1996).

Brown, A., 'Gorbachev and the end of the Cold War', in R. K. Herrmann and R. N. Lebow (eds), *Ending the Cold War: Interpretations, Causation, and the Study of International Relations* (New York, Palgrave, 2004), pp. 31–57.

Bruce, J. B., 'Dynamic adaptation: a twenty-first century intelligence paradigm', unpublished paper, Washington, DC (2004), pp. 4–5.

Bumiller, E., and Sanger D., 'Bush, as terror inquiry swirls, seeks cabinet post on security', *New York Times*, 7 June. 2002.

Burrough, B., et al., 'The path to war', *Vanity Fair*, May 2004, pp. 100–17, 169–82.

Butler, R., *Review of Intelligence on Weapons of Mass Destruction, Report of a Committee of Privy Counsellors*, HC898 (London, The Stationery Office, July 2004).

Button, M., *Private Policing* (Cullompton, Willan, 2002).

Buzan, B., *People, States and Fear*, 2nd edn (Hemel Hempstead, Harvester Wheatsheaf, 1991).

Buzan, B., Wæver, O., and de Wilde, J., *Security: A New Framework for Analysis* (London, Lynne Riener, 1998).

Cahn, A. H., 'Team B: the trillion dollar experiment', *The Bulletin of the Atomic Scientists*, 49, 3 (1993), pp. 22, 24–7.

Callaghan, J., and Phythian, M., 'State surveillance of the CPGB leadership: 1920s–1950s', *Labour History Review*, 69, 1 (2004), pp. 19–33.

Cameron, I., 'Beyond the nation state: the influence of the European Court of Human Rights on intelligence accountability', in H. Born et al. (eds), *Who's Watching the Spies: Establishing Intelligence Service Accountability* (Dulles, VA, Potomac Books, 2005), pp. 34–53.

Caparini, M., *Media and Security Governance* (Münster, Nomos Verlagsgesellschaft, 2004).

Cart, J., 'US scientists say they are told to alter findings', *Los Angeles Times*, 10 Feb. 2005.

Carter, D., *Law Enforcement Intelligence: A Guide for State, Local, and Tribal Law Enforcement Agencies* (Michigan State University and US Department of Justice Office of Community Oriented Policing Services, 2004), <http://www.fas.org/irp/agency/doj/lei/>, accessed 1 Dec. 2005.

Castells, M., *The Rise of the Network Society*, 2nd edn (Oxford, Blackwell, 2000).

Central Intelligence Agency, *A Consumer's Guide to Intelligence* (Washington, DC, CIA Office of Public and Agency Information, 1995).

Central Intelligence Agency, *Iraq's Weapons of Mass Destruction Programs*, <http://www.odci.gov/cia/reports/iraq_wmd/Iraq_Oct_2002.htm>, accessed 1 Dec. 2005.

Cepik, M., 'The Brazilian intelligence system', in T. Bruneau and K. Dombrowski (eds), *Reforming Intelligence across the World: Institutions and Cultures* (Austin, University of Texas Press, forthcoming 2007).

Cerny, P. G., 'Globalization and the disarticulation of political power: towards a new middle ages?', in H. Goverde, et al. (eds), *Power in Contemporary Politics* (London, Sage, 2000), pp. 17–86.

Chapman, J., *Licence to Thrill: A Cultural History of the James Bond Films* (New York, Columbia University Press, 2000).

Chesterton, G. K., *The Man Who Was Thursday* (Harmondsworth, Penguin, 1986; originally 1908).

Chief Surveillance Commissioner, *Annual Report 2004–2005*, HC444 (London, The Stationery Office, 2005); <www.surveillancecommissioners.gov.uk>, accessed 1 Dec. 2005.

Cilluffo, F., Marks, R. A., and Salmoiraghi, G. C., 'The use and limits of US intelligence', *Washington Quarterly*, 25, 1 (2002), pp. 61–74.

Clarke, R. A., *Against All Enemies: Inside America's War on Terror* (London, Simon & Schuster, 2004).

Clegg, S., *Frameworks of Power* (London, Sage, 1989).

Clegg, S., 'Power and authority, resistance and legitimacy', in H. Goverde et al. (eds), *Power in Contemporary Politics: Theories, Practices, Globalizations* (London, Sage, 2000), pp. 77–92.

Cobain, I., et al., 'Destination Cairo: human rights fears over CIA flights', *Guardian*, 12 Sept. 2005.

Cogan, C., 'Hunters not gatherers: intelligence in the twenty-first century', *Intelligence and National Security*, 19, 2 (2004), pp. 304–21.

Coll, S., *Ghost Wars: The Secret History of the CIA, Afghanistan, and Bin Laden, from the Soviet Invasion to September 10, 2001* (New York, Penguin Press, 2004).

Cooper, C. L., 'The CIA and decision-making', *Foreign Affairs*, 51, 1 (1972), pp. 223–36.

Copeland, M., *Beyond Cloak and Dagger: Inside the CIA* (New York, Pinnacle, 1975).

Cory, P., *Cory Collusion Inquiry Report: Patrick Finucane*, HC470 (London, The Stationery Office, April 2004).

Cowan, R., 'Unmasking leaves Provos seething with mutual suspicion', *Guardian*, 12 May 2003.

Cowan, R., 'CCTV captures July 7 terrorists staging a dry run before attacks', *Guardian*, 21 Sept. 2005.

Cowley, C., *Guns, Lies and Spies* (London, Hamish Hamilton, 1992).

Cox, R., 'The covert world', in R. Cox and M. G. Schechter, *The Political Economy of a Plural World* (London, Routledge, 2002), pp. 118–38.

Cumming, A., and Masse, T., *FBI Intelligence Reform since September 11, 2001: Issues and Options for Congress*, RL32336 (Washington, DC, Congressional Research Service, 2004).

Curtis, A., 'Fear gives politicians a reason to be', *Guardian*, 24 Nov. 2004.

Curtis, A., *The Power of Nightmares*, first broadcast in the UK Nov, 2004, <http://news.bbc.co.uk/1/hi/programmes/3755686.stm>, accessed 1 Dec. 2005.

Dahl, R. A., *Modern Political Analysis*, 5th edn (Englewood Cliffs, NJ, Prentice-Hall, 1991).

Dandeker, C., *Surveillance, Power and Modernity* (Cambridge, Polity, 1990).

Danermark, B., et al., *Explaining Society: Critical Realism in the Social Sciences* (London, Routledge, 2002).

Davies, M., 'Guarding the Guardians: The Evolution of Parliamentary Oversight of British Intelligence', unpublished Ph.D. thesis, University of Wales at Aberystwyth, 2002.

Davies, P. H. J., *MI6 and the Machinery of Spying* (London, Cass, 2004).

Davies, P. H. J., 'Intelligence culture and intelligence failure in Britain and the United States', *Cambridge Review of International Affairs*, 17 (2004), pp. 495–520.

Davis, J., 'Tensions in analyst–policymaker relations: opinions, facts, and evidence', *Sherman Kent Center for Intelligence Analysis Occasional Papers*, 2, 2 (2003), <http://www.cia.gov/cia/publications/Kent_Papers/pdf/ OPV2No2.pdf>, accessed 1 Dec. 2005.

Dearlove, J., and Saunders, P., *Introduction to British Politics*, 2nd edn (Cambridge, Polity, 1991).

Deibert, R. J., 'Deep probe: the evolution of network intelligence', *Intelligence and National Security*, 18, 4 (2003), pp. 175–93.

Dennis, M., *The Stasi: Myth and Reality* (Harlow, Longman, 2003).

Der Derian, J., *Antidiplomacy: Spies, Terror, Speed, and War* (Oxford, Blackwell, 1992).

Der Derian, J., 'Anti-diplomacy: intelligence theory and surveillance practice', *Intelligence and National Security*, 8, 3 (1993), pp. 29–51.

Dinges, J., *The Condor Years: How Pinochet and His Allies Brought Terrorism to Three Continents* (New York, New Press, 2004).

Dodd, V., 'Officials missed clues to trap July 7 bomber', *Guardian*, 26 Oct. 2005.

Doig, A., and Phythian, M., 'The national interest and politics of threat exaggeration: the Blair Government's case for war against Iraq', *Political Quarterly*, 76, 3 (2005), pp. 368–76.

Donovan, M., 'National intelligence and the Iranian revolution', in R. Jeffreys-Jones and C. Andrew (eds), *Eternal Vigilance? 50 Years of the* CIA (London, Frank Cass, 1997), pp. 143–63.

Dorn, N., 'Proteiform criminalities, the formation of organised crime as organisers' responses to developments in four fields of control', in A. Edwards and P. Gill (eds), *Transnational Organised Crime: Perspectives on Global Security* (London, Routledge, 2003), pp. 227–40.

Dorril, S., *MI6: Fifty Years of Special Operations* (London, Fourth Estate, 2001).

Dorril, S., and Ramsay, R., *Smear! Wilson and the Secret State* (London, Fourth Estate, 1991).

Dowding, K., 'Model or metaphor? A critical review of the policy network approach', *Political Studies* 43, 1 (1995), pp. 136–58.

Draper, T., 'Is the CIA necessary?', *New York Review of Books*, 14 Aug. 1997.

Drew, E., 'Pinning the blame', *New York Review of Books*, 23 Sept. 2004.

Drum, K., 'Political animal', *Washington Monthly*, 1 Sept. 2001, <www. washingtonmonthly. com/archives/individual/2005_09/007023.php>, accessed 1 Dec. 2005.

Dycus, S., 'The role of military intelligence in homeland security', *Louisiana Law Review*, 64 (2004), pp. 779–807.

Dyer, C., 'Finucane widow urges judges to shun inquiry', *Guardian*, 14 Apr. 2005.

Dziak, J. J., *Chekisty: A History of the KGB* (Lexington, MA, Lexington Books, 1988).

Economist, 'Torture: ends, means and barbarity', 9 Jan. 2003.

Economist, 'Can spies be made better?', 19 Mar. 2005.

Edelman, M., *The Symbolic Uses of Politics* (Urbana, University of Illinois Press, 1964).

Edwards, A., and Gill, P., 'After transnational organised crime? The politics of public safety', in A. Edwards and P. Gill, *Transnational Organised Crime: Perspectives on Global Security* (London, Routledge, 2003), pp. 264–81.

Eggen, D., 'FBI taps campus police in anti-terror operations', *Washington Post*, 25 Jan. 2003.

Eggen, D., and Pincus, W., 'Ashcroft's efforts on terrorism criticized', *Washington Post*, 14 Apr. 2004.

Ellsberg, D., *Secrets: A Memoir of Vietnam and the Pentagon Papers* (New York, Viking, 2002).

Enloe, C., *Bananas, Beaches and Bases: Making Feminist Sense of International Politics* (Berkeley, University of California Press, 1990).

Epstein, E. J., *Deception: The Invisible War between the KGB and the CIA* (London, W. H. Allen, 1989).

Erskine, T., ' "As rays of light to the human soul"? Moral agents and intelligence gathering', *Intelligence and National Security*, 19, 2 (2004), pp. 359–81.

Evans, R. J., *In Defence of History* (London, Granta Books, 1997).

Evans, R. J., *Lying about Hitler: History, Holocaust, and the David Irving Trial* (New York, Basic Books, 2001).

Eyre, R., 'Ballot-box blues', *Guardian*, 26 Mar. 2005.

Eysenck, M. W., and Keane, M. T., *Cognitive Psychology: A Student's Handbook*, 4th edn (Hove, Psychology Press, 2000).

Farson, S., 'Old wine, new bottles and fancy labels', in G. Barak (ed.), *Crimes by the Capitalist State* (Albany, State University of New York Press, 1991), pp. 185–217.

Federation of American Scientists, 'Signals intelligence in the Gulf War', at <http://www.fas.org/spp/military/docops/operate/ds/signals.htm>, accessed 1 Dec. 2005.

Fenwick, H., *Civil Liberties*, 2nd edn. (London, Cavendish Publishing, 1998).

Ferris, J., 'Netcentric warfare, C4ISR and information operations: towards a revolution in military intelligence?', *Intelligence and National Security*, 19, 2 (2003), pp. 199–225.

Fine, S., 'Anarchism and the assassination of McKinley', *American Historical Review*, 60 (1955), pp. 777–99.

Firestone, D., and Risen, J., 'White House, in shift, backs inquiry on 9/11', *New York Times*, 21 Sept. 2002.

Flood, B., 'Strategic aspects of the UK national intelligence model', in J. H. Ratcliffe (ed.), *Strategic Thinking in Criminal Intelligence* (Sydney, Federation Press, 2004), pp. 37–52.

Flood, P., *Report of the Inquiry into Australian Intelligence Agencies* (Canberra, Australian Government, July 2004).

Foot, P., *Who Framed Colin Wallace?* (London, Macmillan, 1989).

Ford, H. P., 'Revisiting Vietnam: thoughts engendered by Robert McNamara's *In Retrospect*', *Studies in Intelligence*, 39, 5 (1996), <http://www.odci.gov/csi/ studies/96unclass/ford.htm>, accessed 1 Dec. 2005.

Ford, H. P., 'Unpopular pessimism: why CIA analysts were so doubtful about Vietnam', *Studies in Intelligence*, 1 (1997), <http://www.odci.gov/csi/studies/97unclass/vietnam.html>, accessed 1 Dec. 2005.

Ford, H. P., 'The US Government's experience with intelligence analysis: pluses and minuses', *Intelligence and National Security*, 10, 4 (1995), pp. 42–3.

Foreign Affairs Committee, *Sierra Leone*, 2nd Report, Session 1998–99, HC116-I (London HMSO, 1999).

Foreign Affairs Committee, *The Decision to Go to War in Iraq*, HC 813-1 (London, HMSO, 2003).

Foreign and Commonwealth Secretary, *Review of Intelligence on Weapons of Mass Destruction: Implementation of its Conclusions*, Cm 6492 (London, The Stationery Office, March 2005).

Foucault, M., 'Governmentality', in G. Burchell et al. (eds), *The Foucault Effect: Studies in Governmentality* (London, Harvester Wheatsheaf, 1991), pp. 87–104.

Frances, J., Levačić, R., Mitchell, J., and Thompson, G., 'Introduction', in G. Thompson et al. (eds), *Markets, Hierarchies and Networks: The Co-ordination of Social Life* (London, Sage, 1991), pp. 1–19.

Freedman, L., 'The CIA and the Soviet threat: the politicization of estimates, 1966–1977', in R. Jeffreys-Jones and C. Andrew (eds), *Eternal Vigilence? 50 Years of the CIA* (London, Frank Cass, 1997), pp. 122–42.

Freedman, L., *The Official History of the Falklands Campaign, i: The Origins of the Falklands War* (London, Routledge, 2005).

Friedrich, C. J., *Man and His Government* (New York, McGraw-Hill, 1963).

Fry, M. G., and Hochstein, M., 'Epistemic communities: intelligence studies and international relations', *Intelligence and National Security*, 8, 3 (1993), pp. 14–28.

Gaddis, J. L., 'Intelligence, espionage, and Cold War origins', *Diplomatic History*, 13, 2 (1989), pp. 191–212.

Gaddis, J. L., 'Intelligence, espionage, and Cold War history', in J. L. Gaddis, *The United States and the End of the Cold War: Implications, Reconsiderations, Provocations* (New York, Oxford University Press, 1992), pp. 87–104.

Gardiner, L. K., 'Dealing with intelligence–policy disconnects', in H. B. Westerfield (ed.), *Inside CIA's Private World: Declassified Articles from the Agency's Internal Journal, 1955–92* (New Haven, Yale University Press, 1995), pp. 344–56.

Gates, R. M., *From the Shadows: The Ultimate Insider's Story of Five Presidents and How They Won the Cold War* (New York, Simon & Schuster, 1997).

Gellman, B., 'Arms inspectors "shake the tree" ', *Washington Post*, 12 Oct. 1998.

Gellman, B., 'Annan suspicious of UNSCOM role', *Washington Post*, 6 Jan. 1999.

Gellman, B., 'Secret unit expands Rumsfeld's domain', *Washington Post*, 23 Jan. 2005.

Geraghty, T., *The Irish War: A Military History of a Domestic Conflict* (London, HarperCollins, 1998).

Giddens, A., *The Nation State and Violence* (Berkeley, University of California Press, 1985).

Gill, P., 'Symbolic or real? The impact of the Canadian SIRC, 1984–88', *Intelligence and National Security*, 4, 3 (1989), pp. 550–75.

Gill, P., *Policing Politics: Security Intelligence and the Liberal Democratic State* (London, Frank Cass, 1994).

Gill, P., 'Reasserting control: recent changes in the oversight of the UK intelligence community', *Intelligence and National Security*, 11, 2 (1996), pp. 313–31.

Gill, P., ' "Sack the spooks": Do we need an internal security apparatus?', in L. Panitch (ed.), *Are There Alternatives? Socialist Register 1996* (London, Merlin Press, 1996), pp. 189–211.

Gill, P., *Rounding up the Usual Suspects? Developments in Contemporary Law Enforcement Intelligence* (Aldershot, Ashgate, 2000).

Gill, P., 'Policing in ignorance?', *Criminal Justice Matters*, 58 (2004–5), pp. 14–15.

Gill, P., 'The politicisation of intelligence: lessons from the invasion of Iraq', in H. Born et al. (eds), *Who's Watching the Spies: Maintaining Accountability over the World's Secret Agencies* (Washington, DC, Potomac Inc., 2005), pp. 12–33.

Gill, P., 'Not just joining the dots but crossing the borders and bridging the voids: Constructing security networks after 11 September 2001', *Policing & Society*, 16, 1 (2006), pp. 26–48.

Gill, P., 'Keeping in touch with "earthly awkwardness": failures of intelligence analysis and policy in the UK', in T. Bruneau and K. Dombrowski (eds), *Reforming Intelligence across the World: Institutions and Cultures* (Austin, University of Texas Press, forthcoming 2007).

Gimenez-Salinas, A., 'New approaches regarding private/public security', *Policing and Society*, 14, 2 (2004), pp. 158–74.

Godfrey, E. D., 'Ethics and intelligence', *Foreign Affairs*, 56 (1978), pp. 624–42.

Godson, R., 'Intelligence for the 1990s', in R. Godson (ed.), *Intelligence Requirements for the 1990s* (Lexington, MA, Lexington Books, 1989), pp. 1–29.

Godson, R., *Dirty Tricks or Trump Cards: US Covert Action and Counterintelligence* (Washington, DC, Brassey's Inc., 1995).

Goldenberg, S., 'Ex-CIA chief eats humble pie', *Guardian*, 29 Apr. 2005.

Goldenberg, S., 'More than 80,000 held by US since 9/11 attacks', *Guardian*, 18 Nov. 2005.

Goldsmith, S., and Eggers, W. D., *Governing by Network: The New Shape of the Public Sector* (Washington, DC, Brookings Institution, 2004).

Goo, S. K., 'List of foiled plots puzzling to some', *Washington Post*, 23 Oct. 2005.

Gordievsky, O., *Next Stop Execution* (London, Macmillan, 1995).

Gordon, M. R., 'Poor intelligence misled troops about risk of drawn-out war', *New York Times*, 20 Oct. 2004.

Gormley, D. M., 'The limits of intelligence: Iraq's lessons', *Survival*, 46, 3 (2004), pp. 7–28.

Goshko, J. M., 'Annan: US spying charge could hurt disarmament', *Washington Post*, 3 Mar. 1999.

Gow, D., 'Bush gives green light to CIA for assassination of named terrorists', *Guardian*, 29 Oct. 2001.

Greenberg, K. J., and Dratel, J. L. (eds), *The Torture Papers: The Road to Abu Ghraib* (Cambridge, Cambridge University Press, 2005).

Gregory, F., and Wilkinson, P., 'Riding pillion for tackling terrorism is a high-risk policy', ISP/NSC Briefing Paper 05/01, (London, Chatham House, July 2005), <http://www.riia.org/pdf/research/niis/BPsecurity.pdf>, accessed 1 Dec. 2005.

Grice, E., 'Dossier a mistake – Rimington', *Daily Telegraph*, 13 June 2004.

Grieve, J., 'Developments in UK criminal intelligence', in J. H. Ratcliffe (ed.), *Strategic Thinking in Criminal Intelligence* (Sydney, Federation Press, 2004), pp. 25–36.

Haggerty, K. D., and Ericson, R. V., 'The militarization of policing in the information age', *Journal of Political and Military Sociology*, 27 (1999), pp. 233–55.

Halliday, F., 'The end of the Cold War and international relations: some analytic and theoretical conclusions', in K. Booth and S. Smith, *International Relations Theory Today* (Cambridge, Polity, 1995), pp. 38–61.

Handel, M. I., 'Surprise in diplomacy', in R. L. Pfaltzgraff, Jr, U. Ra'anan and W. Milberg (eds), *Intelligence Policy and National Security* (London, Macmillan, 1981), pp. 187–211.

Harnden, T., and Ansari, M., 'Pakistan: the incubator for al-Qaeda's attacks on London', *Sunday Telegraph*, 24 July 2005.

Hay, C., *Political Analysis: A Critical Introduction* (Basingstoke, Palgrave, 2002).

Heldon, C. E., 'Exploratory analysis tools', in J. H. Ratcliffe (ed.), *Strategic Thinking in Criminal Intelligence* (Sydney, Federation Press, 2004), pp. 99–118.

Henderson, P., *The Unlikely Spy: An Autobiography* (London, Bloomsbury, 1993).

Herbert, I., and Sengupta, K., 'Revealed: how Aldgate bomber became a single-minded jihadist killer', *Independent*, 10 Sept. 2005.

Herman, M., *Intelligence Power in Peace and War* (Cambridge, Cambridge University Press, 1996).

Herman, M., *Intelligence Services in the Information Age* (London, Frank Cass, 2001).

Herman, M., 'Threat assessments and the legitimation of policy?', *Intelligence and National Security*, 18, 3 (2003), pp. 174–78.

Herman, M., 'Ethics and intelligence after September 2001', *Intelligence and National Security*, 19, 2 (2004), pp. 342–58.

Hersh, S. M., *Chain of Command: The Road from 9/11 to Abu Ghraib* (London, Penguin/Allen Lane, 2004).

Hersh, S. M., 'Behind the "Mushroom Cloud"' (interview), *New Yorker Online*, 23 Oct. 2003, <www.newyorker.com/printables/online/031027on_onlineonly01>, accessed 1 Dec. 2005.

Hibbert, R., 'Intelligence and policy', *Intelligence and National Security*, 5, 1 (1990), pp. 110–28.

Hill, E., *Joint Inquiry Staff Statement*, Part 1, 18 Sept. 2002, <www.fas.org/irp/congress/2002_hr/091802hill.html>, accessed 1 Dec. 2005.

Hill, M., *The Policy Process in the Modern State*, 3rd edn (Hemel Hempstead, Harvester Wheatsheaf, 1997).

Hitchens, C., 'Who runs Britain?', *London Review of Books*, 8 Dec. 1994.

HMG, *Central Intelligence Machinery*, (London, HMSO, 1993).

HMG, *Iraq's Weapons of Mass Destruction: The Assessment of the British Government* (London, HMSO, Sept. 2002).

HMG, *National Intelligence Machinery* (London, HMSO, 2005), accessible at <www.cabinetoffice.gov.uk/intelligence/>.

HMIC, *A Need to Know: HMIC Thematic Inspection of Special Branch and Ports Policing*, Home Office Communications Directorate, Jan. 2003, <www.inspectorates.homeoffice.gov.uk/hmic>, accessed 1 Dec. 2005.

Hoare, O. (ed.), *British Intelligence in the Twentieth Century: A Missing Dimension? Intelligence and National Security*, 17, 1 (2002) special issue.

Hogan, M. J., *Cross of Iron: Harry S. Truman and the Origins of the National Security State* (Cambridge, Cambridge University Press, 1999).

Hollingsworth, M., and Fielding, N., *Defending the Realm: MI5 and the Shayler Affair* (London, André Deutsch, 1999).

Holsti, K. J., *International Politics: A Framework for Analysis* (Englewood Cliffs, NJ, Prentice-Hall, 1967).

Holt, T., *The Deceivers: Allied Deception in the Second World War* (London, Weidenfeld & Nicolson, 2004).

Home Office, *Guidelines on Special Branch Work in Great Britain* (London, Home Office, July 1994).

Home Office, 'Anti-terrorist legislation must balance public protection with individual rights', press release 072/2004, 25 Feb. 2004.

Hooper, J., 'Italy demands US explanation over kidnapped cleric', *Guardian*, 1 July 2005.

Hooper, J., 'Kidnap probe reveals CIA modus operandi', *Guardian*, 2 July 2005.

Hoy, C., and Ostrovsky, V., *By Way of Deception: An Insider's Exposé of the Mossad* (London, Arrow, 1991).

Hulnick, A. S., 'Controlling intelligence estimates', in G. Hastedt (ed.), *Controlling Intelligence* (London, Cass, 1991), pp. 81–96.

Hulnick, A. S., *Fixing the Spy Machine: Preparing American Intelligence for the Twenty-First Century* (London, Praeger, 1999).

Human Rights Watch, 'Statement on US secret detention facilities in Europe', Nov. 2005, <http://www.hrw.org/english/docs/2005/11/07/usint11995.htm>, accessed 1 Dec. 2005.

Hutton, B., *Report of the Inquiry into the Circumstances Surrounding the Death of Dr. David Kelly CMG*, HC 247 (London, HMSO, 2004).

Ignatius, D., 'Can the spy agencies dig out?', *Washington Post*, 15 Apr. 2005.

Ingram, M., and Harkin, G., *Stakeknife: Britain's Secret Agents in Ireland* (Dublin, The O'Brien Press, 2004).

Intelligence Services Commissioner, *Report for 2004*, HC548, <www.statewatch.org/news/2005/nov/int-rep-2004.pdf>, accessed 1 Dec. 2005.

Interception of Communications Commissioner, *Report for 2004*, HC549, Nov. 2005, <www.statewatch.org/news/2005/nov/teltap-2004.pdf>, accessed 1 Dec. 2005.

ISC, *Annual Report 2001–2002*, (Cm 5542 June 2002), <www.cabinetoffice.gov.uk /intelligence>, accessed 31 July 2005.

ISC, *Inquiry into Intelligence Assessments and Advice Prior to the Terrorist Bombings on Bali 12 October 2002*, Cm 5724 (Dec. 2002), <www.cabinetoffice.gov.uk/intelligence>, accessed 31 July 2005.

ISC, *Iraqi Weapons of Mass Destruction – Intelligence and Assessments*, Cm 5972 (Sept. 2003), <www.cabinetoffice.gov.uk/intelligence>, accessed 30 Sept. 2003.

ISC, *Annual Report 2003–2004*, Cm 6240 (June 2004), accessible at <www.cabinetoffice.gov.uk/intelligence>, accessed 31 July 2005.

ISC, *Handling of Detainees by UK Intelligence Personnel in Afghanistan, Guantánamo Bay and Iraq*, Cm 6469 (March 2005), <www.cabinetoffice.gov.uk / intelligence>, accessed 15 June 2005.

ISC, *Annual Report, 2004–05*, Cm 6510 (April 2005), <www.cabinetoffice.gov.uk/ intelligence>, accessed 10 May 2005.

Janis, I. L., *Victims of Groupthink: A Psychological Study of Foreign Policy Decisions and Fiascos* (Boston, Houghton Mifflin, 1972).

Jay, A. (ed.), *The Oxford Dictionary of Political Quotations* (Oxford, Oxford University Press, 1996).

Jeffreys-Jones, R., *Cloak and Dollar: A History of American Secret Intelligence* (New Haven, Yale University Press, 2002).

Jeffreys-Jones, R., *The CIA and American Democracy*, 3rd edn (New Haven, Yale University Press, 2003).

Jehl, D., 'New CIA chief tells workers to back Administration policies', *Los Angeles Times*, 17 Nov. 2004.

Jehl, D., 'New spy plan said to involve satellite system', *New York Times*, 12 Dec. 2004.

Jensen, J. M., *Army Surveillance in America, 1775–1980* (New Haven, Yale University Press, 1991).

Jervis, R., *System Effects: Complexity in Political and Social Life* (Princeton, Princeton University Press, 1997).

Jessop, B., 'Interpretive sociology and the dialectic of structure and agency', *Theory, Culture and Society*, 13, 1 (1996), pp. 119–28.

Johnson, C., *Blowback: The Costs and Consequences of American Empire* (London, Little, Brown, 2000).

Johnson, L. K., *A Season of Inquiry: The Senate Intelligence Investigation* (Lexington, University Press of Kentucky, 1985).

Johnson, L. K., *America's Secret Power: The CIA in a Democratic Society* (New York, Oxford University Press, 1989).

Johnson, L. K., 'On drawing a bright line for covert operations', *American Journal of International Law*, 86 (1992), pp. 284–309.

Johnson, L. K., *America as a World Power: Foreign Policy in a Constitutional Framework*, 2nd edn (New York, McGraw-Hill, 1995).

Johnson, L. K., 'Intelligence', in B. W. Jentleson and T. G. Paterson (eds), *Encyclopedia of US Foreign Relations* (New York, Oxford University Press, 1997), pp. 365–73.

Johnson, L. K., *Bombs, Bugs, Drugs, and Thugs: Intelligence and America's Quest for Security* (New York, New York University Press, 2000).

Johnson, L. K., 'Spies', *Foreign Policy*, Sept.–Oct. 2000, pp. 18–26.

Johnson, L. K., 'Bricks and mortar for a theory of intelligence', *Comparative Strategy*, 22 (2003), pp. 1–28.

Johnson, L. K., 'Preface to a theory of strategic intelligence', *International Journal of Intelligence and Counterintelligence*, 16 (2003), pp. 638–63.

Johnson, L. K., 'Spymaster Richard Helms: an interview with the former US Director of Central Intelligence', *Intelligence and National Security*, 18, 3 (2003), pp. 24–44.

Johnson, L. K., 'Lawmakers and spies: congressional oversight of intelligence in the United States', paper given to Annual Meeting of International Studies Association, Hawaii, 2005, pp. 4–6.

Johnston, L., *The Rebirth of Private Policing* (London, Routledge, 1992).

Johnston, L., *Policing Britain: Risk, Security and Governance* (Harlow, Longman, 2000).

Johnston, L., 'Transnational private policing, the impact of global commercial security', in J. Sheptycki (ed.), *Issues in Transnational Policing* (London, Routledge, 2000), pp. 21–42.

Johnston, L., and Shearing, C., *Governing Security: Explorations in Policing and Justice* (London, Routledge, 2003).

Jones, T., and Newburn, T., *Private Security and Public Policing* (Oxford, Clarendon Press, 1998).

Jordan, L. J., 'Homeland security faces massive overhaul', *San Francisco Chronicle*, 17 June 2005.

Kahn, D., 'An historical theory of intelligence', *Intelligence and National Security*, 16, 3 (2001), pp. 79–92.

Kampfner, J., *Blair's Wars* (London, Free Press, 2004).

Kaplan, A., *The Conduct of Inquiry: Methodology for Behavioral Science* (New York, Transaction Publishers, 1998).

Kean, T., and Hamilton, L., *9/11 Commission Report: Final Report of the National Commission on Terrorist Attacks upon the United States* (New York, W. W. Norton, 2004).

Keegan, J., *Intelligence in War: Knowledge of the Enemy from Napoleon to Al-Qaeda* (London, Hutchinson, 2003).

Kegley, C. W., *Controversies in International Relations Theory: Realism and the Neoliberal Challenge* (New York, St Martin's Press, 1995).

Kegley, C., and Wittkopf, E., *American Foreign Policy*, 5th edn (New York, St Martin's Press, 1996).

Keller, W. W., *The Liberals and J. Edgar Hoover: Rise and Fall of a Domestic Intelligence State* (Princeton, Princeton University Press, 1989).

Kent Center for Analytic Tradecraft, *Making Sense of Transnational Threats*, Sherman Kent School, Occasional Papers, 3, 1 (2004).

Kent, S., *Strategic Intelligence for American World Policy* (Princeton, Princeton University Press, 1966; 1 pub. 1949).

Kent, S., *The Law and Custom of the National Security Estimate: An Examination of the Theory and Some Recollections Concerning the Practice of the Art*, June 1975, <http://www.odci.gov/csi/books/shermankent/making.html>, accessed 1 Dec. 2005.

Kern, G., *A Death in Washington: Walter G. Krivitsky and the Stalin Terror* (New York, Enigma Books, 2003).

Kerr, S., 'Turning knowledge into wisdom: British and American approaches', paper given to Intelligence Studies Panel, International Studies Association, Portland, Oregon, Mar. 2003.

Kessler, R., *The CIA at War* (New York, St Martin's Griffin, 2004).

Kickert, W., and Koppenjaan, J., 'Public management and network management: an overview', in W. Kickert et al. (eds), *Managing Complex Networks: Strategies for the Public Sector* (London, Sage, 1997), pp. 35–61.

Kitson, R., and Kelso, P., 'England hunt rugby spies', *Guardian*, 18 Nov. 2003.

Kitson, R., 'All Blacks discover spies in the bushes', *Guardian*, 16 Nov. 2005.

Klerks, P., 'The network paradigm applied to criminal organisations, theoretical nitpicking or a relevant doctrine for investigators?', in A. Edwards and P. Gill (eds), *Transnational Organised Crime: Perspectives on Global Security* (London, Routledge, 2003), pp. 97–113.

Kliem, G., 'The spy who loved her', *Guardian*, 18 Nov. 2004.

Knightley, P., *The Second Oldest Profession: The Spy as Patriot, Bureaucrat, Fantasist and Whore* (London, André Deutsch, 1986).

Knightley, P., 'The biggest con-trick', *New Statesman*, 19 July 2004, pp. 14–15.

Knoke, D., and Kuklinski, J. H., 'Network analysis: some basic concepts', in G. Thompson et al. (eds), *Markets, Hierarchies and Networks: The Co-ordination of Social Life* (London, Sage, 1991), pp. 173–82.

Knott, S. F., *Secret and Sanctioned: Covert Operations and the American Presidency* (New York, Oxford University Press, 1996).

Kornbluh, P., *The Pinochet File: A Declassified Dossier on Atrocity and Accountability* (New York, The New Press, 2004).

Krivitsky, W. G., *I Was Stalin's Agent* (London, Hamish Hamilton, 1939).

Laqueur, W., *Terrorism* (London, Abacus, 1978).

Lathrop, C. E., *The Literary Spy* (New Haven, Yale University Press, 2004).

Layder, D., *New Strategies in Social Research* (Cambridge, Polity, 1993).

Le Carré, J., *Absolute Friends* (London, Hodder & Stoughton, 2004).

Leffler, M., *A Preponderance of Power: National Security, the Truman Administration and the Cold War* (Stanford, CA, Stanford University Press, 1992).

Legg, T., and Ibbs, R., *Report of the Sierra Leone Arms Investigation* (London, The Stationery Office, 1998).

Leigh, D., *The Wilson Plot* (London, Heinemann, 1988).

Leigh, D., 'Britain's security services and journalists: the secret story', *British Journalism Review*, 11, 2 (2000), pp. 21–6.

Leishman, F., 'Policing in Japan: East Asian archetype?', in R. Mawby (ed.), *Policing Across the World* (London, UCL Press, 1999), pp. 109–25.

Lichtblau, E., 'Flight groundings lead allies to query Washington', *New York Times*, 3 Jan. 2004.

Linzer, D., 'Two detail Bolton's efforts to punish dissent', *Washington Post*, 29 Apr. 2005.

Lowenthal, M. M., *Intelligence: From Secrets to Policy*, 2nd edn (Washington, DC, CQ Press, 2003).

Lucas, W. S., and Morey, A., 'The hidden "alliance": the CIA and MI6 before and after Suez', *Intelligence and National Security*, 15, 2 (2000), pp. 95–120.

Lustgarten, L., and Leigh, I., *In from the Cold: National Security and Parliamentary Democracy* (Oxford, Clarendon Press, 1994).

Lyon, D., *Postmodernity* (Minneapolis, University of Minnesota Press, 1994).

Lyon, D., *Surveillance Society: Monitoring Everyday Life* (Milton Keynes, Open University Press, 2001).

Lyon, D., *Surveillance after September 11* (Cambridge, Polity, 2003).

MacEachin, D. J., 'Predicting the Soviet invasion of Afghanistan: the intelligence community's record' (2002), <www.odci.gov/csi/monograph/afghanistan/index.html>, accessed 1 Dec. 2005.

MacEachin, D. J., 'CIA assessments of the Soviet Union: the record versus the charges', *Studies in Intelligence*, 1 (1997), <www.odci.gov/csi/monograph/russia/ciasay.html>, accessed 1 Dec. 2005.

MacEachin, D. J., *US Intelligence and the Confrontation in Poland, 1980–1981* (Philadelphia, Penn State University Press, 2002).

McAnulla, S., 'Structure and agency', in D. Marsh and G. Stoker (eds), *Theory and Methods in Political Science*, 2nd edn (Basingstoke, Palgrave Macmillan, 2002), pp. 271–91.

McClintock, M., *The American Connection: State Terror and Popular Resistance in El Salvador* (London, Zed Books, 1984).

McClintock, M., *The American Connection: State Terror and Popular Resistance in Guatemala* (London, Zed Books, 1984).

McCullagh, D., 'Report: anti-terror efforts pinch privacy', CNET News, 3 Sept. 2002, <http://news.com.com/>, accessed 1 June 2003.

McDonald, D. C., *Commission of Enquiry Concerning Certain Activities of the RCMP*, Second Report: *Freedom and Security under the Law* (Ottawa, Minister of Supply and Services, 1981).

McDonald, H., 'Revealed: five British spies inside IRA', *Observer*, 18 May 2003.

McGrew, T., 'Conceptualizing global politics', in T. McGrew. and P. Lewis et al., *Global Politics* (Cambridge, Polity, 1992), pp. 1–28.

McGrory, D., and Reid, T., 'CIA accused of running secret jails in Europe for terrorists', *Independent*, 3 Nov. 2005.

Machon, A., *Spies, Lies & Whistleblowers* (Lewes, The Book Guild, 2005).

Mackay, J., *Allan Pinkerton: The First Private Eye* (New York, Wiley, 1996).

Mader, J. (ed.), *Who's Who in CIA* (Berlin, 1968).

Mandel, R., 'Distortions in the intelligence decision-making process', in S. J. Cimbala (ed.), *Intelligence and Intelligence Policy in a Democratic Society* (Ardsley-on-Hudson, NY, Transnational Publishers, 1987), pp. 69–83.

Mangold, T., *Cold Warrior: James Jesus Angleton: The CIA's Master Spy Hunter* (New York, Simon & Schuster, 1991).

Mann, J., *Rise of the Vulcans: A History of Bush's War Cabinet* (New York, Viking, 2004).

Manning, P. K., 'Policing new social spaces', in J. Sheptycki (ed.), *Issues in Transnational Policing* (London, Routledge, 2000), pp. 177–200.

Manningham-Buller, E., 'The international terrorist threat and the dilemmas in countering it', speech at the Ridderzaal, Binnenhof, the Hague, Netherlands, 1 Sept. 2005, <www.mi5.gov.uk/print/page387.html>, accessed 1 Dec. 2005.

Markle Foundation, *Creating a Trusted Information Network for Homeland Security*, 2nd Report of the Markle Foundation Task Force, Dec. 2003, <www.markle.org/downloadable_assets/nstf_report2_full_report.pdf>, accessed 6 Jan. 2005.

Marrin, S., 'Preventing intelligence failures by learning from the past', *International Journal of Intelligence and Counter Intelligence*, 17, 4 (2004), pp. 655–72.

Marrin, S., and Clemente, J. D., 'Improving intelligence analysis by looking to the medical profession', *International Journal of Intelligence and Counterintelligence*, 18, 4 (2005–6), pp. 707–29.

Marsh, D., and Furlong, P., 'A skin not a sweater: ontology and epistemology in political science', in D. Marsh and G. Stoker (eds), *Theory and Methods in Political Science*, 2nd edn (Basingstoke, Palgrave, 2002), pp. 17–41.

Martin, D. A., *Wilderness of Mirrors* (London, HarperCollins, 1980).

Marx, G., *Undercover: Police Surveillance in America* (Berkeley, University of California Press, 1988).

Mayer, J., 'Outsourcing torture', *New Yorker*, 14 Feb. 2005, <www. newyorker.com/printables/fact/050214fa_fact6>, accessed 1 Dec. 2005.

Mayntz, R., 'Governing failures and the problem of governability', in J. Kooiman (ed.), *Modern Governance: New Government–Society Interactions* (London, Sage, 1993), pp. 9–20.

Mazower, M., *The Policing of Politics in the 20th Century* (Oxford, Berghahn Books, 1997).

Meacher, M., 'Britain now faces its own blowback', *Guardian*, 10 Sept. 2005.

Mearsheimer, J., *The Tragedy of Great Power Politics* (New York, Norton, 2002).

MI5, *The Security Service*, 2nd edn (London, HMSO, 1996).

Miller, G., 'Shades of cover', *Los Angeles Times*, 16 July 2005.

Miller, J., and van Natta Jr, D., 'In years of plots and clues, scope of Qaeda eluded US', *New York Times*, 9 June 2002.

Milne, S., *The Enemy Within: MI5, Maxwell and the Scargill Affair* (London, Verso, 1994).

Morgan, P. M., *Deterrence Now* (Cambridge, Cambridge University Press, 2003).

Morrison, D., 'The story of Stakeknife is full of holes', *Guardian*, 16 May 2003.

Morrow, R. A., with Brown, D. D., *Critical Theory and Methodology* (London, Sage, 1994).

Moynihan, D. P., *Secrecy* (New Haven, Yale University Press, 1998).

Muir, H., 'End of the road for Special Branch', *Guardian*, 9 Sept. 2005.

Müller-Wille, B., *For Our Eyes Only? Shaping an Intelligence Community within the EU*, Occasional Paper, 50 (Paris: Institute for Security Studies, 2004),<www.issseu.org/occasion/occ50/pdf>.

Murphy, D. E., *What Stalin Knew: The Enigma of Barbarossa* (New Haven, Yale University Press, 2005).

Nash, E., 'Madrid begins inquiry into CIA "torture" flights', *Independent*, 16 Nov. 2005.

Nomikos, J. M., 'Intelligence requirements for peacekeeping operations', Research

Institute for European and American Studies (2003), <www.rieas.gr/papers.html>, accessed 1 Dec. 2005.

Norton-Taylor, R., *Truth is a Difficult Concept: Inside the Scott Inquiry* (London, Fourth Estate, 1995).

Norton-Taylor, R., 'Security services face worst scenario', *Guardian*, 13 July 2005.

Norton-Taylor, R., 'There's no such thing as total security', *Guardian*, 19 Aug. 2005.

Norton-Taylor, R., and White, M., 'New intelligence chief fails to meet Butler guidelines', *Guardian*, 17 July 2004.

Nye, J. S. Jr, 'Peering into the future', *Foreign Affairs*, 73, 4 (1994), pp. 82–93.

Oborne, P., 'Butler has found Scarlett guilty – so why has he been promoted?', *Spectator*, 17 July 2004.

Odom, W. E., *Fixing Intelligence* (New Haven, Yale University Press, 2003).

Office of the Inspector General, *The FBI's Efforts to Improve the Sharing of Intelligence and Other Information*, Report 04-10 (Washington, DC, Department of Justice, Dec. 2003).

O'Reilly, C., and Ellison, G., ' "Eye spy private high": re-conceptualising high policing theory', *British Journal of Criminology*, advance access publication (2005).

Oren, M. B., *Six Days of War: June 1967 and the Making of the Modern Middle East* (New York, Oxford University Press, 2002).

O'Shaughnessy, H., *Pinochet: The Politics of Torture* (London, Latin America Bureau, 2000).

Parliamentary Joint Committee on ASIO, ASIS and DSD, *Intelligence on Iraq's Weapons of Mass Destruction* (Canberra, Commonwealth of Australia, Dec. 2003).

Penkovsky, O., *The Penkovsky Papers* (New York, Doubleday, 1965).

Perkovich, G., *India's Nuclear Bomb: The Impact on Global Proliferation* (Berkeley, University of California Press, 1999).

Perkus, C. (ed.), *COINTELPRO: The FBI's Secret War on Political Freedom* (New York, Monad Press, 1975).

Petersen, M., 'The challenge for the political analyst', *Studies in Intelligence*, 47, 1 (2003), <http://www.odci.gov/csi/studies/vol47no1/article05.html>, accessed on 1 Dec. 2005.

Pettman, J. J., *Worlding Women: A Feminist International Politics* (London, Routledge, 1996).

Philips, J., 'Up to 200 Italian police ran parallel anti-terror force', *Independent*, 5 July 2005.

Phythian, M., *Arming Iraq* (Boston, Northeastern University Press, 1997).

Phythian, M., 'Hutton and Scott: a tale of two inquiries', *Parliamentary Affairs*, 58, 1 (2005), pp. 124–37.

Phythian, M., 'Still a matter of trust: post-9/11 British intelligence and political culture', *International Journal of Intelligence and Counter intelligence*, 18, 4 (2005–6) pp. 653–81.

Pincher, C., *Their Trade Is Treachery* (London, Sidgwick & Jackson, 1981).

Pincher, C., *Too Secret Too Long* (London, Sidgwick & Jackson, 1984).

Pincher, C., *The Spycatcher Affair: A Web of Deception* (London, Sidgwick & Jackson, 1987).

Pincus, W., 'Negroponte steps into loop', *Washington Post*, 13 May 2005.

Pincus, W., and Eggen, D., 'Al Qaeda unchecked for years, panel says Tenet concedes CIA made mistakes', *Washington Post*, 15 Apr. 2004.

Pinkston, D. A., and Saunders, P. C., 'Seeing North Korea clearly', *Survival*, 45, 3 (2003), pp. 79–102.

Pollack, K., *The Threatening Storm: The Case for Invading Iraq* (New York, Random House, 2003).

Porter, B., *The Origins of the Vigilant State: The London Metropolitan Police Special Branch Before the First World War* (London, Weidenfeld & Nicolson, 1987).

Porter, B., *Plots and Paranoia: A History of Political Espionage in Britain 1790–1988* (London, Unwin Hyman, 1989).

Poveda, T., *Lawlessness and Reform: The FBI in Transition* (Pacific Grove, CA, Brooks/Cole Publishing Company, 1990).

Powers, R. G., *Secrecy and Power: The Life of J. Edgar Hoover* (London, Hutchinson, 1987).

Powers, T., 'The failure', *New York Review of Books*, 29 Apr. 2004.

Preston, P., 'They miss so much it's spooky', *Guardian*, 21 Apr. 2003.

Priest, D., 'Help from France key in covert operations', *Washington Post*, 3 July 2005.

Priest, D., 'CIA holds terror suspects in secret prisons', *Washington Post*, 2 Nov. 2005.

Prime Minister, *Government Response to the Intelligence and Security Committee Inquiry into Intelligence, Assessments and Advice prior to the Terrorist Bombings on Bali 12 October 2002*, Cm 5765 (London, The Stationery Office, Feb. 2003).

Prime Minister, *Government Response to ISC Report on Iraqi Weapons of Mass Destruction – Intelligence and Assessments*, Cm 6118 (London, The Stationery Office, Feb. 2004).

Randall, V., 'Feminism', in D. Marsh and G. Stoker (eds), *Theory and Methods in Political Science*, 2nd edn (Basingstoke, Palgrave, 2002), pp. 109–30.

Ranelagh, J., *The Agency: The Rise and Decline of the CIA* (New York, Simon & Schuster, Touchstone Edition, 1987).

Ransom, H. H., *The Intelligence Establishment* (Cambridge, MA, Harvard University Press, 1970).

Rathmell, A., 'Towards postmodern intelligence', *Intelligence and National Security*, 17, 3 (2002), pp. 87–104.

Raviv, D., and Melman, Y., *Every Spy a Prince: The Complete History of Israel's Intelligence Community* (Boston, Houghton Mifflin, 1991).

Richelson, J. T., *A Century of Spies: Intelligence in the Twentieth Century* (New York, Oxford University Press, 1995).

Richelson, J. T., *The Wizards of Langley: Inside the CIA's Directorate of Science and Technology* (Boulder, CO, Westview, 2001).

Richelson, J. T., and Ball, D, *The Ties that Bind*, 2nd edn (Boston, Unwin Hyman, 1990).

Risen, J., and Rohde, D., 'A hostile land foils the quest for bin Laden', *New York Times*, 13 Dec. 2004.

Ritter, S., *Endgame: Solving the Iraq Problem Once and For All* (New York, Simon & Schuster, 1999).

Ritter, S., *Iraq Confidential: The Untold Story of America's Intelligence Conspiracy* (London, I. B. Tauris, 2005).

Robarge, D. S., 'CIA analysis of the 1967 Arab–Israeli war', *Studies in Intelligence*, 49, 1 (2005), <http://www.odci.gov/csi/ studies/vol49no1/ html_files/arab_israeli_war_1.html>, accessed 1 Dec. 2005.

Robertson, K. G., 'Recent reform of intelligence in the United Kingdom: democratization or risk management', *Intelligence and National Security*, 13, 2 (1998), pp. 144–58.

Robin, C., *Fear: The History of a Political Idea* (New York, Oxford University Press, 2004).

Rogers, P., *Losing Control: Global Security in the Twenty-First Century* (London, Pluto Press, 2000).

Rouquie, A., *The Military and the State in Latin America* (Berkeley, University of California Press, 1992).

Rudgers, D. E., *Creating the Secret State: The Origins of the Central Intelligence Agency, 1943–1947* (Lawrence, University of Kansas Press, 2000).

Russell, R. L., 'CIA's strategic intelligence in Iraq', *Political Science Quarterly*, 117, 2 (2002), pp. 191–207.

Sanders, D., 'Behaviouralism', in D. Marsh and G. Stoker (eds), *Theory and Methods in Political Science*, 2nd edn (Basingstoke, Palgrave, 2002), pp. 45–64.

Sanger, D. E., 'What are Koreans up to? US agencies can't agree', *New York Times*, 12 May 2005.

Schechter, J. L., and Deriabin, P. S., *The Spy Who Saved the World: How a Soviet Colonel Changed the Course of the Cold War* (New York, Scribner's, 1992).

Schreier, F., and Caparini, M., *Privatizing Security: Implications of Private Military Companies for Effective Security Sector Governance* (Geneva, DCAF, 2005).

Schweizer, P., 'The growth of economic espionage: America is target number one', *Foreign Affairs*, 75, 1 (1996), pp. 9–14.

Sciolino, E., and Van Natta Jr, D., 'June report led Britain to lower its terror alert', *New York Times*, 19 July 2005.

Scott, J., *Power* (Cambridge, Polity, 2001).

Scott, L., 'Secret intelligence, covert action and clandestine diplomacy', *Intelligence and National Security*, 19, 2 (2004), pp. 322–41.

Scott, L., and Jackson, P., 'The study of intelligence in theory and practice', *Intelligence and National Security*, 19, 2 (2004), pp. 139–69.

Scott, R., *Appendices to the Report of the Inquiry into the Export of Defence Equipment and Dual-Use Goods to Iraq and Related Prosecutions Laid Before the House on 15 February 1996 on CD-ROM* (London, HMSO, 1996).

Seifert, J. W., *Data Mining: An Overview* (Washington, DC, Congressional Research Service, 2004), <www.fas.org/irp>, accessed 1 Dec. 2005.

Senate Select Committee on Intelligence and House Permanent Select Committee on Intelligence, *Report of Joint Inquiry into Intelligence Activities Before and After the Terrorist Attacks of September 11, 2001* (107th Congress, 2nd Session, Dec. 2002).

Senate Select Committee on Intelligence, *Report on the US Intelligence Community's Prewar Intelligence Assessments on Iraq* (Washington, DC, GPO, June 2004).

Shearing, C., and Stenning, P. (eds), *Private Policing* (London, Sage, 1987).

Shenon, P., 'Bush names former New Jersey Governor to 9/11 panel', *New York Times*, 17 Dec. 2002.

Sheptycki, J., *Review of the Influence of Strategic Intelligence on Organised Crime Policy and Practice*, Special Interest Paper, 14 (London, Home Office, 2004).

Sheptycki, J., 'Organizational pathologies in police intelligence systems', *European Journal of Criminology*, 1, 3 (2004), pp. 307–32.

Shlaim, A., 'Failures in national intelligence estimates: the case of the Yom Kippur War', *World Politics*, 28, 3 (1976), pp. 348–80.

Short, C., *An Honourable Deception? New Labour, Iraq, and the Misuse of Power* (London, Free Press, 2004).

Shrimsley, R., 'The bogeyman and the fearmongers are out to get you', *Financial Times*, 22 Oct. 2004.

Shulsky, A. N., and Schmitt, G. J., *Silent Warfare*, 3rd edn (Washington, DC, Brassey's Inc., 2002).

Sick, G., *All Fall Down: America's Tragic Encounter with Iran* (New York, Penguin, 1986).

Silberman, L. H., and Robb, C. S., Commission on the Intelligence Capabilities of the United States Regarding Weapons of Mass Destruction, *Report* (Washington, DC, GPO, Mar. 2005).

Sillitoe, P., *Cloak Without Dagger* (London, Pan Books, 1956).

Simpson, C., *Blowback: America's Recruitment of Nazis and its Effects on the Cold War* (London, Weidenfeld & Nicolson, 1988).

Simpson, J., *From the House of War* (London, Arrow, 1991).

Singer, P. W., *Corporate Warriors: The Rise of the Privatized Military Industry* (Ithaca, NY, Cornell University Press, 2003).

Singer, P. W., 'The private military industry and Iraq, what have we learned and where to next?,' DCAF Policy Paper, Nov. 2004, <www.dcaf.ch>, accessed 15 June 2005.

SIRC, *Annual Report 1985–86* (Ottawa, Minister of Supply and Services, 1986).

SIRC, *Report 2001–2002: An Operational Audit of the CSIS* (Ottawa, Public Works and Government Services Canada, 2002), <www.sirc-csars.gc.ca>.

Sparrow, M. K., 'Network vulnerabilities and strategic intelligence in law enforcement', *International Journal of Intelligence and Counterintelligence*, 5, 3 (1991), pp. 255–74.

Special Committee of the Senate on the CSIS, *Delicate Balance: Security Intelligence Services in a Democratic Society* (Ottawa, Minister of Supply and Services, 1983).

Spicer, T., *An Unorthodox Soldier: Peace and War and the Sandline Affair* (Edinburgh, Mainstream Publishing, 2000).

Stack, K. P., 'Competitive intelligence', *Intelligence and National Security*, 13, 4 (1998), pp. 194–202.

Statewatch: Monitoring the State and Civil Liberties in the UK and Europe, Statewatch, PO Box 1516, London. Also at <www.statewatch.org>.

Steele, R. D., *The New Craft of Intelligence: Personal, Public and Political* (Oakton, OSS International Press, 2002).

Steury, D. P., 'How the CIA missed Stalin's bomb', *Studies in Intelligence*, 49, 1 (2005), <http://www.odci.gov/csi/studies/vol49no1/ html_files/ stalins_bomb_3.html>, accessed 1 Dec. 2005.

Stevens, J., *Stevens Enquiry: Overview and Recommendations* (London, The Stationery Office, 2003).

Stevens, J., *Not for the Faint-Hearted: My Life Fighting Crime* (London, Weidenfeld & Nicolson, 2005).

Strohm, C., 'Homeland Security to expand biometric visitor tracking system', 25 Oct. 2005, <www.govexec.com>, accessed 28 Oct. 2005.

Sulick, M., 'Al Qaeda answers CIA's hiring call', *Los Angeles Times*, 10 July 2005.

Sweeney, J., *Trading with the Enemy: Britain's Arming of Iraq* (London, Pan, 1993).

Szikinger, I., 'National security in Hungary', in J. P. Brodeur et al., *Democracy, Law and Security: Internal Security Services in Contemporary Europe* (Aldershot, Ashgate, 2003) pp. 81–109.

Tapia-Valdés, J. A., 'A typology of national security policies', *Yale Journal of World Public Order*, 9, 10 (1982), pp. 10–39.

Terriff, T., Croft, S., James, L., and Morgan, P., *Security Studies Today* (Cambridge, Polity, 1999).

Thomas, E., and Vistica, G., 'A troubled company', *Newsweek*, 13 Nov. 1995.

Thompson, E. P., 'The secret state within the state', *New Statesman*, 10 Nov. 1978.

Thompson, G., *Between Hierarchies and Markets: The Logic and Limits of Network Forms of Organization* (Oxford, Oxford University Press, 2003).

Thompson, G., Frances, J., Levačič, R., and Mitchell, J. (eds), *Markets, Hierarchies and Networks: The Coordination of Social Life* (London, Sage, 1991).

Thucydides, *The Peloponnesian War* (Harmondsworth, Penguin, 1983).

Tomlinson, R., *The Big Breach: From Top Secret to Maximum Security* (Edinburgh, Cutting Edge, 2001).

Travers, R., 'The coming intelligence failure', *Studies in Intelligence*, 1 (1997), <www.odci.gov/ csi/studies/97unclass/failure.html>, accessed 1 Dec. 2005.

Treverton, G. F., 'Intelligence and the "market state"', *Studies in Intelligence*, 10 (2001), <www.cia.gov/csi/studies/winter_spring01/article09.pdf>, accessed 1 Dec. 2005.

Treverton, G. F., *Reshaping National Intelligence for an Age of Information* (New York, Cambridge University Press, 2003).

Walsh, J. (ed.), *The Gulf War Did Not Happen: Politics, Culture and Warfare Post-Vietnam* (Aldershot, Arena Books, 1995).

Walsh, N. P., 'Russia accuses "spies" working in foreign NGOs', *Guardian*, 13 May 2005.

Walzer, M., *Just and Unjust Wars*, 3rd edn (New York, Basic Books, 2000).

Ware, J., 'Torture, murder, mayhem – the dirty war just got dirtier', *Guardian*, 12 May 2003.

Warner, G., 'Transnational Organised Crime and the Secret Agencies', *International Journal of Risk, Security and Crime Prevention*, 3, 2 (1998) pp. 147–9.

Warner, M., 'Wanted: a definition of "intelligence"', *Studies in Intelligence*, 46, 3 (2002), <http://www.odci.gov/csi/studies/vol46no3/article02.html>, accessed 1 Dec. 2005.

Watkins, A., *A Short Walk Down Fleet Street* (London, Duckworth, 2000).

Webster, P., and Bowcott, O., 'Terror suspect turned out to be Welsh insurance agent', *Guardian*, 3 Jan. 2004.

Weisman, J., 'GOP leaders urge probe in prisons leak', *Washington Post*, 9 Nov. 2005.

West, N., (ed.), *The Faber Book of Espionage* (London, Faber & Faber, 1993).

West, N., 'Fiction, faction and intelligence', *Intelligence and National Security*, 19, 2 (2004), pp. 275–89.

Westerfield, H. B. (ed.), *Inside the CIA's Private World: Declassified Articles from the Agency's Internal Journal, 1955–92* (New Haven, Yale University Press, 1995).

Whitaker, R., 'The Bristow affair: a crisis of accountability in Canadian security intelligence', *Intelligence and National Security*, 11, 2 (1996), pp. 279–305.

Whitaker, R., *The End of Privacy: How Total Surveillance is Becoming a Reality* (New York, The New Press, 1999).

Whitaker, R., 'A Faustian bargain? America and the dream of total information awareness', in K. D. Haggerty and R. V. Ericson (eds), *The New Politics of Surveillance and Visibility* (Toronto, University of Toronto Press, 2005), pp. 141–70.

Widgery, Lord, *Report of the Tribunal Appointed to Inquire into Events on Sunday 30th January 1972*, HC 220 (London, HMSO, 1972).

Wilensky, H., *Organizational Intelligence: Knowledge and Policy in Government and Industry* (New York, Basic Books, 1967).

Wilkinson, T., 'Italy seeks former US diplomat in kidnapping', *Los Angeles Times*, 30 Sept. 2005.

Wilkinson, T., and Miller, G., 'Italy says it didn't know of CIA plan', *Los Angeles Times*, 1 July 2005.

Williams, I., 'UNSCOM suffers a terminal blow', *Middle East International*, 15 Jan. 1999.

Wilsnack, R. W., 'Information control: a conceptual framework for sociological analysis', *Urban Life*, 8 (1980), pp. 467–99.

Winks, R. M., *Cloak and Gown: Scholars in the Secret War, 1939–1961*, 2nd edn (New Haven, Yale University Press, 1996).

Winter, G., *Inside BOSS: South Africa's Secret Police* (Harmondsworth, Penguin, 1981).

Wohlstetter, R., *Pearl Harbor: Warning and Decision* (Stanford, CA, Stanford University Press, 1962).

Wolf, M., *Memoirs of a Spymaster* (London, Pimlico, 1998).

Woodiwiss, M., *Organized Crime and American Power* (Toronto, University of Toronto Press, 2001).

Woodward, B., *The Commanders* (London, Simon & Schuster, 1991).

Woodward, B., *Plan of Attack* (London, Simon & Schuster, 2004).

Wright, P., *Spycatcher: The Candid Autobiography of a Senior Intelligence Officer* (New York, Viking, 1987).

Wrong, D. H., *Power: Its Forms, Bases, and Uses* (Oxford: Blackwell, 1988).

Wyden, R., 'Wyden releases additional views on Senate intelligence report', 9 July 2004, <http://wyden.senate.gov/media/speeches/2004/07092004_intelreport.html>, accessed 1 Dec. 2005.

Yasamee, H. J., and Hamilton, K. A. (eds), *Documents on British Policy Overseas, Series II Volume IV: Korea June 1950–April 1951* (London, HMSO, 1991).

Younge, G., and Dodd, V., 'CIA blunder on al-Jazeera "terror messages" ', *Guardian*, 29 June 2005.

Index